# DREAM TEAM

# DREAM TEAM

# TEAM

## LEWIS COLE

WILLIAM MORROW AND COMPANY, INC.

New York                                    1981

*The author would like to express his gratitude for permission to re-print material from the following books:*

*Life on the Run*, by William Bradley. Copyright © 1976 by William Bradley. Quoted with permission of Times Books, New York.

*Miracle on 33rd Street*, by Phil Berger. Copyright © 1970 by Phil Berger. Quoted with permission of International Creative Management, New York.

*W. H. Auden: Collected Poems*, by W. H. Auden, edited by Edward Mendelson. Copyright © 1976. Quoted by permission of Random House, Inc., New York.

*Clyde: The Walt Frazier Story*, by Walt Frazier and Joe Jares. Copyright © 1970, 1974 by Walt Frazier and Joe Jares. Tempo Books, an imprint of Grosset & Dunlap, Inc., New York.

**Library of Congress Cataloging in Publication Data**

Cole, Lewis.
  **Dream team.**

  1. New York Knickerbockers (Basketball team)
I. Title.
GV885.52.N4C64          796.32′364′097471          81-11180
ISBN 0-688-03726-7                                   AACR2

Printed in the United States of America

First Edition

1  2  3  4  5  6  7  8  9  10

BOOK DESIGN BY MICHAEL MAUCERI

*For Cathy,*
*"roving forward"*

# _ ACKNOWLEDGMENTS _

The people who speak in this book all shared their time, thoughts, and memories with gracious generosity. Some deserve special mention. Nate Bowman helped me contact some of his former teammates; Marv Albert let me observe him broadcast a game, a particular treat; Phil Berger and Ira Berkow introduced me to some of the subtleties of the team and its members. The staff of the Knick office assisted me unfailingly with information, tickets, and game films: Jo Anne Farrell, Patty Disken, Carl Martin, Stew Meyer, Kevin Kennedy, Jim Wergeles, Frankie Blauschild, and, of course, Eddie Donovan and Red Holzman. My editor, Jim Landis, and Elaine Markson, my agent, practiced the merciful virtues of patience and trust. I thank them all.

# DREAM TEAM

# __PROLOGUE__

In the spring of 1974, I needed a new devotion. For the previous six years, April and May had been riotous months in my life. A college senior in 1968, I had helped to lead a student strike at Columbia University against the Vietnam war and racism. Afterward I became a "full-time," as the expression went, "Movement person": I organized opposition to the war and support for black and Puerto Rican liberation movements. Strikes and demonstrations in the spring climaxed each season of protest. Now I was politically inactive. The war had ended; Students for a Democratic Society and the Black Panther Party, the two organizations with which I had worked, were hopelessly destroyed, the victims of internal faction fights and government attacks; and for political and personal reasons I wasn't ready to join any of the groups that had replaced them. I was very busy—I was teaching English at a community college, working on a magazine, and writing; but I still missed the passion and drama that had commanded my life each spring. I needed something to seize my imagination. Quite wonderfully and unexpectedly, I found it. I became a fan of the New York Knickerbockers.

Friends regarded my passion as regressive: Thrust into adulthood, I was clinging to a teenager's diversion. I saw things differently. We used an expression then—"the real world." The phrase covered a lot of ground, mostly rocky.

We employed it most frequently in an argumentative or explanatory capacity—"this is the real world, you know?" The rhetorical question implied that whatever had preceded the present predicament—family, campus, a love affair—had been negligible, maybe even false, certainly less than the real world. The phrase also suggested an attitude toward experience, an end to the melodramatic sentiments and expectations of adolescent and student life, and the start of a cooler, more ironic view. "Don't be so shocked, this is the real world, you know?" In all instances, the real world was grim—I can't remember an occasion when anyone ever suggested that happiness might be part of the real world, you know?—excitingly grim, and a certain tough pride was the reward for anticipating and accepting it. "The real world" was our vision of adult life in America, the world outside the shelters in which we had grown up; and for me, basketball—although it ended up disproving this bleakly romantic view—represented the real world.

I never would have imagined this. Professionally successful, radical intellectuals, my parents provided me with material comfort and a sense of special intellectual achievement in my youth, and I grew up believing I would live well and have my ideas treated with sympathy and respect. While attending Columbia, I assumed I would eventually teach English and write fiction and criticism, and was so certain of this future that I didn't consider my academic triumphs as advancements in my career—my successes were merely the way things were meant to be.

I didn't even think my political activities would upset this plan. As a student, I felt ambivalent toward Columbia. In the midst of the war and the black liberation movement, a lot of the research and discussion at the university was frivolous at best and deadly at worst, and many faculty members and students dismissed political involvement with a maddeningly fatuous snobbery. In 1967, before many people opposed the war, a group of poets were touring campuses giving read-ins against it, and I helped arrange a night for them to appear at Columbia. I asked several important Columbia English professors to sponsor the evening, but none agreed, and finally I approached a young teacher, a poet himself with whom I enjoyed a limited friendship. I was certain he would be pleased to help host the event. Instead, he begged off, explaining he was against the war but couldn't devote himself to anything except teaching or writing. "You know," he offered as an explanation, "Rilke once said he couldn't even buy a dog because the animal would fascinate him so much he would stop writing poems."

At the same time, I was proud of my academic record at Columbia; indeed, in my self-serving innocence, I even announced this opinion publicly. During the rebellion, I appeared with several other strikers on the David Susskind show. Susskind argued with us in his usual disingenuous manner, and, to close the show, declared if he were president of Columbia he would expel us all. For some of my colleagues, this end was devoutly to be wished—they were ashamed of their attendance at an elite institution. But Susskind's attitude annoyed and insulted me, and I told him that, with my academic distinctions, Columbia would be loathe to let me go. Susskind's look suggested I had momentarily lost touch with reality and several weeks later, the administration proved him right: They withheld my degree, thereby barring me from their graduate school, into which I had already been accepted, following Susskind's advice to the letter.

I protested this unfair expulsion, but Columbia obdurately refused to give me my degree—and shortly, I came to welcome my release from the academy. Working in the movement, I experienced my equivalent of others' years in the Army. I gained whatever mechanical adeptness I possess, learning how to drive, a miracle for city boys like myself, and dealt with people quite removed from my own background. At the time, the left attracted people from all classes, and before one mass rally in New Haven, a demonstration for the release of Black Panther Party leaders Bobby Seale and Ericka Huggins, I spent a morning speaking to employees at Time-Life, and the afternoon leafleting students at Lafayette High School in Brooklyn. Most of my close friendships were formed then, and some of my understanding of courage, foolishness, and evil. During my first two years as an organizer a week didn't pass without a major demonstration, conference, or rally, protests that often ended with fights or jail. At the same time there were intense personal and political battles within the movement. Some of these were pathetic and weird. I attended one national meeting in which a contingent of gay males argued that all men in attendance should wear dresses. There weren't enough dresses to go around—most of the women, of course, wore jeans—and few of the men fit into the ones available, so the gays and their converts debated the next step for defeating Nixon's Vietnamization plan while wearing sheets draped over them and looking like toga-robed extras from the BBC production of *I, Claudius*. But the internal struggles could also be vicious. In 1971, when the Black Panther Party split up, members from each side went on a vendetta; several were assassinated in ways as brutal as any practiced by the American military in Vietnam.

Some moments suggested adventure and mastery. After the murders at Kent State in May 1970, a group of us decided to buy guns legally. The model I wanted was sold only at a store located in a blighted section of Brooklyn. I drove out with a friend and we searched in vain for the shop; the address listed in the telephone book was occupied by a furniture store featuring a special on rya rugs. Finally I entered and asked the salesman if the gun store had moved. A short, friendly man, he laughed at my confusion and led me through to the rear where the plush couches and heavy coffee tables gave way to bayonets, ammunition, rifles, pistols, flack jackets, helmets, bandoliers, earplugs, targets, handcuffs, bottles of Mace, and dog whistles. I presented myself as a graduate student in political science at Columbia—an outcast's revenge—and imagined it was understood immediately between the owner and me that I was buying the gun because I lived on the border of Harlem and wanted to be well armed if the blacks in my neighborhood ever rioted. Or did he instantly see through my disguise, a shopkeeper who didn't care who bought his wares? I chatted with him as I purchased the gun and filled out the forms, and left that grocery store of death feeling proud, contemptuous, and uncertain that it was indeed I who had managed to pull off this stunt.

Still, I hadn't stepped outside the charmed circle of my life. I went on these adventures because of the movement, and my radical ideology kept me at a distance from events and people. There had always been a tendency in the movement to reduce experiences to their ideological meaning, a kind of iconography in which behavior and points of view were examined for the attitudes they embodied. (Sometimes people competed to see who could recognize the most meanings in the fewest instances.) At first this kind of symbol reading was applied to political events—rallies, demonstrations, positions. But after the killings at Kent State and the rebellion at Attica that followed a year later, fewer and fewer new people joined the movement and the same kind of analysis was applied to films, recipes, rock 'n' roll songs, and of course an entire assortment of unbelievably messy personal relations, relationships that inevitably became more entangled as the movement diminished in power, size, and scope. An extreme moralism accompanied this obsessive detailing of emotion and event. Things were judged good or bad, correct or incorrect, and your opinion of them condemned you or raised you to the status of the elect—by their views shall you know them. The talk didn't sharpen contradictions, it flattened them. It puffed up small differences and shrank big ones until everything more or less was the same size and fit neatly into preconceived judgments. In the end the ideology itself became reduced to a set of narrow standards as obfuscatory and tiresome as any academic jargon, and it was during this period that I found the Knicks.

At first the team served merely as a distraction. Two nights a week, I drove home from school; while roaming for a parking space, I occasionally caught a game narrated over the radio in a wonderfully grave, excitable voice. One evening my search lasted an hour. Toward the end, I tuned in a contest from Portland, a close battle that went into overtime just as I found an opening for my car. After parking I decided to remain seated—the extra period was only five minutes and, though the desire seemed ridiculous to me, I wanted to hear how the game turned out. With a few seconds left, the Knicks trailed by six and I shut off the heater and opened the door. Then they scored a basket and I stayed put, my feet in the street. But what could happen, after all? Only several seconds were left and Portland had possession of the ball. It was cold and the Trail Blazers called a time-out. I closed the door as the voice declared faint hopes in a distinctive way, emphasizing words seemingly at random, giving a breathless and dramatic import to its announcements. Why was I here? I hadn't eaten for the past five hours. Portland inbounded the ball and immediately a Knick stole it and scored. The voice communicated the moment's wonder by repeating the fact in a tone of restrained amazement, creating an air of suspense. Now Portland led by just a basket and I turned on the heater. It was all right to stay—surely this was an extraordinary performance. Portland called another time-out. I didn't mind the minute of advertisements; indeed, I relished the wait because the pause heightened the tension of what would happen next. The Trail Blazers tossed in the ball. In a hushed and somber tone, the voice described the sight of the court. Then it burst into disbelief as a Knick stole the ball again and scored, sending the game into another overtime. Sitting in the cramped seat of my Dodge Colt, I was mystified why I should be thrilled by the performance of several absolute strangers, playing a game I was more or less entirely ignorant about, in a faraway city I had never visited. But I didn't budge. I listened to the Knicks win in the next overtime period, and when I finally shut off the set and opened the door to the chilling air I only regretted I had no reason to stay longer. The win and the voice (I later found out that it belonged, of course, to Marv Albert) were a miraculous moment, and I suppose my insistence on rooting for the Knicks ever since is partly a consequence of associating them with that first game: I expect them to pull things out in the final six seconds. Certainly, the game made me a fan. The next night I was watching the news when some clips from the game appeared on the screen. I looked at them with fascination and pride; because I had listened to the Knicks winning the game, I felt that somehow the triumph belonged partly to me.

Shortly after, the play-offs began. The Knicks were matched against the Capital Bullets—perpetual orphans, the Bullets have shuttled back and forth from Baltimore to Washington—and the series was the first I followed. The games absorbed me utterly. I waited impatiently for them to begin, scheduled all social engagements around them; when there was a conflict I broke the date if the person didn't want to watch.

The final contest was a magical evening. The two teams had split the first six games, New York coming back whenever the Bullets threatened to oust them from the series. Now the teams were playing in New York and a group of us agreed to meet at a bar that had cable television, then a rare item. I arrived forty-five minutes before the opening tap. The bar was already jammed. Men and women filled a noisy and smoke-ridden wood-lined room which was alive with anticipation; the owner was turning away all customers whom he didn't know on a first-name basis. My companions weren't there and I was stymied—I would miss the crucial game and the thrill and fun of the bar's excitement. I accidentally ran into a friend who was waiting for mutual acquaintances, and we bit our nails and talked distractedly until our parties arrived. By then there were almost twenty of us and what would we do? One had cable at his house. We raced uptown in cabs and sat in a semicircle before his set, turning off the audio and putting on the radio so that we could hear Albert's perfect narration. The only thing needed to make the evening perfect was for the Knicks to win, and eventually they let us celebrate.

The Celtics beat the Knicks in the next round, but that summer was no respite for me. I checked the daily paper for news, delighted at the first off-season story, and read the small box in little print titled Transactions that listed each team's latest trades and acquisitions. On the courts where I played ball, I essayed my first fans' conversations, those obsessive exchanges of names, statistics, famous occasions, and other facts and half truths. At nights I traveled uptown to the City College's large, bleak gym where little-known professional players performed with athletes still hopeful of getting NBA jobs. Frequently the games were so chaotic that the public-address announcer would insult the players rather than report the score and number of fouls. Teams usually chant "Defense!" after huddles, a battle cry as they march back onto the court. My first evening at CCNY one team was losing by forty or fifty points and called a time-out. "Defense!" they shouted loudly, ending their conference. "Defense! they cry!" mocked the announcer. "But there is no defense!" The crowd enjoyed it all. They shared a rare fraternity, loving the game and rooting for their favorites with a fine sense of humor. And, for me, they possessed another special quality. During my second or third night there, I strolled around the court at half time. I felt easy and familiar with the people around me and also sensed being in a new and different environment. I couldn't figure out the cause for this double sensation and looked around me. I am tall—close to six feet six—and realized as I scanned the crowd that more men were at my eye level than below it. For the first time in my life, I was congregating with people of equal height.

When the season started, I went to the Garden and bought tickets for an exhibition doubleheader, my first pro game. The seats were at the end of the court, in the rafters. Could I actually see the players' faces or was I so familiar with them from television that I merely imagined their features? The team played sloppily and the fans around me shouted insults, dampening my eager enthusiasm. But, more than the actual contest, I loved the arena, a vast, brightly lit, and airy oval that widened upward from the court into row after row of every conceivable kind of New Yorker. Black kids strutted down the halls with picks in their hair, yelling after their buddies or laughing at jokes. Slick-haired white kids from the suburbs rushed after Dad to get two dollars for a yearbook. Gorgeous young black women, wearing tropically colored lipsticks and extravagant hairdos, and young white secretaries, their hair flipped, bobbed, or shagged strolled in pairs past businessmen in pinstriped suits and workingmen still dressed in heavy construction boots and flannel shirts, none of them having the time to change between getting off the job and coming to the game. In a way, it didn't matter whether or not the Knicks won. They had already achieved a kind of wonder simply by bringing all these people together.

But of course their winning mattered; it mattered more and more. The team kept claiming a larger share of my sympathy and imagination. I imagined there would be a natural limit to my pursuit. But some reason for devoting more of my time always suggested itself. One player was a rookie and the next few games would prove whether or not he could succeed as a pro. Another player was performing brilliantly: Could he keep it up? Tonight they were playing Detroit with Bob Lanier at center: Would they contain him? Next week they were matched against Chicago with Jerry Sloan and Norm Van Lier in the backcourt: Could they match their hustle? When they won, I remembered their flawless plays. When they lost, I was haunted by their mistakes and bad luck. I watched all their television games, bought all the papers for their coverage. At times my constancy impressed even myself. One day,

talking to a woman friend, I suggested my concern was
a little odd. "Not at all," she replied, naming for me in a moment the state of mind that had ruled me for the last eight
months, "you're in love."

Of course that was it! I was in love! But what a rotten team
to love! And what a rotten time to pick to love them! From
'69 to '73, they had reigned as modern basketball's most be-
guiling squad, a mix of masters and hard workers who won
with stylish courage and intelligence. But after the '74 play-
offs, my initiation into their mysteries, they lost several key
players. They started the '74–'75 season, my first full term as a
fan, with a brilliant debut, posting an 18–8 record, their rookies and substitutes shining, the veterans in perfect form. Then
they collapsed. They lost one game after another, lost badly,
and just as I thought that surely they would win against their
next opponent, they would lose again, lose soundly, no match
at all for their competition. For them comebacks lasted
one game. In February they traded one player for two, a
move hailed as a clever maneuver when they won several
nights later. Then they lost nine of their next thirteen games
—eighteen out of twenty-six hours spent watching my heroes
being hopelessly humiliated. Finally, toward the end of the
season, they settled into a comfortable mediocrity, split the
balance of their contests, and, through an essentially proce-
dural sleight-of-hand, qualified for the play-offs. Now, as they
played the hitherto obscure and lowly Houston Rockets, in a
best-two-out-of-three series, I entertained high hopes for
them, certain they would reclaim their former glory. They
lost the first contest in Houston. Shaken, they returned to
New York for the second. The night of the game, I re-
proached them in my mind—Now maybe, darling, you'll pull
yourself together?—and hurried from school to the same bar
where I had rooted for them the season before. Just like old
times, the place was packed, and the Knicks won neatly. They
were back on track, and the following Sunday afternoon,
with a friend, I returned to the bar, expecting them to wrap

up the series and challenge Boston or Washington. Outside, the early spring day was fresh and beautiful, but the glorious weather only made viewing a basketball game seem wrong: The bar was empty except for us, and the color of the television screen that shined brilliantly at night was diffused by the strong afternoon sunlight. Halfway through the third period the game was tied and I told the team to exert a little more pressure; the Rockets moved ahead, and I cautioned the Knicks not to disregard their competition; then—very quickly, as is always true for bad basketball teams—they were down by twenty, twenty-four, twenty-eight, beaten and finished. When the final buzzer sounded, they trailed by thirty-two. Depressed and dulled, my friend and I bestirred ourselves to walk outside. The opportunity of ending the affair presented itself, I suppose—winter was over and I had five months to break the habit before next season started. But the team and basketball had become synonymous to me. "It is the same in life," writes Proust. "The heart changes, and that is our worst misfortune; but we learn of it only from reading or by imagination; for in reality, its alteration, like that of certain natural phenomena, is so gradual that, even if we are able to distinguish, successively, each of its different states, we are still spared the actual sensation of change." Even if I wanted to say good-bye to the Knicks, to leave them meant giving up the game, and I couldn't do that. However they frustrated and disappointed me, I was wedded to them. I spent the rest of the afternoon figuring out with my friend how they could improve for the coming season.

But they were even worse the next year. They were a bad team and the worst kind of bad team, not an inexperienced one that eventually betters itself, but the remnant of a once brilliant unit now going to pieces. Made up of wasted and mediocre talents, at their best they played .500 ball, winning and losing games evenly, poised between the cautious hope they would win ten games in a row and the paralyzing fear they would fall apart and lose forever. No margin for error existed for them, no relief from the urgency to triumph in every contest. They could always do either better or worse, and occupied a no-man's-land, a high unpromising plain of mediocrity, a barren plateau of futility.

Still, for all that, my fascination deepened. Watching them was an education in the characters of the players and the game itself, and in a way their season-long sideways march to oblivion—or was this merely the argument an overintellectual fan used to justify his passion?—was as tantalizing as a champion's progress.

The team hosted four stars: Walt Frazier, Earl Monroe, Bill Bradley, and the coach, Red Holzman. It was painful to watch as the best attempts of these fine talents were constantly (and unintentionally) botched by their teammates. After a while their performances became caricatures. Frazier and Monroe were the team's only offensive threats and the constant pressure to score tired and frustrated them. Frazier had been a wonderful clutch shooter, a study of deliberation as he took his jumper, the ball always filling the net. Now his coolness appeared caution or confusion, the ball often bouncing off the rim or missing the mark altogether. Monroe used his old fakes and spins, a series of suspenseful gestures that let him get closer to the basket and was supposed to free him from his defender. Now two or three men played against him and frequently his elaborate dance of preparation would end with one defender slamming the ball back at him, a maddening moment, often followed by Monroe retrieving the ball and irrepressibly shooting and missing once more. Bradley was a cipher. He couldn't demonstrate his offensive tricks without the help of his old teammates, and the tactics that had gotten him points in the past now seemed aimless. Holzman, the coach, was reduced to the role of a stage manager in a Busby Berkeley movie, calling in one replacement after another to save the failing show, a Bonnard drawing with a pencil.

Of the substitutes, my favorite was a young forward named Mel Davis. A local product, famous high-school player in

Brooklyn, and leader of a team at St. John's, one of the city's Catholic colleges and an annual basketball power, Davis was a well-muscled rebounder called "Killer," a nickname coined by teammates after one rookie practice in which Davis performed with particular rambunctious enthusiasm. The Knick management, New York fans, and he, all expected him to become a starter. But he never made the grade. His own successes overwhelmed him. Once, while the Knicks were struggling, Davis played exceptionally well and Holzman named him a starter: The team was embarking on a road trip in which they played three poor squads in four nights and Holzman hoped the sudden promotion would help them return with a good record. Davis failed the test almost before it began. He shot every time he touched the ball, never scored, and rarely rebounded, and the experiment ended immediately. Such defeat was common to him. He constantly collided with his own insufficiencies. His inability to meet the high standards he set for himself baffled him, and his performances were playlets of despair and triumph which left you keenly experiencing his pride and humiliation. During one contest, he kept missing his shots and tossing his arms in the air after every try. His failure was agonizing to see, but he didn't stop shooting—the player who stops shooting when he misses isn't meant for basketball—and finally one jumper fell through the net. Elated, Davis pummeled the air one final time, his fists doing a war dance over his head. The gesture was so violently explosive that he tripped over his own feet and almost fell flat on the floor.

Not all the players were so spirited. The Knicks had two centers. John Gianelli had played several years for the team. He had been chosen to replace Willis Reed, the gloriously gifted, heroically inspiring center of the championship teams. Gianelli was an unlikely substitute. Tall, thin, diffident, he played in an anxious and resentful manner, a sharp contrast to his shorter, powerfully built, black, enormously proud, and straightforward predecessor. Gianelli's talents were always debated. To this day, Holzman insists Gianelli's a good ballplayer. But for many Knick fans he was, at best, a sometimes decent performer for whom the game seemed to be more exercise than pleasure. He had a nice, soft shot and practiced fundamentals; but he lacked authority on court, the prime quality a center needs. The fans booed him mercilessly and he griped about them. Finally, the Knicks traded for a backup, a journeyman, named Neal Walk. A prized college player when he entered the pros, Walk had shone in his first seasons, then undergone a change of heart, grown a beard, and turned vegetarian, questioning his previous love of competition. He and Gianelli vied for the starting position and for a while the rivalry resulted in excellent performances. When Walk finally replaced Gianelli as a starter, the daunted Gianelli entered the game as a sub and immediately slam-dunked the ball, an exciting and unusual display for him. But, eventually, the strategy of pitting one against the other failed: Instead of the friction between them producing sparks that would fire the team, it just wore the two of them down. They ended the season as twins, each reflecting the other's commendable but uninspiring virtues, and understandable but unforgivable faults.

The Knicks' troubles on the court led them into other difficulties. In the championship years, the Garden had often been packed: The Knicks had been one of pro basketball's first teams to enjoy frequent sellouts. With the team's decline, fans stayed away—even the black teenage scalpers who loudly shout, "Tickets! Got tickets?" every fifty feet on the way to the box office complained about the poor attendance. The team needed to upgrade itself to attract crowds and made a series of deals to acquire better players.

These transactions were as dramatic as any good game. Details of domestic life attended each exchange—a player was traded to New Orleans after he had just purchased a house in New Jersey—but the public stories of the athletes were more intriguing than their private ones. These men were like natural resources: The exploitation of their talents generated wealth. The heart of the whole industry, they were fought for with money, influence, and the law. The stories chronicling the legal and corporate struggles to control them were a daily education in business, and not just basketball. In the early seventies many sports reporters sought to describe the athletic world realistically and not, in Red Smith's words, "God up the ballplayers." They often offered startlingly complete accounts of the personalities, transactions, and negotiations determining the future of the team. Such accounts included a good deal of business information—tax write-offs, city bond issues, congressional lobbies, power structures in major American cities—and discussed these items with less respect and more common sense than they received in the business section of the same newspapers.

Greedier and richer than most other teams, the Knicks were in the midst of these frays, and you couldn't properly root for them without receiving instruction in contract law, NBA politics, and the psychology of young millionaire players and their older and richer millionaire owners. Practically every player they acquired arrived with a history of legal entanglements. At the age of twenty-two, one had already starred in college, signed with a team that folded, jumped leagues, and was the subject of a threatened suit. Another was so highly prized that the Knicks paid him a substantial bonus to sign a multimillion-dollar contract; the contract was contested by another team, but the money was for him to keep even if the court eventually ruled against the Knicks. (They did; the team lost everywhere those days.) The purchase of several players demanded elaborate negotiations in which the participants abruptly ended and resumed the talks more frequently than any grandstanding corporate attorney hoping to impress a recalcitrant labor-union leader, and, in one instance, a lawsuit that threatened to change the rules governing the NBA and all organized sports. And the men fighting these battles were often from the elite of the financial and legal world. In the latest match—a no-time-limit affair that has continued for close to three years—some of the legal actors include Louis Nizer; Larry O'Brien, the Kennedy pol and current commissioner of the NBA; and Telford Taylor, the prosecutor at Nuremberg who now oversees any league decisions concerning players.

I also learned about the athletic problems of building a team. At first, I imagined a few stars could end the team's troubles and with fellow fans invented trades that all led to championships. These discussions were fun but pointless. Teams are delicate mechanisms, requiring a neat balance of skill and character to function well, and the Knicks proved this: In the next couple of years, they acquired several prominent players and each worked out unhappily. One was Spencer Haywood, a high-scoring, tough rebounding forward. He seemed to fit the needs of the team but played only one good year for them. His problems were social and psychological. A prideful and talkative man, á la Reggie Jackson, he was too eager to please, too quick to take offense. A knee injury hampered him during his second season as a Knick, and afterward he worried that any time he made a sudden move he would hear cartilage tearing and crumple on the floor, a fear as paralyzing as the injury itself. He claimed the injury was healing slowly; the team management implied he was malingering; the fans booed him; and disappointment ran the circle round until he was traded. Another was Bob McAdoo, one of the game's great shooters, the league's leading scorer for the previous three seasons. McAdoo is a taciturn, unsmiling, tall, lean man who prizes his privacy. Once I observed him as he was leaving the Garden. Kids seeking autographs surrounded him and he signed their ticket stubs and yearbooks while distractedly trying to hail a cab. By the time he had satisfied the last fan, he had missed all the cabs and started to walk up Eighth Avenue, a block populated by transients—hookers, dope dealers, junkies, and commuters. He wore nondescript clothing, covering his head with a green wool sailor's cap and carrying his playing gear in a plain over-the-shoulder bag, but his height called him to people's attention and he was instantly recognized by passersby. With unseeing eyes, he walked through the crowd and past his audience, a young black man worth over half a million a year whose deadly neutral, straight-ahead gaze kept all lookers and admirers away. Fans argued about him. For all his scoring, was he a winner? His admirers—I am one—praised his shot and claimed the team relied on him too much. His detractors said he was greedy, a coward who disappeared when the last shot needed to be taken or choked at the foul line. Certainly his presence gave the team a respectability they lacked entirely without him. But his position was always a difficult one, fans and other teammates wanting him to be a leader and, at the same time, resenting his authority. In the end management decided against him, trading him for three draft picks.

Upon arrival each of these players raised my hopes for the team. My enthusiasm exaggerated their virtues and minimized their faults. Many fans decide after only one or two games how a player will disappoint them, adopting the attitude of classic Greek playwrights: Players are stamped with character and can't escape their natures. Conclusions are a joy for these fans and they don't hesitate to jump to them, even though the history of the game records lots of players whose qualities emerged slowly, seventh-round draft choices who ended up stars, and eleventh-man bench warmers who established themselves as starters. I suffered an opposite fault, clinging to my hopes too long, and looking on the development of players romantically: Character and circumstance suggested endless possibilities. I encountered this desperate attitude in others as well as myself. Several years after the Houston Rockets beat my Knicks, I traveled with the Texas squad. The club had aged into a respectable team with gifted but mismatched guards who duplicated the other's abilities rather than complementing them. The coach kept juggling with the line-up but no pair worked well for more than a game, and he resorted to increasingly bizarre and pointless combinations. The last night of the trip, the team was defeated badly and I sat with the coach as the team bus drove back to the motel from the arena. The bus was dark and the highway lights flashed periodically across his face as, in a hushed voice, he told me his latest plan, the most ill-conceived coupling yet. I asked him why he didn't just stop and let things be. He had a decent team; they would win a lot of games; why didn't he just let them play within their range? A sophisticated and ironic man, the coach looked shocked at the suggestion. "*You* can think like that," he answered bluntly, "I can't. I've got to give myself something to do with these guys for the next four months." In similar fashion, but without his financial considerations, I had to find something to root for among my Knicks.

In time, being a fan created problems. I wanted to attend more games than I could afford—all of them. Visiting the Garden, I experienced the same excitement that had thrilled me on my first trip. Usually I sat in the upper rows, the blue seats, from which the game is a ballet viewed from above. The escalator takes a good minute to reach this heaven. No matter how calmly I had left the subway station five minutes before, I would grow impatient to join the noise I heard from the arena as the escalator moved past the upper balconies. I would jump the last few steps, then hurry past the ticket-takers and down the round, wide hallways filled with strolling kids and adults, until I turned into one of the gateways leading to the arena, the noise and smell meeting me as I neared the opening of the tunnel-shaped walkway, its portals framing the disgruntled fans, chatting women, aged ushers who were the familiar characters of the evening. The last step I always hurried, not from habit, but need: the eagerness to see the game. Then I crossed into the aisle of the arena. The buzz and color of the fans surrounded me; the bright lights shone over the court; and, far below, the players performed to the cheers of the crowd. In that instant I enjoyed the relief and excitement one experiences when arriving home.

I didn't only want to attend more games. I also wanted to sit elsewhere. In the balcony there were some curiosities. One ravaged-looking man with a stark Marine crew cut used to shout out what zone defense the other team was using; another kid hated a particular referee and yelled insults and threats at him before the ref even had a chance to make a bad call. But the fans there were generally both knowledgeable and witty and showered the team with the cleverest comments and loudest boos and applause in the arena. Still, I wanted to be far away from them, down below, sitting with the men whose business had become such a source for romance in my life.

During half time, I descended to observe them at courtside. In the ten rows nearest the court, the general managers, scouts, assistant coaches, press agents, agents, and broadcasters moved around in a closed community, hailing each other, introducing wives and kids, exchanging confidences and jokes. Mostly twice my age and utterly removed from my life or background, they dressed in surburban clothes and seemed exotic and appealing to me, figures out of a modern folklore who had started the first franchises, spotted historic players before they were known, attended legendary games. In the center of the hubbub were the players. Seen from close up, the bodies that looked more or less the same from above took on distinct features: a veteran's knee was gnarled from surgery, a college kid had tree-trunk-thick thighs, a center's vast torso tapered into a wasp waist. They walked on court, out from the locker rooms where the coach had preached, pleaded, or praised them, and were greeted by girlfriends sitting in the front-row seats or old college friends or admirers standing at the press tables. They nodded and waved, a flirtatious twenty-two-year-old telling his girlfriend where to meet him after the game, and a responsible adult making sure his aunts, uncles, nieces, and nephews had gotten the seats he had left for them at the box office. They picked up a ball and started shooting, warming up with a relaxed repetition of shots. The crowd gathered around the court, jammed up at either side under the basket, taking photos and asking for autographs, sometimes one of them catching an errant ball and throwing it back, any contact with a player thrilling them, the player's recognition a kind of benefice. Then the buzzer sounded and they retired to the bench, only one player who had missed several shots in a row staying on the court, superstitiously, insistently taking jumpers until he filled the net. Before everyone in the arena had begun to return to their seats, a guard inbounded the ball, and by the time I had climbed all the way back up under the rafters, so far from all the intimacy and excitement of the court, the players whom I had observed being lovers, family, friends, and men at work were now magicians at whose tricks the audience chanted and clapped, gasped and sighed.

I envied them, envied even the hapless members of the team I taunted from above. There were players I didn't like or approve, ones uncomfortable with their talent, foolish, or mean. But even they had a certain admirable clarity to their lives. They played a kid's game but their concerns were adult: They pursued talent and success without reserve, worked daily and hard, and received the rewards or sufferings of triumph or defeat.

I rarely followed my envy of the players to its logical conclusion and imagined my life as one of them; my background was too distant from basketball for me ever to think seriously that I deserved their situation. But their example did make me question my own. Partly I had become a fan because I missed the action of the Movement. Jumpy and unpredictable, basketball is tailored for nervous types like myself, and days have a certain purpose when you root for a team and are waiting for a game to start, worrying through it, and repeating it in your mind. But in the end the players made me impatient with this satisfaction. What are you doing up here? I would think as I reached my seat. You should be *down* there, with those guys, *doing* something. The desire was a metaphor for me to exert in my life the single-minded pursuit of career and talent that they demonstrated and to do it in the same world they occupied, the world represented in that courtside confusion of

deals and budgets, high-sounding talk and low-minded principles, old friendships, new talents, and common compromises, a
world that I could no longer conceive of as alien, for it was
the only one that mattered—the real world. And so I quit
teaching to write for a living, especially writing about basketball, the simple game that taught me a lot. Through writing, I
came to attend as many games as I wanted; sat courtside
where the players loom over you and you smell the fresh talc
they rub on their hands before entering games; and met many
of the men whom I had come to admire from afar.

In the course of my work, the idea for this book was suggested to me. I eagerly seized it. I hadn't rooted for the
1969–70 Knicks—they preceded my discovery of the game—
but I had come to know them later as players and people. Together they had created the great myth of modern basketball;
after the title, the team split up and its members led every
conceivable kind of career, a patchwork quilt of distinctly
American lives that included a bouncer in a bar and a United
States senator. This book tells their story—the tale of their
triumphant collaboration on court and the individual fates
they pursued upon leaving the game of my (and their) devotion and entering the real world.

# 1969

# 1

When the New York Knickerbockers won the 1970 National Basketball Association they gained two titles. The first was titular and ephemeral. They entered the record book as the season's best professional basketball team. The second was permanent and actual. They became the game's dream team, the instance of how basketball should be played and why it should be watched, the moment of superb mastery in the sport.

Several factors combined to produce this result.

Aesthetically, the Knicks were flawless. They played textbook basketball—high-school and college coaches said a good game by the Knicks was an education for young players—and were exciting to watch. Against first-rate competition and without a spectacular physical specimen, such as Wilt Chamberlain, to overwhelm other teams, they outplayed their opponents, using all five men in the floor play, passing the ball smartly, taking advantage of their opponents' defensive lapses, and shooting with a pleasing accuracy. Upon their triumph, Leonard Koppett, sportswriter for the *New York Times*, wrote: "Rarely has a team won a championship with such a purity of accomplishment." There have been teams with greater single stars, teams that won more games and more championships, but no squad ever performed with such consistent intelligence as the Knicks, ever fulfilled more completely the ideal of collective grace and execution to which the game is devoted—was ever, in short, more a team.

Commercially, they elevated the game from a regional and seasonal sport to the status of a national pastime that commanded prime-time ratings and the front pages of the country's leading newspapers and magazines. Before the Knickerbockers, the Boston Celtics with Bill Russell had dominated professional basketball, winning eleven championships in thirteen seasons, but the game's appeal had remained limited to a few cities—the Celtics didn't sell out even in Boston. The Knicks won when the league was expanding and they attracted celebrities, crowds, and publicity. During the championship season, Madison Square Garden sold out thirty-seven times and the team drew almost a half a million customers on the road. They changed the image of basketball from an athletic contest performed in grungy arenas before cigar-smoking bettors to a fashionable entertainment featuring skilled craftsmen and attended by such stars as Robert Redford, Woody Allen, Elliott Gould, and Zero Mostel. They were the subject of serious articles in such periodicals as the *New York Times* Sunday Magazine and *Esquire*, and after the team clinched the championship at least three members published autobiographies and there were two book accounts of the season. Largely because of the influence of the team, basketball was acclaimed to be the sport of the seventies.

Culturally, they became one of the year's monuments and mementos. The year was climactic politically and socially. Nixon had just assumed the presidency, and as he introduced his domestic and foreign policies, the most dramatic features of the counterculture appeared and were widely adopted. The *Times* Sunday Magazine entered the new decade with four main articles: One concerned the making of a Chinese Red Guard, another was a portrait of the Charlie Manson family, a third on the war in Laos, and the last about Weatherman, the underground faction of Students for a Democratic Society that had disappeared and was soon to be credited with a series of bombings. That spring National Guardsmen shot four students at Kent State University, the killings precipitating student strikes across the country. Later one of the students at Kent State, a Vietnam vet, said: "I don't know where I'll be [in the future], but I hope I'm not in the same shoes my father's in right now. Because the world he's given me to grow up in hasn't worked for him, and we can't go downhill much further." Along with mobilizations against the war, all-night communal criticism-self-criticism sessions, and new albums by the Rolling Stones, the Knicks were one of the symbols for the period. Indeed, the team is often one of the few items remembered unequivocally from then because while people still laugh embarrassedly at the mention of their first acid trip or resent a political leader who manipulated them, they associate the Knicks with one emotion solely: pleasure.

The men who collaborated to produce this triumph were a diverse and uniquely American crew. There were five whites, all bred in the Midwest, a Jewish coach and Irish general manager representing the eastern metropolises, and seven blacks who came from regions as varied as the Oak Cliff section of Dallas and Far Rockaway, Queens. All but one had strict proletarian origins, their athletic mastery sparing them the anonymous lives of their parents. Their fathers included a Gary steelworker, a Detroit barkeeper, an Atlanta dude, a woodcutter in a Louisiana sawmill. The one exception was the president of a bank in Crystal City, Missouri, who had worked his way up from railroad ticket seller and yard clerk: "The feel of money seemed to appeal to me," he once said to explain his financial success, sounding as though he were a player describing a favorite shot.

Their player-sons differed widely in their experience off the court. Bill Bradley, the son of the banker, distinguished himself as a Rhodes scholar Princeton graduate—he opens his book about playing basketball with a quote from F. Scott Fitzgerald—and even as an undergraduate was so accomplished and respected that his college coach predicted the star would govern his home state before reaching forty. Willis Reed, the team's captain and spiritual leader, grew up on his grandparents' farm in Louisiana chopping cotton and picking watermelon, and took pride in the patience and skill he displayed as a hunter, a craft he had begun to master even as a young child. Red Holzman, the coach, lived as a proper suburbanite on Long Island. On days when he wasn't leading the team through a scrimmage, looking at films of games and players, traveling with the team, or coaching his players, he went to the track or played tennis. Nights after games he enjoyed exotic New York restaurants—"Scungilli," he once answered a reporter who inquired where he had first heard the news of an important trade, "I was eating scungilli"—and caught late-night television movies. One of the team's youngest members, Phil Jackson, was the son of Pentecostal ministers; during the championship season he experienced a religious crisis in his search for the nature of being and reality.

Even their experience of the game they shared varied. Bradley once practiced on the *Queen Elizabeth*, daily dribbling a ball down the lower corridors of the luxury liner while accompanying his mother on an ocean voyage. Walt Frazier, the son of the Atlanta hustler, worked out on dirt courts in the segregated city park near his home. Reed played college ball in relative obscurity; the star of a local all-black school, he discovered he was ranked a possible All-American by browsing through some basketball magazines while waiting at a small-town bus depot. For Cazzie Russell, the team's top substitute, and Dave DeBusschere, its star forward, talent brought acclaim. Russell attracted a national following as a college star and a two-hundred-thousand-dollar contract as a rookie in the pros. DeBusschere was such a local favorite in Detroit that soon after joining the city's professional team, the Pistons, he was named the squad's player-coach. For others, the sport was an experience of profound and pleasurable isolation. "What attracted me was the sound of the swish," Bradley once said, "the sound of the dribble, the feel of going up in the air. You don't need eight others, like in baseball. You don't need any brothers or sisters. Just you." The night of his senior prom, Dick Barnett practiced on the court outside the school, playing in the darkness. "I saw [my classmates] but they couldn't see me because it was dark. After a while, you'd adjust to the darkness and could play. You had a comfortable feeling about where you were. . . . Even when they couldn't see me, they could hear the ball and they knew that it was me, Barnett, alone, shooting on Roosevelt playground."

In one season, these young masters—Barnett, the group's veteran was but thirty-four—achieved more success than most people claim in a lifetime. Their triumph lasted for only an instant—the team was being dismantled less than a month after it had won the championship—but their collective deed transformed them into unique personages: the creators and objects of a moment when all elements combined to produce perfection.

# 2

The center of the team, both literally and figuratively, was Willis Reed. He played the position and was the team's indispensable leader.

Center is the dominant position in basketball. When you watch a game, the center is often the tallest player on the court—in several instances also the widest—and he usually stands close to the basket. The team's offense and defense revolve around him.

Like quarterbacks and pitchers, the center performs a unique offensive function. He is the only member of the team to play with his back to the basket. This position affords him numerous ways to score: hooks, turning to take a short jumper or lay-up, or, if he's a player blessed with strong knees he can stuff the ball (only sometimes breaking the backboard, à la Darryl Dawkins). At the same time, he also threatens to pass the ball to a teammate, all of whom, on a good squad, constantly circle around him, their paths drawing more or less imaginary ellipses, every several seconds one of them escaping from the opponent guarding him and running toward the basket, a particle flying off from the nucleus of an atom. If the play is executed correctly, the moment will be magical: The player moves suddenly toward the basket, the center bounces the ball behind his back at exactly the right instant, and the player picks up the ball and deposits it off the backboard into the hoop.

Similarly, centers can dominate a game defensively. Sometimes merely their presence changes another team's offensive tactics. Their height, width, and strength will scare opponents away from the hoop, force them to pass too much, shoot from beyond their normal range, or vaingloriously decide to challenge the center once and for all, matching their speed or cleverness against the big man's bulk and pride, creating a momentary clash of arms, legs, and ball most notable for its use as a blowup picture demonstrating the action in the game.

Reed's specialty as a center was to combine both offensive and defensive skills. In the universally respected judgment of Red Auerbach, the architect of the Boston Celtics, Reed was "perhaps the most versatile of all the great, big men." Enjoying a variety of shots, he scored regularly and impressively, hitting almost 50 percent of all his tries, making his neat, soft, left-handed jumper even at considerable distances from the basket. His marksmanship made him troublesome to guard. If you played him closely, trying to block his shot, he might move around you, and barrel his way past other defenders on a scoring trip to the basket; if you stayed away from him, prohibiting a drive to the hoop, he would probably make his shot. He collected rebounds methodically, often gathering over twenty for several consecutive games. His accurate outside shooting drew opposing centers away from the basket, opening up the hoop for other Knicks; and, a massive and mobile six feet nine, he guarded his basket, allowing his teammates to gamble on defense, trying to steal the ball without worrying if the man they were guarding passed them: He would only meet Reed on any journey inside the key. Finally, he set immovable picks, planting his huge, thick body in an opponent's path and freeing a teammate for an uncontested shot.

Reed's strength was prodigious. In one of the less glorious seasons that preceded the Knicks' championship year, Reed fought with the Los Angeles Lakers. Phil Jackson recalled the impression the fight made on him in a book he wrote in 1975, after eight years on the team. At the time Jackson was a senior at the University of North Dakota. Drafted by the Knicks, he received a game film from his new team, one of the black-and-white, 16-millimeter reels that constitute the main visual record of the sport. Jackson called up some friends, bought a keg of beer, and held a party. After a while he and his friends began to laugh at the film because they found the players' performances stupid and selfish, much inferior to the "intelligent style of ball we had been taught." Then "there was a jump ball . . . the next thing we saw was the Knicks' Willis Reed being attacked by every Laker in sight. Three players jumped on his back and somebody else was grabbing him and hitting him in the face. Willis was knocked to the floor and had all of these guys hanging on him, when he seemed to get an infusion of energy and strength. He just stood up and shook everybody off. At that point, it ceased to be a fight and became a massacre. Willis punched John Block in the nose, hit Henry Finkel in the head, and dumped Rudy LaRusso onto the floor. Another Knick, Emmette Bryant, was running around jumping on people's backs and kicking players in the head, but I couldn't take my eyes off Willis. He was a huge, barrel-chested man who weighed at least 250 pounds. He was shrugging 230 pounders off of him like a bear shaking off the rain. We ran the entire episode back and forth about five times in disbelief . . . I had never seen anybody that strong in my life."

Of course, there were men stronger than Reed, even players: Jackson had never heard how a busboy at Kutscher's country club named Wilt Chamberlain used to change flat tires by lifting the car while a co-worker took off the wheel. But Reed's strength was formidable because it was matched by a seemingly indomitable will. As a college graduate, he had been rejected as a first-round draft choice by the NBA clubs; after playing his rookie season at center, he had suffered the humiliation of the Knicks acquiring another player for the position and being transferred to forward. Still, he persevered. His premiere season in the NBA, he won the Rookie of the Year award; after being switched to play forward, he was voted an all-star at the position. "I played as if every game were a war," he once told Pete Axthelm, the author of *The City Game*, one chronicle of the Knicks' championship year. "Let's face it; if I didn't make it here, where would I have gone?" He was the "captain," the man who had experienced all the slow progress and hard times of the team's journey toward the crown, counselor to other players, intimidator of opponents, public spokesperson for the team, an exemplary player who succeeded by sheer insistent labor. "I feel better," wrote Bill Bradley on playing with Reed, "for being part of his effort."

The team's next key defensive player was Dave De-Busschere. DeBusschere was the strong forward for the Knicks. Forwards are the corner men in basketball. They stand shorter than centers, taller than guards, and share the talents of both. Strong forwards are distinguished by their rebounding and defense. They are among the specialists who have taken over basketball in the past decade—small forwards, defensive centers, dominating centers, and a veritable plague of guards, shooting, tall, lead, and penetrating. These titles often mask an overall ineptitude—some penetrating guards can't hit the rim from more than five feet out. But power forwards are exempt from the criticism. The term was invented to describe DeBusschere's play—"he was the epitome of the position," says Paul Silas, a veteran forward who shares some of DeBusschere's talents. Study the criteria used to determine whether or not a player is a power forward and after diligent comparison of physical specifications, minutes played, rebounds caught, shots taken, and all the facts that draw a player's profile, and you will still find that the answer to only one question satisfactorily decides the issue: Does the player remind you of DeBusschere?

DeBusschere displayed both special physical and mental qualities. "I had in mind," wrote James Naismith, the inventor of the game, "the tall, agile, graceful, and expert athlete." DeBusschere fits the description. A physical talent who took naturally to sports, he played both professional basketball and baseball his first four years after graduating college. He stood six feet six, but appeared, and, as they say, *played* taller because his height was honest: His neck wasted few inches. He was broad and powerful, weighing almost as much as Reed, a muscular 230 pounds that he threw around in games—as he wrote in a published diary of the team's championship year, he enjoyed contact on the court. Finally, he enjoyed the coordination of men smaller and slighter than himself, performing honorably at guard in college and when he first entered the pros, dribbling, passing, and shooting from the outside with a unique ability for a man his size.

But DeBusschere's most memorable quality was his mental attitude: the concentration, effort, and enthusiasm he brought to the game. Offensively, he was no slouch—for his professional career average, he scored sixteen points per game, and though he wasn't the most reliable shooter, hitting only a little more than 40 percent of his shots, he always threatened to score, taking his shot approximately fifteen times a game. Still, the Knicks, with some of the game's all-time great shooters, didn't particularly need his scoring power. They relied on him for defense: not fancy steals or dramatically blocked shots, but a steady pressure that nabbed key rebounds and forced the other team's leading scorers into bad shots. Defense is the part of basketball that depends on will. It's sad but true that you can't become a great shooter or shot blocker simply by applying yourself: You need the gifts of instinct, daring, and touch. With defense it's the other way around. Even possessing all of nature's talents, you'll still lose your man and give up two points if your attention flags. At his best, DeBusschere remained vigilant throughout a game, his intelligence and effort upsetting the offensive mechanism of the other team. Bill Bradley, in his book *Life on the Run*, says there was always contact between DeBusschere and the man he was guarding, and one of the team's rookies told another writer that when DeBusschere entered a game, "for six, seven, eight minutes . . . you don't even see the man he's guarding. He cuts him off from the ball, takes him right out of the game." In one late-season contest, he shot two for seventeen, a truly nightmarish performance, but got twenty-six rebounds. Afterward, Holzman commented on DeBusschere: "He is a great all-around player. He played thirty-four minutes just on the strength of other contributions—defense, rebounding, and knowledge of the game. Few other players could have stayed in there with such a poor shooting night."

Frequently his skills won games. One memorable Knick accomplishment in the championship year was a record-setting eighteen-game winning streak. (Though everyone tramps in once you open the door. The next year the Bucks won twenty, and the Los Angeles Lakers passed them in the following season with a still unsurpassed thirty-three). The night the Knicks went for the record, they trailed a mediocre Cincinnati squad by five points with sixteen seconds left. By his own account, DeBusschere had played badly, Holzman even benching him through most of the fourth quarter. Desperate to reclaim his pride and save the winning streak, DeBusschere figured the options as Cincinnati prepared to inbound the ball. Correctly predicting the receiver, he intercepted the pass and scored on a breakaway dunk. The play saved the day: Rattled, the Cincinnati players lost the ball again and the Knicks won by a point. Such efforts are memorialized in the photographs of the man. Even in the shots of him on the bench, he never appears distracted or relaxed. Eyes squinting, he looks at the court or the twenty-four-second clock or the scoreboard overhead; the corners of his mouth are turned up in pain or just from the dryness that makes your throat ache when you've run too hard, and his meaty, thick legs are stretched out before him in exhaustion and relief.

Complementing DeBusschere in the other corner was Bill Bradley, the team's small forward. Bradley stood an even six feet five and weighed a little over two hundred pounds. Dressed in street clothes, he looked like a college letterman turned businessman and not a celebrated professional athlete. In college, his physique didn't hinder him; he ran his Princeton team, leading the squad in every offensive category. But he floundered during his first pro seasons because he couldn't play a complete game either at guard or forward. He was taller but slower than most backcourt men, and quicker but shorter than most forwards; and he couldn't leap an inch—the Knicks joked that even at the height of his jump you could still slip an average *New York Times* between the soles of his sneakers and the floor. Then he was paired with DeBusschere and the bigger man's abilities freed Bradley to concentrate on his own strengths. Never an altogether commanding performer, he became a player whose contributions, as the commentators say, couldn't be found in the box scores. He played a nagging, distracting defense, pulling and picking at the other player. He ran constantly, moving, as the expression goes, without the ball, rather than waiting for a pass from a teammate, overcoming his slowness with an endurance that eventually wore down his opponent. He shot a consistently accurate jumper, releasing his high-arching shot with a quick flick. And, with his alertness, he interrupted plays, batting the ball away from an opponent, and made them, passing promptly to a teammate. Presently the small forwards in the league all possess more spectacular physical talents than Bradley, and manage, for him, unimaginable feats—rebounding, dunking, and freeing themselves for shots rather than needing their teammates to secure for them the grace of a moment's clear view of the basket. But Bradley was one of the most successful pioneers of their position, and with DeBusschere combined to create the mobile and combative front court that remains the ideal toward which teams strive.

Bradley was the most prestigious member of the team. He was a legendary college player. As a junior he led the Olympic team to victory in Japan. As a senior he took a group of scantily talented Princeton undergraduates into the final rounds of the National Collegiate Athletic Association championship, and, though his team lost, won personal honors as most valuable player, the tourney's player of the year, and unanimous All-American. He was the fourth highest all-time college scorer, averaging 30.1 points a game, and received the Sullivan Award, an annual honor given by the Amateur Athletic Union to the nation's outstanding athlete, a distinction the organization had never before bestowed on a basketball player.

In themselves, the number and variety of these testimonials separate Bradley from the average college star who surfaces with crocus-like predictability each year at play-off time in March. But Bradley won honors besides these that set him apart. He turned down numerous scholarship offers, paying to attend Princeton instead. He graduated a Rhodes scholar and went on to Oxford. At twenty, he was granted the respect usually reserved for men three times his age, and a normally sober-minded journalist on the *New York Post* once wrote that as he contemplated this uncertain world he was comforted by the fact that in just twenty-five years Bradley could run for President. He was wealthy, famous, white, and Christian—as an undergraduate he addressed groups as a representative of the Fellowship of Christian Athletes—and he embodied the middle-class notion of the way a knight-errant should behave: Diligent, courteous, modest, he made his privilege seem a burden while never giving it up.

Even so normally reliable a witness of human imperfections as John McPhee, the *New Yorker* writer, idolized Bradley. When Bradley was a senior, John McPhee profiled him in the *New Yorker*. (The piece was later expanded into a book entitled *A Sense of Where You Are.*) The piece fashioned Bradley's public image. McPhee had played basketball himself, but the work is remarkably innocent. One afternoon, McPhee watched Bradley shoot hoops at a new neighborhood gym. Bradley kept missing and, after several of these inexplicable goofs, he commented the basket was an inch and a half low. Some weeks later, McPhee returned with a ruler and found Bradley was right. McPhee uses the incident to suggest Bradley's scientific exactness as a player, but basketball players aim at baskets hundreds of times daily and knowing that the rims are high or low or loose or tight is no more a major deductive feat for them than a mechanic guessing the firing order of your spark plugs. Similarly, McPhee quotes Bradley describing his shots—the five elements that compose his hook, his reverse pivot, the trick he uses not to drift on his jumper—and we are meant to admire the delicacy of his analysis. But when this sort of minute inspection is practiced by kids on city playgrounds —albeit not as grammatically—it is considered a reflection of their lack of intellectual development. McPhee converts Bradley into an Ivy League Lone Ranger taming the town of Basketball, and moving on. ". . . basketball," he wrote, "was more a part of him than he a part of basketball." Referring to Bradley's decision not to sign with the Knicks and study at Oxford instead, a commitment that then seemed to preclude any professional career for Bradley, McPhee wrote: "The most interesting thing about Bill Bradley was not just that he was a great basketball player, but that he succeeded so amply in other things that he was doing at the same time, reached a more promising level of attainment, and, in the end, put basketball behind him because he had something better to do."

Actually what was most interesting about Bradley was his continuing attachment to basketball. Like a true romantic hero, he remained loyal to his childhood love, even when admirers, such as McPhee, cheered him for leaving her. In his book he discusses his return to the game. He reports that in Oxford he had begun "to see how far I had to grow and change if I was to become a person that even I would like to know." After not touching a basketball for nine months, he went to the Oxford gym one afternoon "simply for some long overdue exercise. There I shot alone—just the ball, the basket, and my imagination. As I heard the swish and felt my body loosen into familiar movements—the jumper, the hook, the reverse pivot—I could hear the crowd though I was alone on the floor. A feeling came over me that stirred something deep inside. I realized that I missed the game and that . . . never to play again, never to play against the best, the pros, would be to deny an aspect of my personality perhaps more fundamental than any other."

He returned to New York and signed an enormous contract for a rookie, the Knicks believing he would win games and attract fans. Again, he proved his human frailty. On his first circuit around the league, Bradley drew satisfactorily large crowds but played disappointing ball and not until his third season did he begin to contribute substantially to his team's success, though he never fulfilled the promise of his college career.

Indeed, the man's most legendary quality became his dogged, contradictory individuality. Among the club's flashy dressers, he wore almost theatrically threadbare clothes. While the team once waited for their luggage at an airport, DeBusschere noticed a small toilet case bumping down the conveyor belt with the trunks and valises. He asked Barnett why its owner hadn't just stuck the small item in his back pocket. "Ask Bradley," replied Barnett, "he's got his whole wardrobe in there." At a time when commercial endorsements were starting to pay big money to athletes, he refused to put his imprimatur on anything sold for profit. When Robert Lipsyte, sports columnist for the *Times*, inquired about his interest in penal reform, Bradley responded testily: "Well I don't run around looking for a television camera and when the red light goes on deliver my three minutes package on penal reform." But when Lipsyte asked him whether or not he was simply having fun playing with the Knicks, Bradley replied with a thesis. "I'm having fun playing the game now," Bradley said, "because we approach at times the ideal of how basketball should be played: as a real unit with unselfishness, complete cooperation, and the use of techniques to bring out these attitudinal factors—hitting the open man, helping out on defense, knowing what to do on offense and taking advantage of a situation because we know each other so well. There's a great deal of exhilaration and contentment quick on its heels. After a good first quarter, we can step back and look at it. There are not too many aspects of life where contentment follows so quickly the exhilaration of a total coordinated effort." Nicknamed "Dollar Bill," a pun noting both his parsimonious public behavior and his privilege, he became famous for his tactical cleverness and deliberation in a game usually marked by its spontaneity and simplicity. After the Knicks lost an important play-off game, he planned a strategy for the team, a complicated reordering of offensive and defensive forces that he explained to some teammates at midnight in a hotel room. "He didn't have any notes," one of the listeners admiringly told Phil Berger, the author of *Miracle on 33rd Street*, one of the books about the '69–'70 season. "He had it all in his head."

# 3

The experience of Dick Barnett, the team's backcourt veteran, was totally different from Bradley's. He was the son of a black steelworker in Gary, Indiana, a graduate of an all-black school in Tennessee, and his career was a search for recognition and reward. In 1959, he had been drafted by the Syracuse Nationals on the first round, a compliment then paid to few black players. Two years later, Abe Saperstein, a promoter who founded the Harlem Globetrotters, became miffed at his NBA friends because they reneged on their promise to give him the league's first West Coast franchise. In revenge, Saperstein founded his own American Basketball League, a short-lived organizational mishmash headed and paid for by Saperstein that operated in cities without NBA clubs. The Cleveland franchise was called the Pipers, the first professional squad to be coached by a black man, a legend named John McLendon, who won 800 of his college games and had trained Barnett in school. Barnett played in Cleveland until the ABL folded, then announced he wouldn't return to the Nats, who, suffering financially, sold him off to the Los Angeles Lakers for a then unheard-of thirty-five thousand dollars. (This sort of auction happens periodically in sports and is a good guide to inflation. During the last of these fire sales in 1976, the Knicks bought a backup center who lasted but several games; the price for gambling he would make the team was one hundred thousand dollars.) Barnett lasted two seasons in Los Angeles; an explosive scorer, he found himself stuck on the bench behind the team's offensive duo of Jerry West, commonly considered the second greatest guard ever to play the game, and

Elgin Baylor, the sport's premier offensive forward, the Dr. J. of his time. Then traded to New York, Barnett finally received some long-due praise, Holzman calling him one of the game's most consistent guards and the most underrated performer in the league.

Barnett's peripatetic journey is now more the rule than the exception: Players change teams with the insouciance of belles switching partners at a dance. But back in the sixties, before court decisions forced sports to operate as a business that didn't just profit the owners, Barnett's frequent transfers of loyalty were uncommon and he came to be seen as a mercenary, an opportunist who was as solely concerned with his own advancement as Bradley presumably was oblivious of it.

Barnett did little to dispel the image. Physically, he was unimpressive, a rangy six feet four, lacking the bulk of either Reed or DeBusschere or the exquisite proportions of other guards. His face was a mask of raised arches—high cheeks, drooping eyes, domed forehead. He did not reveal himself to reporters. "Like what the writers do is get all these anecdotes about you," he told Phil Berger, who came to admire his cynical honesty, "most of them boolshit, so that you come out like one big anecdote, like a clown." His comments during interviews were always mild, colorless. In one decisive play-off game, he scored twenty-seven points. Did you ever have a more satisfying game? asked one reporter. "Yeah," Barnett replied, ending the session.

Even as a player, Barnett didn't attract favorable attention. He was the shooting guard, also called the off-guard, the one whose primary responsibility was to score. Barnett performed this task methodically—upon retirement he was the league's all-time fourteenth highest scorer—but the honor was dubious. Everyone loves to get points in basketball—filling the hoop is the game's singular thrill—but few fans like to admire scorers. Scorers are considered showboaters and grandstanders, selfish players who lack the devotion and discipline of their teammates. Their success seems testimony to their self-

ishness, and our admiration of them appears to reveal an at-
avistic narcissism in us that we would prefer kept hidden.
Like all great masters of style, they are expendable, and no
player thrills the fans and is forgotten by them as quickly as
a great shooter.

Barnett particularly suffered this unenviable reputation.
Dressed like a dude before the style became fashionable, the
owner of a night spot called "Dick Barnett's Guys and Dolls,"
nicknamed "Skull" by the fans for his closely cropped hair,
Barnett, during his L.A. days, was considered exotic and arrogant. He was known mainly for his shot, a left-handed jumper
during which he leaned back at a slight angle and tucked his
legs under him, spasmodically jerking them after releasing the
ball. Unique and accurate—Barnett could hit from twenty-
five feet out—the shot was called "Fall back, baby" because
Barnett would sometimes challenge his opponent with these
words while shooting. Variously interpreted over the years,
the phrase is a taunt: Most obviously it means the player
should give up defensively because the shot will be good.
Players talk a lot on the court. Bradley used to confuse rookies by speaking gibberish with a teammate; trying to understand the double-talk, the rookie would be distracted and
fooled. Frazier used to yell, "Press!" making a player who was
inbounding the ball think he was about to meet pressure; the
player would become startled and Frazier would go for a
steal. Barnett's line was a direct put-down, a cousin to the cur-
rently popular "Face!"—the epithet uttered by street players
after they made a shot in your you-know-what. The challenge is annoyingly childish and Barnett's repartee, though
more clever, didn't win him many friends. (Sometimes he said
"Too late" instead, and won over even fewer allies.) He received the traditional rap against shooters—he was an incomplete and lazy ballplayer—and was named only once to the
league's annual All-Star game, not even judged worthy of the
honor during his first year in New York, when he averaged 28

points a game, fourth highest among all players for the season. This estimation of him overlooked his considerable craft. He wasn't deficient defensively. Actually, he often guarded the other team's top backcourt scorer, and while there are no exact statistics in basketball to measure defense, he was an integral part of the team's defensive machinery, the best in the league. His offensive achievement is also admirable. For fourteen years, Barnett played approximately one hundred games per season. In this time, he was paired with teammates of widely differing talents and characters, including most of the premier backcourt performers, and against players of equally various gifts, performing in gyms as discrepant as the players, before crowds that ranged from familiar hometown rooters to racist hecklers, and in game situations that changed according to the weather, schedule, referees, and emotional climate of both clubs. Throughout all this and working with and against all these curious peers, Barnett was assigned to one task—to score. And he succeeded, hitting almost one of every two shots for 15 points a contest. As Holzman implied, this was a considerable record of consistent achievement, as solid, in its way, and certainly as necessary for the triumph of a team, as the work performed by a steady rebounder.

The image of Barnett as a trigger-happy shooter also didn't square with some of his other qualities. He trained exceptionally hard. He exercised after every game, to ease the pains that were his inheritance from his professional career; and after ten years in the league, he spent a summer playing ball to get in shape for the season. His assessments of situations were invariably realistic. At Syracuse, he understood he would never receive top dollar because he was a substitute and demanded to be traded; in Los Angeles, he realized he would never receive the star billing he deserved because he couldn't compete with West and Baylor. Forgetting the general pieties, he insisted that winning mattered most in one's career. After the Knicks took the championship, people said Barnett had improved defensively. Barnett disagreed. "Winning is the cure for everything," he explained about the change of opinion. "All faults are forgiven . . . I thought I played the same defense ever since I came into this league."

He was also an ironist. During one game, he got the ball at midcourt and forgot which basket was his. He promptly passed the ball to Frazier. "I figured I couldn't lose that way," he explained later. "I knew I had to get credit for an assist and if that was the wrong basket Frazier would be the goat." One day DeBusschere appeared in an oversized raincoat. "London Fog?" intoned Barnett, "that sucker cover all of London." He invented a cry (Boo-ay!) the Knicks used in the locker room to shame a teammate, and he was unsparing in his critique of the social life of his comrades. During training camp, he criticized Reed's attentions to a woman: "Back in New York, you don't know her; out here you act like she was Hedy Lee-mar or something." To Berger, he said: "After you leave that arena you just another brother out there." And he was equally honest about his abiding and finally inexplicable commitment to the game. "I don't know what it does for me," he told one interviewer, talking about his habit during the off-season of playing for a couple of hours to "revive" himself. "Only . . . when I start to play nothing else exists. Call it an escape from reality if you want."

Even after the championship, critics knocked him. In 1970 the NBA created three new teams. To stock them, each club performed a triage, selecting its most expendable players and casting their names in a lot from which the new club owners formed their squads. It is, of course, an insult to be picked for this sacrifice, but several New York sportswriters suggested Barnett's name be included. But for others he was an existential hero, sworn to truth, a willing victim of his own bad faith, a stylist shorn of pretense, a heroic lumpenproletariat.

Paired with Barnett in the backcourt was Walt Frazier, the team's guiding genius. He was the club's playmaking guard, the one assigned to set and execute the unit's offensive patterns. He distinguished himself in this role and became one of the game's finest performers. In the championship year, he averaged close to 40 minutes a game, made over half of all his attempted field goals to score 20.9 points a game, and was credited for 6 rebounds and 8 assists in each contest. He was never rated as the game's greatest guard—that honor belongs unequivocally to Oscar Robertson, and, after him, Jerry West —and, essentially a suggestible person, Frazier never became the court general people expected him to be. Still, almost from the start with the Knicks, he was charged with the team's success or failure. "Actually, the unheralded giant of the Knicks' revival has been Frazier," wrote one *Times* reporter explaining the team's 1969 winning streak that presaged their championship season. "There is an adage that statistics don't lie. Frazier's value to New York can best be demonstrated by the scoring, rebounding, and assist figures in the last three games." And, a year later, when the Knicks momentarily waffled going toward the championship, he was blamed. "When Walt Frazier is tired or uninspired," wrote Robert Lipsyte, "the Knicks do not look like the world's greatest basketball team . . . Willis Reed may be the only indispensable Knick, but Frazier is the ignition key to the smooth running mechanism at its best."

Frazier was the most magical player on the team, the one whose performances seemed inexplicable. The points, rebounds, assists, and minutes played of the others appeared the result of effort; to some extent, all conscientiously presented their mastery as a prize won only through hard work. Frazier had labored as studiously as any of them. Of his attributes as a player only his hand-eye coordination was a gift; the rest had been acquired through practice. But publicly none of his strenuous exertion showed. Instead Frazier projected an image of effortless, commanding grace.

Simply put, Frazier was beautiful to watch. His physical appearance was entrancing: brown, flawless skin, a compact, lithe body, the curved, vast, broad eyelids of an Assyrian statue, and a beard that changed seasonally from sideburns to muttonchops to a kingly bushiness. He moved with cunning, ease, and immense self-possession, the sort of studied gestures movies have taught us to associate with bullfighters and samurai swordsmen. During a game every act was deliberate. He started under the basket, inbounding the ball. Was the other team pressing his teammates? Frazier waits calmly until one gets clear. At his discretion, he bounces a neat pass to his man, gets the ball back, and begins his journey, his eyes set ahead on the players downcourt as they circle around the perimeter of the basket. At half court his opponent meets him. Looking straight at the man, Frazier dribbles behind his back, now controlling the ball with his other hand, unexpectedly advancing on the side of the court opposite from the one he was approaching. In the clear now, he begins his play. He flips a short behind-the-back pass; dribbles the ball, and spins out a pass, his arm sweeping behind him, the ball flying off to his side as he continues to run forward; shovel passes the ball, his hand scooping up the leather on the bounce and flinging it toward a teammate downcourt. Or he takes his jump shot, holding himself steady in the air, his forearm set directly toward the basket, his body, for one moment, suspended above the court, then releasing the ball in a smooth arch that one out of every two times ends by plopping through the net at the same time that his feet softly touch wood. The next time down, his opponent expects him to shoot and, knowing this, Frazier fakes him out. Crouching, he leans forward and pumps his torso upward. Thinking Frazier's about to jump, the man guarding him flies into the air to block the shot and Frazier releases the ball as the patsy crashes into him. The trick provides him with three possible benefits: The opposing player is called for the foul; Frazier goes to the line to shoot free throws; and, sometimes, the ball, really just tossed up by Frazier right before the collision occurs, finds its home and falls into the basket. This time, it misses the mark but Frazier goes to the foul line, taking his time as he shoots his free throws, bending low, the line of his arms a perfect parallel to the angle of his legs, the muscles in his body sculpting the air around him. Now it is the fourth period and Frazier is tired. Going for a rebound, he falls and lies stretched out on the floor, hands at his side, knees bent, slowly regaining his breath, taking the full twenty-second injury time-out. He leaves the game and sits on the bench wearing the same undistracted, straight-ahead stare he dons during games, his hooded eyelids masking every expression but concentration and acceptance, until Holzman summons him for service again. Then he strides slowly to the scorer's table, says "sub" while pointing a finger to indicate he's going back onto the court, tucks his shirt into his shorts, and joins his teammates. The crowd cheers his return, but Frazier doesn't acknowledge their happiness, looking impassively at the baseline where his opponent prepares to inbound the ball. He sets himself and, as the opposing guard dribbles upcourt, Frazier suddenly slaps at the ball, pokes it free, and runs downcourt to his own basket, chased by the victim and the cheers of the crowd. There, alone, he rises in the air for an uncontested lay-up. He is in the clear, his opponent having already ceded the basket, but as he extends his hand toward the hoop he transforms one fundamental bit of caution all coaches insist on into a balletic gesture and turns his head majestically to make sure no one will interfere with his offering. Then he places the ball softly off the glass—again, just the way you're taught in school—and resumes his defensive position as soon as he touches the floor. The game has been won.

Frazier was lauded for his defense. He was picked for the league's all-defensive team six times and made fashionable the notion that stopping a player from getting points is as valuable as scoring some yourself. Later in his career, younger players said Frazier had always been overrated defensively, arguing he was slow, and that most guards could drive by him. Indeed, Frazier never was particularly speedy—it's hard to tell how fast NBA guards are playing because all are so quick—but he compensated for his slowness with intelligence. He forced opponents into troublesome areas of the court or left his man altogether, beating him to where he wanted to go. He also made steals a dramatic and significant part of the game, his sudden thefts of the ball not only adding to the Knick point total but also frustrating and confusing the opponents. The year after the championship, he wrote a book and discussed his craft. He often kept a little distance between himself and the man he was guarding, he explained, calling this tactic a phantom defense. "I try to keep the dribbler in suspense about where I am. I don't crowd him and this way he has to keep feeling for me, looking to see where I'm lurking." He noted the peculiarities of their play, when and how they passed, and the rhythm of their dribble—"I want to learn the cadence, so I can flick my hand in there at just the right time." Never lunge, he cautioned, because the sudden move will leave you out of position (and, the constant corollary in Frazier's lessons, doing something wrong always makes you look bad). Finally he catalogued all the different steals he made—the guard-to-guard-pass steal; the not-meeting-your-pass steal; the dribbling-the-ball-without-protecting-it-with-your-body steal; the possum-game steal, where you knock the ball from behind; and the majority of steals, the lying-in-wait-as-the-opposing-unsuspecting-guard-goes-around-your-man's-pick steal. To Phil Berger, he added one other. "A lot of guys get careless on the inbounds pass," he explained. "And sometimes they'll just get mad because their man just scored a basket. So my theory is that just like in football when you go for the bomb after an interception. You catch them when they're still unsettled. It's all in figuring how you would feel in that position, you'd feel the same way."

Off the court, Frazier conducted himself with a mannered self-assurance and puppyish enthusiasm. Born and raised in

Atlanta, the oldest male in a house of women, he spoke in a soft and inquiring voice—even when refusing a request he sounded as though he were politely asking a question. He dressed brilliantly. Early on, he wore the mode sixties' fashions, buying so many outfits that he eventually had to put a clothes rack in the otherwise nondescript hotel room he used as his home during the season. He dated beautiful women, displaying them at the various night spots he frequented after games. His enthusiasm for the game and his performances were infectious, even when silly. In the locker room, he invented little quips for the reporters. He told them he was so fast he could steal hubcaps off a moving car and caught so many flies in midair the insects now stayed out of his way. "Fast hands, fast feet," he said, "I'm so fast I scare even me." The reporters took everything down including his almost mystical accounts of victories: "If I make a few steals, get a few passes going really well, hit a few jumpers, I get that feeling that it's going to be one of those beautiful nights. We all start moving in the right groove, the fans get behind us, and something really very special happens out there. After a while I feel I can do anything." He was dubbed several names. Nate Bowman, the team's substitute center, nicknamed him Clyde, after the character in Warren Beatty's film. But Holzman perhaps more correctly called him his key man. "Every time we'd leave a hotel, he'd sneak all the room keys in my pocket," Frazier wrote. "I'd come home and have maybe eight keys weighing me down. Like he'd get all the reporters' keys, too, and dump them in my coat. I'd have them falling out of every pocket." In the coach's understated fashion, the phrase referred obliquely to Frazier's central importance to the team. Prodigious and mercurial, Frazier, more than any other player, stamped the club with his personality—its reputation for cool responses under pressure, style rather than strength, and intelligence instead of sheer insistence was an extension of the qualities he brought to the court.

# 4

Part of the Knick style was the club's second team. Basketball squads are commonly composed of twelve players—five starters, three frequently used subs, and four bench warmers, sparring partners for the starters during practices and understudies during games. The three subs, the second team, are vital for a club to enjoy a winning season. The demands of the pro game, with its long, cross-country, three-season schedule, will burn out the emotional and physical resources of even the most resilient players and a club must have substitutes who can spell the starters, coming off the bench and keeping a lead or reversing a losing score, shooters and skilled defensive performers who will accept their supporting roles and can bring their skills to bear immediately in tense situations. Teams blessed with such athletes fulfill a requisite of triumphant squads, winning the games they need to and not losing the ones they shouldn't, a feat the Knicks accomplished regularly. Their second team would have been starters on most other clubs—nine out of their twelve players that year were first-round draft choices—and in time fans came to say that the club's subs won games for the team. This was an overstatement because the bench only ensured victory, but each member did play as distinct a role and present as sharply defined a character as any of the club's starting five.

Mike Riordan was the club's third guard, usually replacing Barnett. "One of the things that helped Barnett throughout the season," Frazier wrote coyly in his book, "was Riordan coming in for him and playing good ball. That way Dick could get a longer rest on the bench, come back in fresh and get us lots of points in a short time." Riordan was the protagonist of one of pro basketball's exemplary tales. Born in New York, graduate of Providence College, he had been picked by the Knicks in the eleventh round of the draft. He had worked his way onto the team after two years as a player in the Eastern League. Pro basketball's equivalent of baseball's minor league, an organization of players, owners, and referees, all eager to join the big time, the Eastern League more often serves as a pathway to defeat rather than a stairway to success. The life is largely degrading—fans who spit on you, incompetent referees, showers that don't work, the sort of humiliations that make nice memories only if you eventually become a star —and the athletic competition is basically unrewarding. Now serious players who don't make the pros bypass the league completely, going to Europe where stardom, tax-free incomes, and a certain social notoriety await them. In 1970, this option didn't exist and Riordan's passage from the crummy arenas of his apprenticeship to an average playing time of twenty minutes a game in the Garden became a favorite sentimental tale for fans.

Riordan was a scrapper. His face displayed a nervous and pugnacious intelligence—eager eyes, a sharp chin, thick hair. He read papers constantly and slept with the windows wide open during winter. ". . . he buys papers and papers," Phil Jackson complained to Phil Berger about him, a country boy discussing the quintessential New Yorker. "He'll buy a *Times* coming [into the city], a *Post* while he's in the city, and the *Daily News* going home from a game. He reads four papers a day—he gets the Long Island paper delivered to his house . . . it's like he doesn't ever sit back and think to himself and close his eyes and relax, you know." His roommate, another country fellow named Bill Hosket, who came from Ohio to play for the Knicks, repeated the charge. "He thinks just because I like to sit down and eat a meal like DeBusschere or Bradley or anybody—any normal individual like yourself—he thinks that I'm lazy and fat, calls me Burly Bear because I like to sit down and wait on food. He's probably the most impatient person I've ever met."

As a player, Riordan first claimed attention by giving fouls. Because of a rule later changed, a team sometimes benefited by hacking an opposing player. Riordan, then the team's most expendable talent, would be called on by Holzman to do this job. Occasionally the opposing team, trying not to give the Knicks the tactical advantage, would pass the ball quickly from one man to the next, making it hard for Riordan to foul a player. To the cheers of the crowd, Riordan would success-fully pursue the ball, ultimately doing his job, a good actor turning a piece of necessary stage business into a theatrical moment and sometimes stealing the limelight from his more celebrated peers. Later in his career he was trusted to dribble and shoot and the fans learned that he loved to drive to the basket—Frazier called him one of the great drivers in the game. There's a picture of him that suggests his quality. Rior-dan is underneath the basket, his body stretched in the air. One arm is bent, the shoulder keeping away a Celtic who is jumping up with Riordan, trying to block his shot. The other arm is reaching high toward the basket, the hand about to lay the ball off the glass. Riordan's head is tilted slightly and his face is grimacing, the eyes shut tight and the lips curled above the teeth, a kid eagerly taking on a challenge he knows might do him in. "Sometimes you start to drive and say to yourself, 'I'm going in there if I have to jump over the big man and float in backward,'" he told Pete Axthelm. "Then your pro-fessional instincts get the better of you and you look for the open man to pass to. But if you don't see him, well, you just keep flying."

Phil Jackson, the Westerner who had been sent the film of Reed's fight, was supposed to have been the team's reserve forward. Lanky and bony-shouldered, long-armed, Jackson had come to the Knicks two years before as an offensive player—he had averaged 28 points a game during his senior year in college and twice had scored over 50. In New

York, he appeared to be a perpetually uncomfortable man; nothing quite jibed with him. The experience of moving to the big city and becoming a professional ballplayer on a winning team unsettled him—by his own account, he found it hard to make friends on the team or maintain a happy marriage. On the court, he got a bad reputation as a dirty player because of a fight he unintentionally helped to cause in Atlanta. Still, he had begun to emerge as a steady substitute during his second year, when he suffered an injury to his back on a winter road trip. Injuries to players are like broken engagements—nobody feels the other party has acted right. The athlete accuses the management of mishandling him; the management accuses the athlete of exaggerating his complaint. No one is certain of the problem's cause and everyone is unsure about how to cure it. Jackson's injury was no exception. For several weeks, he received discomforting and vague suggestions about the pain he felt in his back; finally he was told he had to undergo a spinal fusion operation, a procedure which left him strapped in a brace for the next six months, and unable to play for the following, the championship, season.

His place was taken by Dave Stallworth. Like Jackson, Stallworth had also come from the West, a black who had grown up in Dallas and been named an All-American at Wichita State College. Six feet seven, weighing 210 pounds, he played a decent defense and was best known for his inside moves, a loosey-goosey forward who feinted and drove for the basket. He was an enthusiast who carried a portable stereo with him into the locker room and wore a white star on a gold front tooth—Berger reports that other members of his family sported hearts, quarter moons, and stars when they smiled. Like Jackson, he had performed promisingly in his 1965 rookie season, scoring 11 points a game, and improved during his sophomore year, upping his average to 12, becoming the first substitute off the bench, and later a starter.

Then, like Jackson, he had suffered a calamity. On a West Coast trip, Stallworth felt a pain in his chest; when the team returned to New York the doctors diagnosed him as the victim of a heart attack. The attack did not incapacitate him, but the doctors warned him never to play ball again and hospitalized him for a little over a month. Stallworth was twenty-four. When he left the hospital, he returned to Wichita, coaching an amateur team there and working in the Parks Department. Slowly, and against the doctor's orders, he began to play ball again; tentatively, he exerted himself. After almost two full years of not playing pro ball he was announced fit enough to try out again for the team. His return couldn't have occurred at a more perfect time. An experienced player who knew the intimate peculiarities of the team, he filled the void created by Jackson's absence, and Pete Axthelm suggests that fans saw his arrival at the beginning of the season as an omen signaling a glorious year. The night of his second debut, the announcer said his name and he ran onto the court dressed in the team's sparkling white warm-ups, a towel wrapped around his neck. While shaking hands with Reed, who headed the line of players standing there to greet him, he looked straight out at the cheering crowd with a joyful, amazed, and questioning stare—all right, life, we'll try this once more. "You feel like doing something other than standing there," he told Berger. "But you also feel that anything you do, it might be out of place. I felt like screaming, I really did, I felt like screaming, just screaming along with them, I really felt that good. I could feel my insides turning, and just felt like letting it out."

The last and most important member of the Knicks' second team was Cazzie Russell. He was the team's sixth man, the first substitute off the bench. Traditionally sixth men play both guard and forward and are noted for their offensive ability. The position was created and championed by the Celtics (in basketball, tradition thy name is Boston!) and has come to symbolize all the virtues of basketball—its demand for versatility, stamina, physical and emotional courage, grace, and sacrifice, the noblest virtue of them all in the world of sports.

As a player Russell met the demands of the position. He

was a sturdy six feet six—his wide shoulders made his torso a neat isosceles triangle. And he could shoot. Indeed, he loved to shoot. "He kneels at the scorer's table like a pinch hitter in the batter's circle," starts one description of him entering a game. "He goes through a nervous routine of straightening his uniform. First he tucks his shirt into his basketball shorts until it looks as though it were pressed to his body. Then he tugs at each sock. Expressions roll on and off his rubbery face each time it appears as if there will be a break in the play that will enable him to get into the game. If the break fails to material- ize, he starts tucking and tugging all over again."

By all rights, Russell, like his predecessors in the position, should have been a starter. During his freshman year, he had starred at the University of Michigan, leading the team to the Holiday Festival championship, the Big Ten title, and third place in the NCAA national tourney. He continued this suc- cess throughout college and was named college Player of the Year after his senior season. A first-round draft pick of the Knicks, he signed a then record-breaking three-year, two- hundred-thousand-dollar contract, and worked as a starter for a year and a half, often scoring in spectacular bursts. "When he's in a streak," Holzman said, "there's no better shooter in the league." He was also an accurate one. During one play- off, he hit seven for seven. But the feat was considered so ordi- nary by one New York newspaper that they didn't mention Russell's achievement in any of the four stories it printed on the game. Then he broke an ankle and Bradley replaced him in the lineup. Upon his return, Russell became the team's sixth man.

But psychologically, the role was unnatural to Russell and he never appeared altogether comfortable in it. He seemed an hon- est and vain man, not merely eager for attention, but desperate for it, innocently and charmingly in love with his own excel- lence. When he entered college, he was asked why he had elected to attend the University of Michigan rather than Cin- cinnati, then the national champion. "I chose Michigan because

I always had some feeling for the underdog," Russell replied. "Michigan's basketball team was down and Cincinnati's was up. I thought I just might be another player at Cincinnati. At Michigan I had a chance to be a star." He prided himself on his physical appearance. He played for hours every day as a high-school kid in Chicago—"Another thing that helped my career were some friendly janitors," he once remarked. "If it weren't for them letting me practice, I might have wound up driving a cab or working in the steel mills or pushing rocks on a construction gang"—and continued the regimen as an adult, even supplementing the team's practice sessions with workouts on his own at the YMHA at night, a devotion unheard of among the pros. "It's not just for basketball," he explained. "One, your clothes look better. Two, it helps you resist sickness. Three, it's good for your complexion. And four, it can't hurt for later on in life." He also ate health foods and on road trips carried a bag filled with vitamin pills, dietary supplements, jars of wheat germ and honey, and an exercise device he used to keep his hands strong and waistline trim. His teammates called him Max Factor because of the oils he used on his body, and also Cockles 'n' Muscles, Wonder Boy, and Stillman's Gym. Barnett, his roommate, advised Berger that admission to their room was by pharmaceutical note only. Performing well meant so much to Russell that in basic training he rehearsed for the Army's physical training test, practicing all the procedures on his own the night before the exam. "I maxed the test," he boasted to Berger. He enjoyed a deep, sonorous voice and liked to pretend he was a radio announcer interviewing players in the locker room after the game, and sometimes amused his teammates by imitating a DJ and calling himself "Jazzy Cazzie." Even his devotion to God —he had been raised in a pious home and Reverend Cazzie was another Knick nickname for him—was subject to the pleasure he took in himself. Recounting a bizarre childhood incident to Berger, Russell offered a theological justification for vanity. "Okay, now here's a girl. She's going to crawl on the floor back to my seat to put lipstick on me, see. So I said, 'If you put that lipstick on me, I'm going to slap you, you know.' This is seventh grade, man, and I said, 'The devil doesn't like ugliness, and if you do that something terrible is going to happen to you.' " Later during the championship season, Bradley was injured and Russell took his place. "God moves in mysterious ways," he told one reporter, while splashing himself with cologne. "Maybe He sprained Bill's ankle." The reporter mischievously inquired about the Bible's attitude toward vanity. "Of course vanity is a sin," Russell answered, "but cleanliness is next to Godliness."

Russell rarely expressed public dissatisfaction at his role as the team's sixth man, but he wasn't happy with it. In the books written after the championship, he is frequently quoted saying he is misused on the team. Playing time is the chief reward coaches give their athletes—p.t., as they call it. Basically starters are assured a certain p.t., the amount varying only if they get into early foul trouble or can't guard their opponent that night. But Russell's p.t. fluctuated constantly. In some games he performed a vital function and played a good thirty minutes; in others his services were simply a bonus, and Holzman, a coach who employed his players with a strict economy, would call upon him only for six minutes out of the full forty-eight. DeBusschere, in his book, remarks that Russell often complained about his playing time. After a hard loss in Los Angeles during the final series, "Cazzie was fuming because he felt he hadn't played long enough. 'Every time I make a mistake,' he said, 'Red yanks me. He won't give me a chance.' " He told Berger that Holzman considered him only an offensive ballplayer and lacked confidence in his ability to rebound and stop his opponent from scoring. "I said [to Holzman], 'You don't have no confidence in me?' Then he started B-sing because he really had no answer. A guy don't have to try to bullshit me, man, to make me think. That's when I told him I didn't think I fitted in his plans for the ballclub. He looked very startled."

He was also sensitive to racial slights. He accused Riordan of not passing the ball to two black players when they were open, but hitting two white ones on the same play a little later; he insisted one white player didn't throw the ball to him correctly when the team ran lay-ups during practice—"he waits till I get right up on him and he drops the ball." Most troubling was Russell's belief that Bradley would get mad when he would replace him. ". . . when DeBusschere comes in for him, I detect no reaction, none whatsoever. Why me? . . . You understand what I'm saying," he asked Berger. "Now, OK, so I get ready to come in for Bradley, he gives me this frown when he passes me. I got out on the floor and I happen to turn and I glance at him going to the bench and I see him muttering and all this, so he's not really mad at Red. So I asked him about it, so he says, 'I'm sorry.' I said, 'Bill, don't give me a song and dance.' I said, 'You can continue to do it but I'm aware of it and I don't really care.'"

Bradley's starting role was particularly insulting to Russell because it was Bradley with whom he had been constantly, unfavorably compared to as a player since his college days. Bradley was seen as the consummate team player, a man skilled in all the demands of the game, a white, selfless, and almost naggingly self-denying ballplayer. Russell was viewed as the essential showboater, a shooter who tried to turn rebounds into spectacular displays instead of simple catches and consequently often missed the ball, a player who didn't move unless he held the ball, a selfish, black narcissist. While both were in college, they led their teams to a match against each other in the Garden Holiday Festival. The game was to decide who was the better player, but the contest settled nothing: Bradley, the team player, was the game's high scorer and won the tourney's Most Valuable Player award, while Russell, the individualist, led his team to victory. When both ended up on the Knicks the rivalry continued, a match sponsored largely by the press and fans which neither of the players could ignore. Late in the '69–'70 season,

Bradley injured himself and Russell momentarily resumed his old starting position. He scored well and hoped perhaps he would win back his old role. But Bradley drove himself to be in shape for the play-offs and when the post-season started Russell again sat on the bench watching Bradley get the nod. Russell's publicly calm acceptance of this bitter disappointment was so palpable that it touched even one sub on the team who didn't like Jazzy Cazzie and his ways. "At times," the player confided to Berger, "I admire the guy because I know for him not to start is the biggest crush."

The last major substitute on the team didn't get even this respect. He was Nate Bowman, the backup center who replaced Willis Reed whenever the captain was tired or got into foul trouble. Bowman was a figure of fun. The tallest Knick on the court—he topped even Reed by a good inch—he was wiry and thin instead of massive, and lacked both Reed's graceful moves and accurate shooting. Like Stallworth, with whom he had played in college, he was a Texan, but appeared foreboding rather than charming—no one was ever particularly frightened of Bowman evidently, but when he was annoyed or disgusted he could turn his face into a frown, a series of downward lines signifying massive disapproval and scorn, and the fans who had nicknamed Stallworth "Dave the Rave" called Bowman "Nate the Snake." He played 744 minutes that season, approximately half the time accorded the members of the second team, and performed only decently: In most games he merely didn't help the team lose their advantage.

His body betrayed him. He was a notoriously bad shooter, hitting only two out of every five shots. ". . . my fingers are, I don't know, they're kind of screwed up, y'know," he told Berger, "cause . . . like my fingers at the ends they curl up, y'know, like they can't lay flat on the table." Playing defense, he too frequently anticipated his opponent's move, and couldn't control his large arms and legs, often getting called for fouls and developing a reputation as a dirty player. He seemed to attract trouble without ever taking responsibility for it. "A lot of people," he told Berger, "look at a tall guy and say . . . I mean, like a little short guy or something, like a lot of times can be just standin' around or something, and a little short guy say five-seven or five-eight will walk up to me . . . 'What are you looking at, you . . . big . . .' A lot of guys just walk up to you and say things to get you to . . . to fight 'em or somethin'."

He was a major participant in one famous court fray pitting the Knicks against the Atlanta Hawks. The Hawks were then coached by Richie Guerin, a combative, direct man who had been an important Knick player. (Now Guerin broadcasts Knick games with Marv Albert; on the air, he knocks and praises players with the same forthrightness with which he used to beat them on the court.) The two teams had skirmished before, and the night of the big fight Guerin reportedly spent half time lambasting his players for letting the New York team dominate them. As soon as play resumed, a scuffle started between Willis Reed and one of the Hawk players. The battle redounded to Willis's credit (another testament to his strength and fury), but Bowman became its unfortunate victim. Several Hawks surrounded him and held him down over a gate while a Hawk fan—God help some sports enthusiasts—mercilessly pounded the big man's head. One of the Hawk culprits was a player named Paul Silas. In the ten years since the battle, Silas has become a renowned figure, a player still active at thirty-six, and the only grandfather in the league; he still claims the fight with the Knicks was the best free-for-all in which he ever participated and says the vision of Bowman stretched helplessly over the fence remains his warmest memory of the moment. Indeed, Bowman was considered the team's clown, but the happy times and memories he gave others were always touched with some nastiness because too frequently the pleasantries were at his expense.

The last three players on the team were the bench warmers and almost entirely anonymous. Two of them were white, a tandem from Ohio named Bill Hosket and Donnie May, well-scrubbed, thick-shouldered fellows who had played together in high school and college. Stars back home, they were unknowns in New York. "The first night I played in the Garden," Hosket told Berger, "I looked up at the scoreboard and it flashed a message that said, 'Welcome Bob Hosket, number 20.' They couldn't even get my name right. I knew then that all that All-America and Olympic stuff didn't mean a thing." The change in status depressed Hosket. In training camp, Holzman removed him from a group portrait of the squad, replacing him with Stallworth; Hosket went on an eating binge that resulted in Riordan's nicknames for him—Burly Bear and Wally Walrus. Twenty-three years old, a business major from Ohio State with a degree in marketing, married and a father, Hosket was paid thirty-five thousand dollars by the Knicks and appeared in but twenty of the team's first sixty-one games. "After about two months of the season," he told Robert Lipsyte, "you see your relative position on a team and accept it. You try to keep yourself ready on the bench, actively interested in the game . . . but now I've watched Dave DeBusschere against every forward in the league, maybe five times each, and my learning curve has tapered off."

His compatriot, May, fared a little better. His entry in the authoritative compendium *Who's Who in Basketball* neatly summarizes his fortunes. "MAY, DON B. 1/3/46, Dayton, Ohio. College: Dayton. 6'4", 200/ Forward. Dayton's greatest scorer with 1980 points. Received All-America mention three years (1966–68). NIT's MVP as Flyers dominated tournament, 1968/ New York (NBA) pick on third round. Participated only occasionally with Knicks but enjoyed celebrity status through role in Vitalis commercial." The commercial was the only time he got to be a starter. In it, he is starting his first game and runs out to greet Barnett, DeBusschere, Reed, and Frazier, who are all being introduced and slapping hands, the fraternal ritual that begins every basketball game. Willis notices his hands are greasy after May slaps him five, and touches May's hair to discover that he's using greasy kid stuff. We can't play with you, the stars tell the rookie, you'll make the ball slippery. They send the downcast May back to the bench and Mike Riordan replaces him. Frazier claims that the advertisers picked May instead of Stallworth or Russell because he was white. Another reason might have been his practiced look of dejection. During the season, May revolted against his infrequent appearance in games. When Holzman would call for Bradley to go back into a contest, May would stand up smartly, looking at Holzman hopefully and pretending he misheard the coach; as Bradley walked to the scorer's table, May would sit down again wearing the despairing look he later was paid for by Vitalis. The ruse, he claims, got him into a couple of games.

The last, most junior member of the whole partnership was a slight, unassuming New Yorker named John Warren. Warren's father had made his living dredging Rockaway Bay, and Warren had played ball locally at St. John's University in Queens. He hadn't ever really anticipated a professional career. Unlike Hosket and May, his presence on the Knick bench pleased and surprised him—he considered it an honor to be allowed into this fraternity of masters and told reporters he didn't terribly mind not playing because at least he had such a good seat for the game. He roomed with the captain, Willis Reed, learned his lessons during scrimmages, and occasionally fantasized about successes on the court. ". . . last night," he told Berger, ". . . I saw myself blocking Jerry West's shot. Like, I never saw anybody block his shot, but I saw myself blocking West's shot, and I stole the ball from West a couple of times, it was outasight." He explained to Berger that his dreams were never two-sided; he only saw himself doing everything correctly. Of the three, he played in the most games, 44 regular-season contests altogether, more than half of the total number, and performed for 272 minutes, almost a full half hour more than either Hosket or May did for the entire year. But their collective low estate on the team can be seen by the fact that all three played only one minute more than Nate Bowman did for the whole season, and that the columns alongside their names in the box score of the last triumphant championship game inform us that even then, in the team's moment of triumph when it was winning by twenty, they "did not play."

# 5

Essentially, the team was the creation of two men, Eddie Donovan, the general manager, and the coach, Red Holzman. They headed the Knick "front office," the collection of secretaries, scouts, and publicity people who administer a team—from paying the players to sending the uniforms to the local dry-cleaning establishment. The Knick front office is a small community with a long history, and the careers of its staff are Hindu-like: the same people keep returning in a different form. Diffident, handsome Dick McGuire, brother of Al McGuire, the famous coach and television commentator, first played for the team, becoming one of the NBA's original all-stars, a guard known for his passing and, in the words of Leonard Koppett, "one of the most reluctant shooters of all times"; later McGuire coached the squad, unsuccessfully, and now scouts college players. Fuzzy Levane is also a scout at present and has been paid previously as a coach, scout, and assistant coach. The public-relations men have shifted positions with every change in the coaching staff, Jim Wergeles and Frankie Blauschild, the two men who have occupied the office, working above or below one another depending on whether their friends or foes were directing the team.

Donovan and Holzman haven't been immune from these

changes in fortune. Originally, Donovan came to the Knicks from St. Bonaventure's, an upstate New York college that was a perennial favorite in the Garden-sponsored annual National Invitational Tournament. Donovan coached his team to ninety-nine straight wins and the distinction of being the nation's highest-scoring unit, and was appointed coach of the Knicks, a position at which he seemed to show no aptitude whatsoever, whereupon he was named general manager. Holzman followed a more tortuous route. When the league was first founded, Holzman played on the Rochester Royals with Fuzzy Levane. In 1953, Levane coached the Milwaukee Hawks (a franchise that later moved to St. Louis, where it became one of the league's greatest teams.) Levane hired Holzman as his assistant and when Levane had won but eleven games midway through the season, Ben Kerner, the team's owner, replaced him with Holzman. Time passed. Levane was hired by the Knicks, and Holzman was fired by the Hawks. In 1957, the coach of the Knicks quit, and Levane was appointed to the job. He needed a scout and named Holzman, who continued happily in this capacity until ten years later, when he was called to take leadership.

Together, Donovan and Holzman shaped the team. Donovan headed the group of men who made the draft choices and trades that resulted in the team's roster. He brought together the individual talents who joined to form the team, choosing from the pool of available players those athletes whose attributes would effect the right blend, the winning combination. Holzman was responsible for seeing that each performed to maximum ability. It was his job to adjust the balance of the team, practically working out the most effective groupings of players. The two worked as a team—agreement in principles and practice was mandatory for success—and complemented one another as neatly as the squad that was their mutual handiwork.

Donovan was a traditionalist. His values were simple. He

wanted to bring a winning team into New York, though that
didn't mean necessarily a championship one: He was a realist
and knew the combination of factors that produce champs
occurs but rarely. He worked hard, researching players and
teams thoroughly. He kept his life private and didn't intrude
on others' privacy, never publicizing information he might
have gathered about a player's business or personal life. He
was devout and appreciated piety in others, but also respected
diversity. There were qualities about players that Donovan
didn't approve, especially their increasing tendency to view
basketball as a job rather than a profession demanding dedication, but he was never ungenerous with his praise of players
and rarely discounted talents too quickly. He didn't possess a
shred of egotism. ". . . shy, sincere, simply motivated, Eddie
never really did become part of the New York scene," his admirer, Leonard Koppett, wrote about him in March 1970
when Donovan announced his retirement from New York to
work in the new Buffalo franchise. ". . . the dazzling successful Knicks of today owe their existence more to his quiet
work than to any other factor . . . He scouted (with Holzman's help) all the players . . . developed in his own coaching
days, the pressing defense philosophy and techniques that
Holzman has installed so well . . . and had the courage to
stick by policies he believed in whether they involved playing
the rookies or making trades."

Perhaps his most important virtue was also his least noticeable one. He was patient. General manager is a job in which
people gain recognition by making deals—a farsighted draft
choice or the acquisition of a crucial player for a cheap price.
The emphasis on this part of the job has grown recently; fans
confuse change with progress and express a general admiration
for the general manager who's always on the move and taking
a gamble. But frequently the most critical aspect of building a
team is knowing when not to make a deal. More impressive
than the deals Donovan did make and the players he selected

were the trades he refused and the choices he dismissed—for five years while under terrific pressure to produce a winner he acquired talent for the Knicks without once committing a major error.

Holzman, the coach, was equally old-fashioned, but hailed from a different tradition. He grew up in New York during the twenties, when basketball was just becoming a business. Then the famous professional team was the Celtics, who barnstormed through the Midwest playing local favorites and featured Nat Holman, the game's first superstar, a dapper matinee idol paid close to $10,000 a year (draining the team's profits until its owner, a promoter named Jim Furey who was also the head cashier at Arnold Constable, embezzled $187,000 from the store, a charge to which he pled guilty and for which he served two years in Sing-Sing). Meanwhile college teams from the West played at the Garden against the local powers of NYU, St. John's, CCNY, and LIU. Started as a regular attraction in 1934, college doubleheaders at the Garden always premiered new developments in the game, from the first radio broadcast to the first accurate jump shot. The game came to be associated with New York, a big-city sport played by children of working-class white immigrants and enjoyed by cigar-smoking bettors who clapped when players for losing teams hit a lucky basket at the end of the game and beat the point spread. (A morally sanitized—but physically riskier —version of this phenomenon has recently appeared in the NBA. Fast-food joints now sponsor promotions for themselves at games, giving away free orders of french fries, chicken, milk shakes, and candy when the local teams perform such wonders as scoring over 130 points or keeping their opponents under 100.) Holzman matured in this world. As a teenager he performed for an amateur group at game and dance nights. In the early forties he played under Holman, who then coached the CCNY team, and appeared twice in the NITs. Later, in 1950, CCNY gave New York basketball fans their greatest thrill and tragedy. The team won both national collegiate tournaments in one season, and six months later most of its starting members were arrested for fixing games. The scandal ruined college basketball in New York, casting a stain on all the heroes of its halcyon days. Coincidentally, it also allowed the growth of the professional game, and twenty years later one of Holman's most apt students helped return a championship to New York in the new version of the arena in which the game had first begun to turn into a million-dollar business.

Holzman presented a more complex public character than Donovan. Holzman was a slight, trim man, always neatly attired in sedate Ivy League clothes. The young Frazier, the Beau Brummel of the team, wrote: "He dresses okay for a coach, not sloppy, you know, with baggy pants and ties and shirts cousins give you for a birthday. Red looks pretty sharp even if he is a conservative dresser." In the locker room, he joked with some players, asked others perfunctory questions about their family, and bored all of them with pregame warnings to watch out for one player or another who could really score. During games he commanded the team, but never took attention away from his players with tantrums directed at the crowd or referees. Instead he worked diligently, kneeling most of the time in front of his chair, studying the action on the floor, calling out instructions through his cupped hand—see the ball, what have we got?—and, when the team was losing, sitting back and squinting at the scoreboard while wondering what was wrong. After games, he met his dutiful wife, Selma, in the Garden press room with the punctuality of a commuter stepping off his nightly train home from the city. Intelligent, clever, hard-working, and vain, he received more attention the less he asked for it and became almost a controversial figure for the writers who covered the team. The daily reporters, such as Leonard Lewin, lionized him. They credited him with the team's success, and presented his public diffidence as a sort of heroic simplicity of character. The younger writers who worked mainly for magazines distrusted him. They circulated stories about him: He was jealous of Bradley; he babied Frazier; he could only teach defense; he was paranoid.

Occasionally he played games with them, mocking the importance they attached to him and their attempts to make him reveal his inner self. One writer for the *New York Times* Sunday Magazine accompanied the team on a road trip. At first, Holzman dismissed his request for an interview; then on a plane ride he said, "Grab your book, I'm going to give you lots of quotes tonight." They spoke for half an hour and discussed everything but basketball. "What the hell can I say?" Holzman asked rhetorically about the team's success. "We're not doing a single thing that hasn't been done before." He was a professional. He had never earned a living at anything but the game, never anticipated victories or defeats. He always found something to praise about a player, a reason for every loss. Above all, he knew the game was a business and that his success depended solely on winning and attracting customers. At the height of his fame, he said he followed three rules of life. "First never worry about something you can't control. Second, never argue about money before going to bed. Third, never make a point with your finger when the waiter is coming with the check." To Robert Lipsyte, he said, "I never did anything spectacular or even really smart. At best, a good job. I just try to stay cool. I never thought getting an ulcer made you a more dedicated man. Is a fighter better because he has a cauliflower ear? I will watch any movie on television, especially if there's a horse in it. I will smoke anything with tobacco in it. I will drink anything with Scotch in it. I would beat my wife if I could but I usually lose when I try. Nothing ever funny or even mildly interesting ever happened to me. I am an ordinary man." Selma agreed. "Red just liked to go about his business. It helps that he's kind of small. He can pass through a crowd."

# 6

There were three stages in the construction of the championship Knicks: the selection of the players from 1964 on who eventually formed the triumphant unit; the naming of Holzman, the coach who finally led them to glory; and the acquisition of DeBusschere, the player whose presence was the last ingredient needed to make the Knicks winners.

This entire process is commonly referred to as the Knicks' "rebuilding" period. The phrase implies an orderliness to the process that didn't exist. Fans invariably find a moral in a team's career. Their attitudes reflect all of humanity's philosophies toward fate. There are optimists who insist a ninth-round draft choice will make a club respectable, and equally insistent pessimists: Bradley tells the story of walking off court during the preliminary play-offs against the Bullets in 1970 and hearing a fan yell that he knew the team would choke, hoping to preclude the dreadful occurrence by acting as though it already had happened. Some fans are conspiracy theorists, arguing that the failure and success of teams is all a master plan, the result of plots among coaches, general managers, and owners, a manipulation of television ratings, markets, players, and league standings. Others are fatalists. For them, teams are stamped with character and relentlessly pursue their destinies through the season.

The privilege of fans, such attitudes hardly reflect the realities of building a team. One adage about coaching holds that you must always know your material, neither forcing your players to perform in a manner inimical to their natural styles, nor surrendering your own vision of the right way to play—

the winning way to play—to the individual predilections of your players. Building a team is similar. The men selecting the players have some ideas about the sort of team they want, and the talents demonstrated by the players help to change this ideal vision; and the coach and general manager seek to influence the players to behave on the court in accordance with their philosophy. The constant and common goal is to win a championship, but innumerable difficulties must be overcome along the way, and the resolution of old troubles creates yet new surprises and impediments. The labor is constant and ceaselessly unpredictable and there is no certain way to achieve the goal. The modesty common to winning coaches and general managers is not false. Schooled in the variety and vagaries of human character and daily circumstances, they know a team reveals itself slowly, and they try to approach the constellation of talents on their club with rational skepticism, neither resigning themselves to preliminary defeat nor basking in premature glory, but experimenting and exploring the relationships between and among players on the club: A rookie plays better opposite one player than another, a star displays previously untapped reserves of strength and coolness, a bench warmer demonstrates he can take charge in difficult situations. Responsible for fulfilling everyone else's dreams, they try to suffer few illusions of their own. Call up a general manager the day after a big trade and he will probably be second-guessing himself, pursuing yet another exchange of players, or worrying about the upcoming draft. Speak to a coach after any win but the one that clinches a championship and he'll tell you that his team's triumph is only another addition in the standing's left-hand column and that a rookie's excellent performance doesn't mean there won't be nights when he will fumble passes and miss foul shots. Their jobs have taught them that the sequence of events climaxing in triumph or failure really contains no innate meaning other than the struggle between mastery and ineptitude, and that the revelation of a team's character only emerges out of this struggle, the sudden and irrefutable knowledge that the team has finally ended its journey toward creating itself and now must live with its nature: hard-luck loser, constant contender but never champion, streaky problem child. For the Knicks the eventual truth was wonderful—they were perfect masters—and, in hindsight, their evolution from performing in reptilian fashion during the early sixties, when the team could barely crawl out of the swamp of a .300 record, to ruler of the NBA, appears calculated and methodical. But actually the success of the team was merely the happy but unpredictable issue of diligent intelligence and chance.

The first bit of luck was the acquisition of Willis Reed in the 1964 draft. The Knicks hadn't intended to pick Reed. They had finished that season thirty-seven games behind first-place Boston, the fifth consecutive year they had posted a losing record and occupied last place, and their miserable showing had won them the year's top draft pick. They had squandered such opportunities before, picking star college players who failed as pros, and they almost repeated the mistake, selecting a center named Jim Barnes on the first round and passing over Reed, seemingly surrendering their claim to him for good since they anticipated one of the other teams would nab him. But to the Knicks' good fortune, Reed was still available when the second round of the draft began, and the Knicks, following the maxim that you take the best athlete and that two centers are better than none, named Reed as their choice. (An instance of pulling victory from the jaws of defeat, since Barnes was later dubbed "Bad News" and spent his professional career shuttling around the league looking for a home.)

The reluctant attitude the Knicks displayed toward Reed might have benefited them. Reed claims their hesitation to proclaim him the premier player of the crop still annoys him and whetted his appetite to prove his excellence. He soon accomplished the test. Reed was present at training camp but Barnes was in Japan with the Olympic team, an honor denied to Reed because a flu kept him from competing for a position on the squad. (What are a hero's victories without such humiliations?) Without a challenger, Reed won the center spot and soon established himself in the position, finishing the season as one of the league's top scorers and rebounders (and foul-happy players, a sign of his future feistiness) and being voted Rookie of the Year.

Reed was the first member of the championship squad to play for the Knicks. The rest joined him in the next three seasons. In '65–'66 Barnett and Stallworth came to the team. In '66–'67 Cassie Russell premiered. The next season the team signed Bradley, Frazier, Jackson, and Bowman. Finally, they added Hosket, Riordan, and May to the roster. Except for DeBusschere, they were complete.

Still, they weren't a winning team until Holzman became coach. Unlike the acquisition of Reed, Holzman's appointment wasn't a matter of chance; it resulted from the sheer exhaustion of other possibilities. Before Holzman, the Knicks had been coached by nine men, and only one, Joe Lapchick, a long and thin-faced man who had played with Nat Holman on the last incarnation of the famed Celtic team and was one of the original stars of pro basketball, had any success. Lapchick joined the Knicks in 1949, two seasons after the team had been founded as one of the charter franchises of the Basketball Association of America, the forerunner of the NBA. The Knicks belonged to Ned Irish, the Madison Square Garden promoter of college basketball and, since Irish was interested in the more profitable amateur games, Lapchick was allowed a free hand in shaping the team. A mediocre collection when he started with it, the Knicks soon became a consistent contender (though loser) for the NBA crown. Then the college scandals made the Garden anathema to college basketball and Irish, deprived of his favorite, tinkered with the team, interfering with Lapchick's decisions. Eventually Lapchick left the Knicks to coach at St. John's. One after another, members of the team were called on to take his place, but Vince Boryla, Fuzzy Levane, Carl Braun, Eddie Donovan,

Harry Gallatin, and Dick McGuire all proved inadequate to the task, none guiding the team toward any distinctive style of play, even while Eddie Donovan, as general manager of the team, began drafting players of true ability. Under McGuire, Holzman's immediate predecessor, chaos reigned, a condition immortalized in an oft-repeated tale from survivors of those days about Knicks sending out a kid to buy hotdogs at the Nedick's stand near the Garden during half time and wolfing down the delicacies while the coach was telling them what to do in the coming twenty-four minutes of play. In late December 1967, the Knicks lost three consecutive games, surrendering to Boston, whom they had won against but twice in twenty-five previous meetings, Seattle, a newly created expansion team that triumphed in but twenty-three games all season, and Philadelphia, whom the Knicks hadn't beaten in almost two years. The team had a 15–22 record, a .405 winning percentage, a hairbreadth away from their division's last place. Some change had to be made and McGuire and Holzman (then the team's chief scout) simply switched jobs. The appointment occurred largely because Holzman was the last man left in the organization who could acquit responsibly the duties of the job, and was so temporary that even after the season ended no one was certain Holzman would return. Nobody anticipated Holzman would become one of the game's great tacticians, and his debut was uninspiring: He lost the first two games he coached, reminding fans of his unenviable 20–83 record as leader of the Hawks back in the fifties. Then his previous apprenticeship began to show some good results. The Knicks started to win, and to win consistently. They finished the season with a respectable 43–39 record, and an auspicious 28–17 mark under Holzman, captured their first play-off berth in nine years, and performed reputably in this unusual bout of postseason play. Altogether, under Holzman, the team had given its most promising performance since Lapchick had left.

The reasons for Holzman's success were less arbitrary than those that led to his appointment.

First he corrected the laxness that had prevailed under McGuire. "I did have one little run-in with Red while he was still Dick's assistant," Jackson remembers in his book. "Nate Bowman was the team's leading observer of young ladies. By half time he would have every good-looking chick in the stands all sighted out. The two of us were messing around in a huddle, and there was something like two minutes left to go in the game. The Knicks weren't far enough ahead or behind for either of us to be used, so Nate was pointing out a few of his favorite sights. All of a sudden Red came over and started busting us. 'How much time is there left on the clock?' he started. We said there were two minutes and four-teen seconds. 'I mean the twenty-four-second clock,' he said. 'Eighteen seconds,' we said. 'No, you fools, it's seventeen. If I ever catch you doing this again, I'll fine you. I want you to pay attention to the ball game instead of clowning around. No wonder we can't win a game.' " Once named coach, Holzman set a system of fines, dunning players for arriving late to prac-tices, departures for road trips, and team meetings, token lev-ies of five and ten dollars that startled the team nonetheless—several players confessed Holzman surprised them and won their respect when three players arrived late at his first team meeting and he announced they would have to render homage to a team kitty.

Next, Holzman demanded discipline on the court. He in-sisted the team play an alert defense and installed a variety of presses, the term that's basketball talk for "pressure": "Press him!" shouts a coach and the player steps up to meet his man. Presses change the tempo of a game. In basketball you wait to inbound the ball or take a foul shot, and dawdle while the other team brings the ball upcourt; the game has its rest peri-ods built into it. Presses forget about these uncalled time-outs, especially the full-court press, when you guard your opponent all the way downcourt, an unnerving and exhausting tactic both to execute and counter that leaves defensive players breathless and offensive ones confused. Presses are the main device a coach can use to make a team work hard—they provide instant (and, in the open range of the backcourt, easily visible) proof of who's goofing off and who doesn't understand the game. They don't instantly win games; indeed, a press can hurt a team: Experienced opponents will know how to "break the press" by passing the ball and will score an easy, uncontested basket. But young, eager, and energetic clubs use presses to demonstrate a crowd-pleasing hustle, and a press will decide some close contests the team might not otherwise count in its win column: With the Knicks, the novelty resulted in doubling the team's triumphs.

Holzman's defense, however, was not just a demonstration of youthful energy. It required intelligence and dominated games. At any moment in a basketball game a team enjoys a variety of offensive options. In one-on-one you must decide whether to shoot or dribble closer to the basket before trying to score; in two-on-two the question becomes more complicated—you can shoot, dribble, or pass; and in a five-on-five, full-court contest these possibilities are of course multiplied many times. Still, in all instances, you follow a simple rule: You make the play that has the best chance of getting you some points. You get as close as possible to the basket because your shot will have a better chance of hitting; you try to get your best shooter the ball because he has a better chance of scoring. Winning teams follow these rules, and the Knicks simply applied them to their defense. When the other team had the ball, the Knicks tried to deny them all but the least promising possibilities of scoring.

They accomplished this in a variety of ways. They hounded players into areas of the court where they'd get into trouble—far from their teammates or close to the sidelines. They played a "sagging" defense, each player shadowing one man, but also leaving him momentarily to help another teammate put pressure on someone else. They forced men away from where they wanted to be, made a guard stop dribbling by getting in his way, convinced someone else not to pass the ball to a man near the basket because there was a good chance it would be stolen, and even sometimes stole the ball directly —a feat that was rarely a matter of chance, though it often seemed that way. With them, every player had a relationship to the ball as it moved from man to man, and Holzman's often repeated yell of "See the ball!" was meant to make them aware of the possible plays that emerged as the players positioned themselves. They forced other teams to change their tactics in an attempt to adjust to the defensive pressure applied by New York, and also created opportunities for their own offense: the steals that made Frazier famous, bad shots that allowed for easy rebounds, sloppy passes that went out of bounds, distracted play that resulted in infractions such as walking or carrying the ball, and finally foolish errors and dispirited play brought about by the frustration and humiliation experienced by their opponents when they couldn't accomplish what they wanted.

Their offense demonstrated a similar discipline. The Knicks weren't a fast-break team: They didn't grab the rebound and move downcourt so quickly that they enjoyed an advantage in men when they took their shot. They couldn't do this because they rarely outrebounded their opponents. (Only one team collected fewer rebounds than they that year.) They also didn't rely on a few masterful performers to score all the points. The year they won the championship, New York had six players averaging in double figures. Again, this was a result of need. No New York player could dominate a game offensively. This want made the Knicks a peculiarly balanced offensive team. They worked for their shots in a beautiful fashion. First, the team was composed of shooters, players who could hit the basket. Second, they worked to get the ball to a player who was momentarily unguarded, the open man—the command in offense equivalent to "See the ball!" on defense. The Knicks devised plays designed to free each player and performed a "patterned offense"—moving the ball until one player was in position for a decent shot, one with a good percentage of scoring. Certainly the Knicks took advantage of fast breaks or one-on-one displays when the opportunities presented themselves—Frazier's steal often started fast breaks, and the other members of the team would sometimes leave Cazzie Russell alone with the ball and the man guarding him —clearing out a side, as it's called—giving him all the space he needed to take his opponent one-on-one and score over him. But these modes weren't characteristic of the team. Instead their hallmark became passing displays and players moving without the ball, offensive designs that revived many fundamental features of the old schoolground plays of basketball— the give-and-go and the pick-and-roll, taking these combinations from the settlement homes where Holzman first learned them, and presenting them in dazzling perfection at the new Garden where young kids marveled at their brilliant simplicity and tried to imitate them on the playgrounds where they performed. The keys to their performance were patience, judgment, and execution, waiting for the opportunity of a good shot, knowing when a decent possibility presented itself, and performing the plays as they had been practiced during scrimmages. Knick players often said that their defense kept them in games and turned them on. "The other thing about defense," Frazier once wrote, "is that it seems to open up every part of basketball for you. There are lots of nights over the course of the long NBA season . . . when you're exhausted from travel and from playing four or five nights in a row. You start the game and you just drag. But you gut it out, play your 'D' and pretty soon you start to get with it. Maybe you make a steal or maybe Willis Reed blocks a shot, we get a basket or two, and suddenly we're rolling. You forget how tired you are, and pretty soon basketball is beautiful again. The shot you missed by three feet five minutes ago all of a sudden is the easiest thing in the world to make." The important role defense played for the team is reflected in their statistics of that year; of all the teams in the league, they had the fewest points scored against them. Still, though their defense is justly lauded, it was the effortless, selfless, consistent execution of one play after another that made the Knicks magical: The most thrilling moment in basketball is when the ball fills the basket touching only the air, and the Knicks performed this miracle regularly.

Finally, Holzman clarified the roles each player filled on the team. Before this happened one last ingredient, Dave De-Busschere, was added to the team. This occurred on December 20, almost exactly one year after Holzman had been named coach of the club, halfway through an unexpectedly rocky season. The addition of DeBusschere transformed the club. After he joined the team, they took eleven games straight, and, except for being ousted by the Boston Celtics for the Eastern Division championships, didn't falter again on their year-and-a-half-long march to the championship. In dealing for him, the Knicks hoped that his talents would supply the element needed to make the team a contender. They bet his gifts and qualities as a player would positively affect the other members of the club, and the gamble worked: Only in DeBusschere's presence did the final characters of the Knicks emerge.

The trade occurred at a difficult time for New York. After their success under Holzman and their play-off drive, the team had started the new season poorly. Their promotional news-letter called them "established" contenders for the Eastern Division title, but Leonard Koppett, the *New York Time*'s inestimable basketball reporter, considered the rating excessive. "Contenders they may prove to be," he wrote, "but established they are not." At the time, Bradley hadn't yet proved he could succeed as a professional ballplayer, the team lacked depth, having lost several key substitute performers to expansion clubs, and they had to show they could win against the many weaker new members of the league. Their premiere offered them an opportunity, a contest against the two-year-old Chicago Bulls, a club that had won only twenty-nine games the previous year. The Knicks lost by four points and Koppett judged their effort "a sluggish and unsatisfactory beginning." They fared worse in their second game, against the Los Angeles Lakers. Koppett wrote: "The New York Knicks, who néeded but only one game this season to go into a slump, fell deeper into it last night as they were crushed by the Los Angeles Lakers, 118–96." He painted a sad portrait of the club's future. "The high hopes of preseason conversations are already chilled by reality and a lot of work lies ahead for a play-off berth." The prediction proved true. The Knicks evened their record, then lost five straight. "Their offense has become completely disorganized and even good shots are not dropping," Koppett reported, "a common condition when players get tight. Defensively . . . they weren't so hot either." Finally, after losing seven of their last eight games, and a visit to San Diego, the newest NBA city, where they entertained the fans with "four fist fights, and one of pro basketball's most awesome sights—an enraged Willis Reed," the team began to win. It put together a genuine streak and reached the .500 mark. Then, just as the team had begun to fulfill its promise, the trade for DeBusschere was announced.

As described by its architect, Eddie Donovan, the exchange was serendipitous. The Knicks had always desired DeBusschere; when DeBusschere was first named coach of the Detroit club, Donovan called to congratulate him and say that he would trade any New York player to get DeBusschere in return. DeBusschere modestly declined the offer. Then Paul Seymour was named coach of the Detroit franchise. Donovan remembered that Seymour seemed jealous of the credit DeBusschere always received and liked two players on the Knick team. The Detroit team started losing badly and needed a change. "I expected Paul Seymour . . . to make a major trade," DeBusschere wrote about the deal. "He had a habit of doing that kind of thing, whether the trade was any good or not." Donovan also anticipated Seymour's worries and suggested the exchange to the coach. The Detroit coach agreed. "Something clicked," Donovan once said about it. "It was lucky. You can never predict these things." Indeed. The day after the trade, New York and the Pistons met in Detroit, DeBusschere receiving a standing ovation and helping lead his new team to a 135–87 victory over his hapless previous teammates.

DeBusschere was traded for Walt Bellamy, a center, and Howie Komives, a guard; and it was as much to rid the team of the influence of these two as to secure DeBusschere's services that New York made the deal. Bellamy was the crucial factor. He was a large man, six feet eleven and 240 pounds, a proven scorer and rebounder, one of the league's all-time leaders in both departments. But he performed mercurially, always working hard when matched against one of the league's better centers, but lackadaisically against weak teams, an honest, but evidently inaccessible, moody and private man whose often passionless performances were simply bad examples for the club. Besides, Bellamy's presence at center forced Reed to play out of position at forward, a frustrating responsibility for the future captain who was simply too slow to keep up with many of his opponents on defense and, out of position, couldn't employ his offensive talents to their best advantage.

Komives, the guard, created just as much confusion. He was a decent scorer and a combative defensive player, known for diving after loose balls and taking a charge. But his abrasive personality created problems on the team and helped to keep Frazier on the bench. Certainly the club's best playmaker, Frazier played after Komives, the club's third guard. ". . . everybody wanted to know a way to correct the situation," a player explained to Berger, "but if you took a guy like [Komives] out of the lineup he would squawk forever. He could create so many problems not starting—like talk of favoritism . . ." Frazier's career had progressed haltingly. The Knicks had drafted him after he had led his Southern Illinois University team to an impressive victory in the 1967 NIT finals, a performance which Holzman judged one of the finest he had ever witnessed by a college guard. But on the team,

Frazier had played unevenly; in his book, he reports he became so disconsolate under McGuire that he sat through games at the end of the bench hoping the coach wouldn't call his name. Upon becoming coach, Holzman made Frazier his favorite. ". . . just after he took over," Frazier remembers in his book, "he pulled me aside on the bus from Philly for a little man-to-man discussion. 'You're a much better ballplayer than you're showing. You can really be great, you've just got to get your confidence.' . . . I started to have good games. My jumper came back and I'd score ten or twelve points. It seemed, bang, just like that I was penetrating, I was hitting, I was running—just overnight . . . I can't explain it fully. I wasn't practicing differently, I wasn't spending any more time after practice, but it just seemed to snap in place. It was the guys having confidence that made me produce." Now, being a sub stunted his natural growth as a ballplayer; he needed to play full games to test and develop his gifts. For all the bravado of his locker-room talk, Frazier has a submissive aspect. Once a player punched him during a game and Frazier didn't return the blow, an act of nonagression that lost him the respect of many fans. Frazier characterizes this part of his nature as his "cool" unflappable self, but it can also be viewed as his passive one. He rose to challenges once they were offered or thrust upon him, and became a masterful clutch performer, calm, resourceful, brave; but he rarely sought duels and never displayed the eagerness for besting others that characterizes other players. As a substitute, he didn't complain about his status, expressing a casual attitude toward starting. He appeared to enjoy his occasional responsibilities and needed to be forced to assume the more demanding ones of a starter.

The arrival of DeBusschere and departure of Bellamy and Komives clarified all these identity problems. Reed returned enthusiastically to center; five days after resuming his old post, he scored twenty-five points, grabbed twenty-eight rebounds, then hit for thirty-four in the next game, and scored on eighteen of twenty shots in a New Year's Day contest.

"It's like coming home," he said about his new responsibility, "like being in a foreign country for a long, long time and coming back to your hometown." Shortly after, he was named to the all-star team, the first player in the league to be so honored at two positions.

Frazier replaced Komives as a starter. At first Frazier figured the trade would be bad for the team. "With Komives gone I knew I was a starter," he wrote, "and I didn't know how it would work out, how it was going to affect my play. I had been happy playing thirty minutes a game . . . Well, my assist and scoring figures doubled and instead of running the team for maybe half a game, I was running things for the whole game and doing a better job of it. I gained confidence; I liked starting. It got so I didn't want to come out of the games more than thirty seconds or a minute at a time. I'd always tell Red I was okay and didn't need a rest." Riordan took Frazier's place as third guard, the proper position for his talents. De-Busschere replaced Reed at forward.

Finally, the last puzzle was answered. Cazzie Russell had played opposite Reed at forward, strengthening the team offensively but weakening it defensively. At the start of the season, Bradley had played guard, where he performed poorly. Then, in a late November game he was switched to forward and scored 21 points and was credited with 7 assists. A week later, as the team started a modest winning streak, Leonard Koppett gave Bradley partial credit for their comeback. The change to forward had given Bradley "a chance to gain the confidence and experience he needs so badly," Koppett wrote. Until two weeks ago, he continued, the "only possible completely honest appraisal of Bradley could have been: So far, he has shown absolutely nothing." Since the change, "he has shown a little relaxation and instinctive movement, without which no pro can operate." Bradley continued to prosper but remained a substitute, shifting from backcourt to forward. Finally Russell missed one game (he had reserve duty for the National Guard) and Bradley took his spot. "Bill was sick and threw up twice during the game," Jackson reports, "but he absolutely refused to come out." The next game Cazzie broke his ankle. Bradley secured his position as starting forward, Russell becoming the team's sixth man. The composition of the team was complete.

# 7

Few teams have entered a season carrying such burdensome expectations as the 1969 Knicks. They were the decided favorites to win their division and the championship, and reporters had already declared them a dynasty, the league's dominating force for years to come. "While the late '50s and the '60s were often called the era of the Celtics," one reporter wrote in a prologue to the season, "the 1970s, at least part of them, may well be the era of the Knicks." Arthur Daley, the famous *Times* columnist, announced the club was "the ultimate in team cohesion." His colleague, the talented Robert Lipsyte, said the team "was a true joy of this writer," and that "they play with a complementary choreography that is breathtaking to see." Joe Lapchick, the old Knick coach, pronounced them "the greatest basketball team I have ever seen." Once the regular season began, opposing coaches joined the chorus. Dick Motta, the coach of the Chicago Bulls, lost his opening game to New York and afterward said the Knicks had played "the finest team effort I have ever seen in the NBA." After the club beat Phoenix a few nights later, Johnny Kerr, the coach for the Arizona squad, said, "[The Knicks] play championship basketball." The coach of their next victims agreed. "At times," he told the press, "the Knicks look unbelievable. Nothing seems to hurt them." By the third week of the season, the team was such a hot property that Mayor Lindsay declared a "Knick week" (his front man did a bad job, selecting a week when the team was on the road), and Adam Clayton Powell had already visited the club's locker room informing the players that he was their official chaplain. "I guess he means well," DeBusschere commented about him in his book.

All the predictions and publicity created an additional difficulty for the team in its quest for the title: Throughout the season, the Knicks not only had to win, but also meet the high standards that had been raised in their name. The task was largely thankless. Victories were mandatory, losses unacceptable. When the Knicks played brilliantly, they were merely performing as they should; when they stumbled through a contest, even winning at the end, they had betrayed themselves and their fans. They became victims of the media. Idealized portraits were painted of them. Athletes were still cast in an old-fashioned mold then; in newspaper stories about the Knicks the players are referred to occasionally as "Red Holzman's boys" as though this elite group of complicated, ambitious young men who were paid hundreds of thousands of dollars to perform crafts they had perfected over years were some group of spirited high-school kids. Other writers tried to balance this sentimental view with the realities of a pro athlete's life: the enormous investment and substantial profit these men represent, the wearying demands made on a celebrity, the aesthetic joy of playing the game, and the personality quirks that often turn membership on a team into a deeply isolating and troubling experience. But in the desire to counter romantic versions of team life, these writers often exaggerated troubles and conflicts. Berger reports various antagonisms—a white bench warmer disliking a black substitute, Holzman nagging Reed or Frazier—as though these predictable and ordinary flaps indicated deep divisions. By the end of the season, DeBusschere was convinced the attention given the Knicks had antagonized other teams. "An athlete has his vanity and when we come in they want to kick the hell out of us. We've done a great deal for pro basketball, we've given it a new national awareness, but the other teams are out to get us." Two opponents didn't deny the charge. "Let's say we feel we owe them something," said Gus Johnson, the great Baltimore Bullet forward whose duels with DeBusschere became a yearly highlight of the play-offs. Earl Monroe smiled when told DeBusschere's statement. "I'm very happy for the Knicks," he answered, and referred to their famous commercial. "I hope they get everything that's coming to them. If they want to use Vitalis, let them use Vitalis."

But the publicity and predictions also helped shape the team's achievement. One of the Knicks' nicest aspects was that its members displayed little false modesty. Athletic competitions always result in heroic triumphs. The odds against an individual or team beating all others to claim the title of being best are so great that they mark those who overcome them as extraordinary. This is particularly true in the pros, where only a remarkable daring and tenacity in purpose and pursuit allow you to survive the physical and mental exhaustion of a season. Still, the ritual occurs every year and, perhaps because it's repeated, teams often seek to portray their own travail and triumph as special. They like to consider themselves underdogs not graced by the gifts and easy schedules of their opponents; and they also will claim their victory is a moral triumph, the sort of jingoism that surfaced, for instance, during the Olympics, when the coach of the '80 American hockey team, Herb Brooks, told President Carter after winning the gold medal that the triumph proved the superiority of our society. The Knicks indulged in very little of this self-serving romance. They couldn't call themselves underdogs. In just the fourth week in the season, the Knicks already led Philadelphia, the next closest team in their division, by five games. They also didn't fake any fellow feeling. Indeed, they insisted that they were not a family, but the members of an enterprise connected to one another only through their common interest in winning on the court. Put in the unenviable position of having to prove themselves by accomplishing a task they had never attempted before, they pursued their goal with an admirably realistic attitude.

The Knicks played out this drama of self-discovery against a tumultuous background of political demonstrations, strikes, bombings, political trials, growing war, and the national conflict over Vietnam and the treatment of black people and minorities in America. The year had begun with a hopeful promise of ending the war. In October a national moratorium was called. Everyone who disagreed with the government's war policy was encouraged to express their opposition in some peaceful way; the resulting protest was so peaceful it seemed a militant act when organizers refused to disavow a letter from the North Vietnamese endorsing the demonstration. The following month, the moratorium organized a demonstration in Washington, attended by over a quarter million people. By then, the friendly feeling of the previous month had disappeared, the Chicago conspiracy trial and the long battle between Bobby Seale, chairman of the Black Panther Party, and Judge Hoffman had commenced, the judge refusing to allow Seale to defend himself, and Seale insisting on speaking in the court, even when he was bound and gagged. A week before the moratorium, Hoffman convicted Seale for contempt of court, and suddenly inquired if there was anything the beleaguered black leader had to say. "What kind of crap is this?" answered Seale. "I have nothing to say. You punish black people all your life. They say you own factories that make things to kill people in Vietnam . . . I'm not in contempt of this court. I know that I, as a human being, have a right to stand up for my constitutional rights." At the demonstration in Washington, several thousand protestors gathered around the Justice Department, chanting "Free Bobby Seale! Free Chairman Bobby!" Police shot canisters of tear gas into the crowd, and Attorney General Mitchell told his wife the scene reminded him of the Russian Revolution. "The police arrested laggards," the *Times* reported about the protest, "and those they believed who looked violent." About the demonstration, Richard Kleindienst said the government had heard there were plans by the group to "invade" the Justice Department, but that the "basic cowardice" of the protestors had asserted itself and the attack didn't materialize. Two weeks later, Lieutenant Calley was indicted for the Mylai massacre, and the father of a soldier under Calley's command condemned the American army. "I sent them a good boy," the man said, "and they made him a murderer." Less than a week later, Chicago police busted into an apartment and shot to death Fred Hampton and Mark Clark, a young leader and member of the city's Black Panther Party chapter. Edward Hanrahan, Chicago police chief and the probable architect of the raid, didn't abide any criticism of the action, even when it was later proved that the victims had not fired a shot at the police, even in their own defense—in short, that they were murdered by law officers acting in the name of the state. "We wholeheartedly commend the police officers for their bravery," he said, "their remarkable restraint and their discipline in the face of this vicious Black Panther attack, and we expect every decent citizen of the community to do likewise." When the date for the December moratorium came around, the organizers of the previous demonstrations admitted that they didn't know how to proceed: Either they had not anticipated the depths of popular antagonism to the war, or they had too easily assumed their success. There wasn't another national demonstration until early May, and by then events had become deadly. The conviction of the Chicago conspirators (minus Bobby Seale) provoked riots in various student communities around the country, including one in Santa Barbara, where the protestors burned down the Bank of America. Ralph Featherstone, a veteran from the civil rights movement, was blown up while driving in Maryland to the site of the coming trial of H. Rap Brown, the leader of SNCC. "Both hands and both arms of the passenger were blown off," read a newspaper report. "This indicated . . . according to the deputy medical examiner of Baltimore that the man was leaning over the device when it exploded." Evidently either Featherstone had been planning to bomb the courthouse or he was the victim of assassins who wanted to kill Brown. With him was another young man named William (Che) Payne. "He did not have a bone in his body left intact," the coroner announced. Another bombing in the news was the explosion of a town house on West Eleventh Street in New York, a blast that destroyed the building. Over the next several weeks, the newspapers reported daily on the police's progress in identifying the remains of the mysterious people who had been inside the house. The details were appropriate to a battlefield. A body was lifted from the rubble with the scoop of a back-hoe machine; the head was badly damaged, both hands missing, the left leg severed. A doctor said that one torso had a number of puncture wounds caused by nails; another reported that short lengths of electrical wire had been removed from the victim's chest cavity. The victims were reported to be members of Weatherman, the underground that had been formed by members of SDS and who had organized to war against the government. "We don't think in terms of being happy," one of the victims was reported to have told a friend when last seen. "We think in terms of being strong people." In New York, a local version of Bobby Seale's fight for legal rights was being enacted with the trial of twenty-one members of the Panther Party who were accused of a plot to attack police stations, railroads, and department stores. Postal workers in the city went on strike and President Nixon sent National Guardsmen in to distribute the mail while also issuing an eight-thousand-word statement on integration and education that said "there are limits to the amount of government coercion that can be reasonably used," and that schools would no longer be expected to achieve "the kind of multiracial society which the adult community has failed to achieve for itself." Plans were begun for a demonstration in New Haven to protest the trial of Bobby Seale and Ericka Huggins for murder. In Cambodia, Prince Sihanouk was deposed, the start of that country's desolating involvement with the Vietnam war. Student protests were found to have occurred at a rate of one a day, faster than the previous year. Major incidents had happened on ninety-two campuses from January through March 23; one in five were violent, and their intensity and duration indicated that the level of protest was rising, not falling. Every area of the country was affected, the highest rate of incidents occurring in New York, Michigan, Massachusetts, California, and Ohio. In Placquemine, Louisiana, blacks protested a desegregation plan, and police invaded their area of town. A white real-estate man commented: "I tell you, I think it's more than the schools. I think it's something else. It's deep-deep. They call it rioting. Hell, it ain't a riot; it's a revolution."

The conflicts touched the players only tangentially. At the first moratorium, the team was in Cincinnati, about to play the Royals, and DeBusschere and Bradley joined a group of protestors. ". . . [we] followed a few thousand Cincinnati college students on a peace march to Government Square here," DeBusschere wrote. "Bradley chatted with a few of the kids, and I relaxed and listened to the peace songs and speeches. I was impressed by how orderly the whole thing was. I imagine some of the kids were just looking for an excuse to get out of classes, but most of them seemed pretty serious." Jackson wrote that his head "was filled with all kinds of socialistic philosophy . . . I was young and I wanted to know why blacks had to live in ghettoes and why there weren't equal opportunities for everybody." Cazzie Russell had to join the Guard sorting the mail, and one day he and Reed tussled over their attitudes toward racism. Driving to a practice in Detroit, Cazzie was stopped by a cop and made to spread-eagle: The police officer had mistaken him for an escaped convict. "That afternoon," Berger writes, "in a team practice . . . Russell and May struck up fighting stances." This wasn't unusual, Berger reports, but then Reed told Russell to save his anger for the game and Russell called Reed an Uncle Tom. "Reed is said to have advised his fellows that Uncle was gonna whoop some ass if he heard more of that kind of talk." Nate Bowman, the substitute center, was the most actively involved in the radicalism of the time, though innocently. Through friends, he had met Rap Brown, and as a favor he often left Brown tickets for games at the box office, the radical leader joining the celebrities (including Woody Allen, who had recently opened in a play called *Play It Again, Sam* with an unknown actress named Diane Keaton) who now frequented the front rows in the Garden. The Knick press man discovered Bowman's largess and remonstrated with him, Bowman claims, even telling Holzman, who evidently didn't know who Brown was. But the problem solved itself: By mid-March, Brown had disappeared.

By then, the team was coasting toward the play-offs, finishing off a triumphant season. They had won their first five games, including one contest against the favored Los Angeles Lakers, a victory that one reporter claimed "sent a shudder through the rest of the NBA." Then they lost to an unimpressive San Francisco team and followed by thrashing the Detroit Pistons, keeping them to less than 100 points, the fourth time in seven contests that they had managed the feat. In their next game, they repeated the trick, holding the Bullets to 99 while scoring 128 themselves, marking the team's eight-hundredth victory, their sixty-first out of their last eighty-one games, and their sixth consecutive triumph against Baltimore, whom they had vanquished in the play-offs the year before. "So devastating do the New York Knicks look when they play their best," wrote Leonard Koppett after the game, ". . . that their ecstatic fans have found a new item to cheer for. They now take victory for granted and root against the other team making 100 points." They did not lose again until November 29, one month and sixteen consecutive wins later.

The string of victories was an NBA record and the highlight of the season until the play-offs. As the team triumphed each of its members assumed his public role. After having scored over thirty points in two back-to-back games, Willis Reed praised the whole club: "We want to win more than most of the clubs we play. And winning all the time, believe it or not, relieves that feeling we had last year—you must win, you must win. That can wear you down." In Los Angeles, on the team's first road trip, DeBusschere jumped for a rebound, collided with another player, and broke his nose. Later, in the team's hotel, a doctor pushed his nose back into place and two days after he was ready for action again in a nose guard, a strip of aluminum taped to his face. In one picture, he is suspended in the air, his arm outstretched trying to block a shot, the pose and nose mask making him look like a Roman centurion halting an intruder at the gate. After playing exceptionally well in a game, Riordan got a whole article to himself. "No one goes to the hoop faster or with more bulldog determination than the sturdily built 200 pounder," wrote the columnist, and said that John Warren didn't mind entering games only to give fouls since Riordan had risen to prominence on the stepping-stone of that modest assignment. Stallworth and Bowman got special notice in Phoenix when a reporter asked the backup center to characterize the team. Pleased by the unfamiliar attention, Bowman grabbed the radio reporter's mike. "I characterize this team as explosive . . . as dynamic . . ." he began. Stallworth imitated Bowman, and Nate told his buddy to shut up; having silenced Stallworth, he turned to find the radio man had slipped away. "Is that all you want?" he asked, wounded. "There's more, more, more." Holzman established his ironic modesty. "Why is the team shooting so well?" asked a reporter in one of the league's new western cities. "How the hell should I know?" Holzman answered. Frazier began to talk with his later characteristic self-assurance. "I don't worry about winning," he told Robert Lipsyte. "I don't look at the schedule anymore. It don't matter where we are playing. I never get excited, I just go along, real passive. The only time I get worked up is at the end when I sense it, the crowd and the noise and I see all the guys running all over the place." Several days later, he demonstrated his genius, performing for thirty-seven minutes, scoring thirty-three points, getting eight rebounds, and making six assists while the Knicks played what Holzman called their best quarter of the season in a 138–108 rout of Atlanta that tied the league's record for consecutive wins and was the team's tenth victory in as many road games. Two nights later, they set a new mark for excellence, in Cleveland, where they played the Cincinnati Royals; DeBusschere intercepted a crucial pass and Frazier hit two free throws that put the Knicks ahead when they had trailed by five but sixteen seconds before. A newsphoto captures the decisive moment. Frazier is leaping in the air as the ball falls through the net. His body is braced in the air, both hands are clenched into fists. In the moment after the photo, his feet will stomp on the floor, an arm will swing downward, and he will express the sheer joy of winning in one unbelieving "Damn!," an exclamation of wonder and certainty at his and his team's greatness. "I knew I had to come through," he told the press afterward. "If I had missed those shots, I wouldn't have gone back to the dressing room. They never touched the net. I've got ice water in my veins." Upon the team's return to their home city, the *Times* devoted a full page to the biographies of the players. "Why Knicks Win Like Clockwork: A Look at the Hands That Make Them Tick," read the headline. That evening the team finally lost, playing sluggishly against the Detroit Pistons, the same team whose defeat had marked the first victory of the streak. The stars reacted predictably to their bad fortune. Reed was stoical. "This team does not depend on one guy to have a good night so we can win," said Reed. "This wasn't our night as a group. We should have stayed home." Bradley was poetic. "Our voyage is over. Now another one is beginning." Holzman, celebrating his twenty-seventh wedding anniversary, was ironic. "I approach this game on a daily basis. Tomorrow is Sunday, a day off. If the streak hadn't ended, I would have had a few drinks and watched the football game on TV. But since the streak is over, I'll have a few drinks and watch the football game on TV." They had done their work. They possessed a 23–2 record, a .920 winning average; they had passed a true test of excellence in the league, triumphing in all ten of their first road games; and they had captured the public imagination in an unprecedented fashion for a basketball team. "It has been taking the Knicks about thirty-six minutes of play to take control of a game and about thirty-seven minutes of talk to explain it," Koppett wrote during the streak about the newsmen who now crowded into the team's locker room.

The streak over, the Knicks continued to prove themselves, albeit less dramatically, for the rest of the season. The sportswriters covering the club kept predicting trouble for the team, but its problems would have been considered blessings by most squads. The sportswriters worried the most around New Year's. "The Knicks seem ripe for a significant slump," warned a *Times* reporter on January 4, "unless they can regain their previous form." Even the players appeared concerned. "You start looking for excuses," DeBusschere explained about the team's sudden ineffectiveness. "It's the holiday season, so much is going on. The schedule is bad; you're not getting any rest. Frazier and Reed are hurt, our big men. The rest of us are important, but basically we supplement around them. And you hope it turns around soon." Usually reserved for five- and six-game losing streaks, in the case of the Knicks these troubled statements had been occasioned by merely two losses. To put things in proper perspective, the losses had been prefaced by wins in three out of the team's last four games, all of them played on the road, the team flying from Detroit to Los Angeles to Vancouver to Phoenix in ninety-six hours, and were followed by another cross-country trek in which the Knicks won six out of eight games and began a new winning streak that ended with but a modest nine triumphs and included another four games in a five-night stretch during which the Knicks dropped but one decision.

The team weathered similarly well the injury to Bradley later on in the year and the periodic absences taken by Cazzie Russell to fulfill his duty in the National Guard. Losing their last batch of games before the play-offs, and posting a 37–21 record for the season after the streak—an unimpressive tally only when compared to record-setting ones—they still ended the season with a league-best 60–22 mark for the year.

# 8

The first round of the play-offs matched the Knicks against the Baltimore Bullets. The outcome was supposed to be decided easily. An excellent team, the Bullets included Earl Monroe, the league's most inventive offensive backcourt performer, Wes Unseld, a mammoth rebounder, and Gus Johnson, a veteran forward whom DeBusschere considered the strongest on any club, plus a combination of other expert players, each performing distinct roles. The year before they had emerged from last place to win fifty-seven games and lead the Eastern Division during the regular season, then lost four straight to New York in the play-offs. The coach was Gene Shue, a handsome man with a casual attitude who had shuttled from team to team as an excellent journeyman guard before arriving in Baltimore and guiding the club to success. "I'm not discouraged," he said early in the '69–'70 season after his team had lost to the Knicks, "I feel in my bones that something nice is going to happen to the Bullets this season." Still, the Knicks had won against Baltimore thirteen of the last fifteen times and appeared to have established a hard-won but unshakable dominance over the other team.

The Knicks won the first two games and, under a picture of

Frazier getting his hair cut by the manager of a salon Frazier had just bought, Koppett declared the Knicks to be "in an all but impregnable position." The Knick victories had come against a primed opponent and they showed "[the team] benefitted from a less noticeable but vital winning factor: the ability to make a tough or opportunistic basket here and there while the opposing team [is] having its hot streak." Then, in Madison Square Garden, the Knicks lost, Unseld, the Bullet center, grabbing thirty-four rebounds, four more than were collected by the entire New York team. "He just did the job," said Reed, who appeared increasingly bothered by a knee injury he had received in November. "I've never seen one man outrebound a team before."

Returning to Baltimore—the sites switched with every contest during the series—the Bullets won again, tying the set. They outrebounded and outshot the Knicks, and Monroe established himself as the dominant single performer in the series, scoring thirty-four points, a surprise to the Knick players who had silenced him during the regular season. Now he sank baskets repeatedly, dribbling the ball until only a few seconds showed on the clock, then turning, faking, and spinning the ball off his hand, producing a deft and accurate shot that couldn't be stopped. Shue lauded the team's defense, and Johnson, who had informed his fellow combatant De-Busschere, while lining up for an inbounds pass, that, unlike the two of them, Monroe wasn't human, claimed the season had started over. Unseld said he refused to get excited until the series was won. Monroe offered the strangest comment of all. Throughout the year the Knicks had claimed their offense was generated by the defense—the proper puritan attitude for a champion team to take. Asked why his team had won, Monroe reversed the equation—the sterling defense of the Bullets, he explained, was a reflection of their brilliant offense.

The win produced other changes. Reed's knee injury hampered his mobility on the court and explained Unseld's domination around the key: The Baltimore center had collected almost twice the number of rebounds as the New York hero. Reed had refused to take a cortisone shot to numb the pain; he dreaded the injections. Now he accepted one and promptly grabbed a hefty thirty-six rebounds and managed the neat trick of scoring an equal number of points. The rebounds were a team record and, as one writer noted, "since this was the 1,844th game played by the Knicks, a club record really means something."

Frazier also altered his play. He had scored sixteen and nineteen points in the Knick victories; in the team's defeats, he had tallied twenty-four and twenty-five. In the practice before the fifth game, Bradley had said "steps had to be taken" to get the team back on track, and Holzman had ordered Frazier to concentrate more on defense and getting the ball to the open man. "I thought I was playing well," Frazier said, evidently somewhat shaken by the adjustment. "I was scoring points, we just weren't winning. I wouldn't have thought to change if no one had said anything." In the following game he scored 16 points and, repeating the feat of the captain, grabbed the same number of rebounds, while helping to hold Monroe below his average and lead the team to a 101–80 victory.

Finally, the Bullet resistance to the Knicks threatened the stature of the New York team. The defeats raised doubts among fans. Perhaps the Knicks weren't extraordinary. Maybe they were simply another commercial sports product sold by Madison Avenue. A year before, Robert Lipsyte had called the Knicks "a true joy of this writer." Now, always quick to call a foul, he wrote a testy column saying the Bullets were "a truly fine team . . . a superb unit, one that might have been acclaimed the best of all times too, if they had played in New York where the magazines and television live." As though to prove his point, the Knicks lost to Baltimore again, Monroe and Gus Johnson starring, leaving the Knicks' hopes for the season resting on one last, seventh game.

But the next night at the Garden, the Knicks answered their

critics. They finally and soundly defeated the Bullets, displaying an offense that Holzman called their best of the season. "We had almost no challenge the final month of the season," DeBusschere said, apologizing for and excusing the Knick performance. "I think it was good for us to get a series like this, to get us up." Shue called the two teams the best in basketball. Monroe, who had scored thirty-two points for his final performance, wished luck to both the Knicks and the Bucks, their upcoming challengers. "I'm not a basketball fan," said the series' premier player. "I hate to watch the game. I just play it." Frazier answered the doubts about the team. "We had this team down 2–0 and let them off the hook. If great champions like the old Celtics had a team down 2–0 they put them away. But we didn't have that championship toughness, and we let the Bullets come back. Then it came down to one game, and we reacted—and I think that shows that we're developing a toughness. The next time we get a team down, we'll finish them off."

It was commonly believed that New York couldn't easily accomplish this task against the Milwaukee Bucks, the team they were to fight for the title of Eastern Division champs. An expansion squad, one of the then yearly additions to the league, the Bucks were a prodigy. Having managed only twenty-seven triumphs in their premiere season, they had been awarded the league's first draft choice and had signed Lew Alcindor (now Kareem Abdul-Jabbar) to a one-million-dollar contract, and with him at center, had gotten the league's second-best record. DeBusschere considered them the toughest opponents they would meet in the play-offs.

Defying predictions again, the Knicks devastated the Bucks in five games, letting them win only one match and displaying a high-spirited ease of mastery throughout the series both on and off the court. Before the first game, Bradley appeared in the Knick locker room wearing a light brown suit cut with fashionable wide lapels, a yellow tie, and suede shoes. Designed for him by Barnett's tailor, his new outfit got applause and cheers from his teammates. "Now that you're a different person," asked Holzman, "do you want me to call you Mr. Bradley?" On the court, the Knicks harassed Alcindor and neutralized his colleagues, Frazier hounding Flynn Robinson, one of the Bucks' outside shooters, who slumped badly throughout the series, and DeBusschere pursuing Bobby Dandridge, later one of the league's finest small forwards, then a rookie from Norfolk State who seemed too slight to last in professional ball.

In the next game, the Bucks put up more of a fight, Alcindor performing mightily, but the Knicks still came out ahead by a point and with a joke. With his team ahead by only a point, DeBusschere stole the ball from Alcindor and passed to Cazzie, who was free downcourt and raced toward the basket for a dunk and a certain two points, except the ball jammed against the hoop and flew off the court. "Caz wears fancy blue and orange sweatbands on his wrists," wrote Frazier, who called the incident the highlight of the series, indicating how seriously he took the Buck threat, "yet he said he missed the dunk because his hands were sweaty." Still, with fifty-two seconds left in the game, the Knicks led only by a point, 110–109, and Reed was called for fouling Alcindor. The rookie—the appellation is an absurd truth—missed both shots. Cazzie Russell redressed his fault by hitting on two foul shots and after Alcindor hit a jumper, the Knicks simply dribbled the ball in open court for the last twenty seconds, while Larry Costello, the Buck coach, yelled at his players to foul one of them. The Knicks won, 112–111, and Russell happily accepted the role of the game's goat, a performance he repeated four days later when the series resumed in Milwaukee and he missed a stuff again, only one of many Knick miscues that resulted in a five-point loss.

Still, it was Russell who answered the Bucks' biggest challenge in the series. During the fourth game, the Knicks led at the half by twenty, but played poorly in the third quarter and Milwaukee came back, pressing and stealing the ball and cutting the lead down to three. Holzman replaced Bradley with Russell. Frazier and Russell had frequently conducted a chicken-and-egg, guard-versus-forward argument, Frazier complaining that Russell shot too much and Russell demanding that the guard give him the ball more. In this instance, Frazier fed him immediately and Russell fulfilled his obligation, hitting his shots. ". . . he even drove straight over Alcindor," DeBusschere wrote about Russell's cameo appearance. "He just roared in, right past big Lew, and laid it in. 'You know that's the way to go on him,' Cazzie told me later. 'You go right at him.'" Later, in the locker room, while the team celebrated its third win of the series, Cazzie fooled with his teammates. "I couldn't give you guys any more to joke about," he said. "I've seen enough imitations of my dunk shots."

The series' last game was played in the Garden, and the Knicks romped. The final score was 132–96, a blowout in which the Knicks performed with such exactness and exuberance that the game remains a pleasure to watch even though it lacks the drama that normally marks fine basketball contests. Every offensive rebound, intercepted pass, stolen ball seems to result in a basket. Leading by thirty-six points, the Knicks— the subs by this time—triple-team a Buck player, forcing him into a corner, hoping to rattle him and get a bad pass. With two minutes left, John Warren steals the ball at midcourt and passes to Riordan, who makes a neat lay-up. Right before the final buzzer, Bowman sets up high, waits until Riordan breaks free, feeds him a pass, and an old schoolyard play has worked again. The only Knick player who didn't get into the action was Hosket, sitting out the game with a twisted ankle. Late in the fourth quarter, when even the most anxious fans had stopped worrying, the New York crowd chanted so insistently for the Ohio State player that Holzman had the P.A. announcer explain the reason for Hosket's stay in the wings; the crowd responded to the information with a large cheer, and Hosket walked up and down the bench, his arms raised high in the air, the crowd loving him, Holzman shouting at him to limp a little more pronouncedly so the crowd wouldn't think him a liar.

Indeed, only for Reed was the series a difficult one. The Knicks outmatched the Bucks easily in all area but one, the pivot, where Reed fought Alcindor. In the first game, Alcindor scored thirty-five points, almost half of them during one ten-minute stretch when the New Yorkers guarded him with only one man instead of the two or three who usually surrounded him whenever he handled the ball. Alcindor's coach, Larry Costello, a pedestrian and mechanical tactician, declared that Alcindor's performance was "lackadaisical" and Alcindor improved upon it during the next game: He scored twenty-eight points, grabbed twenty-three rebounds, and was credited with eleven assists, outplaying Reed in every aspect in a contest that Koppett called the most spectacular play-off game yet and which convinced him that Alcindor "seems destined to dominate pro ball for the next decade." (A correct prediction, Alcindor's prodigious mental and physical gifts and accomplishments making him so influential a talent that he was awarded Most Valuable Player even when performing on a team with an unexceptional record.) The crowd responded to this display with awe and dismay. Because of Alcindor's height, color, dignified manner, and uncompromised excellence as a player, the predominantly white crowd didn't accord him the warm approval and respect that was his due and which they normally gave to athletes whom they could, in some dim way, consider reflections of themselves. Instead, Dick Young, the columnist for the *Daily News*, labeled Alcindor a racist and, as Alcindor left the fifth game, the crowd taunted him, chanting: "Good-bye, Lewie, good-bye, Lewie, we hate to see you go." Reed and the Knicks displayed none of this arrogance. Alcindor's mere presence had forced the team to change its offense, the players shooting mainly from outside and rarely challenging the Buck center with drives to the hoop, a strategy for which the Knicks were ideally suited but which might have cost other teams the title. Reed merely admired him. "I often know what he's going to do," he said at the start of the series, "but that doesn't mean I can stop him." During the course of the games, he habitually referred to Alcindor's height, and the "eyeball to Adam's apple confrontation" that happened when he was matched up against him. "I look like his little brother," he said. "It must be great to be that tall. But I can't stand back and admire him. I've got to take it to him." He outscored him in the last game, the centerpiece of an attack about which the *Times* reporter spoke ecstatically: "Perfection was the only appropriate word for the way the New York Knicks played last night. They crushed the Bucks . . . with so dazzling a display of shooting, passing, moving, sniping and team cohesion that their style overshadowed the significance of an historic victory . . ." But Reed's experience of this excellence and triumph was entirely different. "I'm tired, I'm so tired," he confessed to DeBusschere in the middle of the final game. "I almost felt like I couldn't walk out there."

# 9

The final test of the team was against the Los Angeles Lakers. The club starred three veterans whose careers had set the standards for each of their positions: a guard, Jerry West; a forward, Elgin Baylor; and the center, Wilt Chamberlain. These three highly individual talents had been brought together to form what the Los Angeles owners hoped would be a devastating championship team. Instead the trio had lost to the Boston Celtics in the '68–'69 title series. After this debut they were promptly branded not a true team but merely a collection of superb performers. Fans considered them antithetical to basketball's ideal of teamwork and judged them ill-suited to wear the crown when compared to the selfless Knicks. For this reason the championship mattered dearly to them. The Knicks had to win the title to prove the popular judgment of them was true; the Lakers had to secure it to show the popular judgment of them was false.

The series opened in New York, two days after a mini-riot at the Garden: Six thousand fans lined up at six in the morning for the eight thousand tickets available for the tournament and charged the box office a half hour later when they heard only several hundred were left. The Knicks won the game handily, 124–112. Chamberlain let Reed shoot from outside, not leaving the area around the basket to guard him, and Reed chalked up points and gave the Knicks a nice half-time lead. The team withered under a Laker attack in the third quarter, but revived in the fourth, their defense performing what for them was an ordinary miracle of holding the opposing team to but two field goals in seven minutes and winning the game. Afterward, people speculated about Chamberlain's defense—shouldn't he have guarded Willis more closely? Chamberlain's motives were analyzed. He had suffered a bad knee injury in the fall and made a remarkable comeback. But maybe the knee wasn't completely healed, or was he immobile simply because, deep down, he was really a passive competitor? "Does your knee hamper your style of play?" asked one reporter in the locker room afterward. "My man," replied the seven-footer who could never seem to satisfy people's expectations, "I don't have a style."

The score of the second game was closer, the Knicks losing, 105–103. ". . . the title will cap a season that the stomping, screaming, orgiastic Knick fan—who chants 'defense' when the other team has the ball and cheers Nate Bowman for making it downcourt—knows will never again be approached, not by this team," wrote Robert Lipsyte in anticipation of a victory before the game. But DeBusschere says he could feel something wrong even before the contest started. "Just about everyone wandered in later than usual, even Red, and the room was strangely quiet—not tense quiet, but sort of casual quiet, as though we were playing just another game." From the first the Knicks had planned to capitalize on the age and slowness of Baylor and Chamberlain, figuring to overwhelm strength and accuracy with motion and speed. Instead, they slowed down and found themselves matching baskets with the Lakers while Chamberlain exerted his power defensively, coming out and guarding Willis, not letting him take his shot. "When we move, we win," Holzman shouted at half time. "When we don't, we lose." Still, the Knicks remained slow and Chamberlain won the game, blocking two key shots at the end. "Would you say, Wilt," asked a reporter afterward, "that you came to play?" Chamberlain answered: "Man, I always come to play. Do you think I worked four months on my knee so I could come here and jive?"

The third and fourth games were played in Los Angeles. The team flew in a special chartered jet; Barnett invited some reporters to the upstairs lounge for a wild-card poker game that everyone but he treated frivolously and at which he was the only winner. The next night at the Forum —famous for crowds as soporific as the Garden ones were manic—the Lakers came out strong and ran up a fourteen-point lead at half time. But the Knicks tied the game late in the second half and with only a few seconds left DeBusschere scored to give them the lead. There were so few seconds remaining that Chamberlain threw the ball to his teammate West, and then ran off the court to the locker room. Under the Laker basket, DeBusschere waited for the buzzer to sound. West dribbled the ball a little upcourt, meeting Reed at the foul line on the far end of the arena, and heaved the ball toward the basket, a desperation shot that traveled fifty-five feet and cleanly filled the net, tying the game. DeBusschere toppled over in amazement at the feat. "Nobody hit me. I was so stunned I couldn't keep my feet. It was no vaudeville act. I just collapsed right on the floor." Still, the Knicks recouped to win the overtime session and gain what Koppett called "a realistic mental edge . . . the Lakers had countless opportunities to put the game out of reach after taking their lead, but just couldn't." He called the game a pivotal one; if they won the next contest, they would return to New York with a 3–1 edge. Instead, the Knicks played poorly in the fourth contest, not executing in the third quarter, at one point missing twelve shots in a row and turning the ball over eight times. Reed had been enjoying a fine series thus far, averaging 35 points in the first three games. Now he appeared stiff. He had been taking cortisone pills for the pain in his knee, but their effect had diminished; now the pain immobilized him on the court, making the team's defense lax and their offense predictable. West scored thirty-four points and was credited with eighteen assists. DeBusschere got into early foul trouble and coached Stallworth on how to play Baylor—Baylor always preferred moving to his right, and the trick was to force him left. But the veteran proved too resourceful and ended scoring 30 points and getting 13 rebounds. The game became a sloppy and thrilling contest, equaling the drama of the previous match with another overtime period in which the Lakers outscored the Knicks.

Two days later, on May 4, the fifth and critical contest was held back in New York. It was pre-empted by the news that four students at Kent State University in Ohio had been shot to death by National Guardsmen. The Friday before, students had demonstrated on the campus, symbolically burying the Constitution and that night, upon hearing of the invasion of Cambodia, several thousand of them had smashed windows and burned the ROTC office, four thousand rounds of .22 ammunition exploding in the flames. The Guard had been summoned and on Sunday, after church services, locals had swarmed over the campus to see the wreckage. Monday morning another demonstration was called and as the Guardsmen advanced toward the protestors, the Guardsmen suddenly and inexplicably fired into the crowd. The deaths were entirely arbitrary; the victims weren't even particularly militant in their opposition to the war; one of the young women killed had put a flower in a Guardsman's rifle the day before, telling the soldier that flowers were better than bullets. The news was of particular concern to Marv Albert, the team's radio announcer, whose brother, Steve, attended Kent State. Before the game Marv Albert tried desperately to reach his brother. "The telephone lines were jammed . . . I canvassed the WHN wire service machines throughout the day, but the news was sketchy. I finally went to the Garden with no idea of Steve's whereabouts . . ."

At the arena, opinion divided about which squad was a favorite in the game. Baylor had aggravated an old injury while playing so masterfully in the fourth game and West had jammed his thumb. Keith Erikson, another forward, was suffering a bad ankle and Chamberlain's knee was always questionable. The Knicks were not a formidable force, however. Thus far, the talents of the Laker stars had matched the Knick teamwork, and Reed, without whom the Knicks never performed brilliantly, appeared to be weakening. He had averaged twenty-seven points and seventeen rebounds through the first four games, but in the last the Knicks had been badly beaten off the boards and the *Times* reporter wrote that the center "was in the worst physical shape of the season." He was taking cortisone pills and Vitamin B shots, but told DeBusschere that he had forced himself to play the last game. Finally, the special quality of the Knicks had been lacking throughout the series. Before the fifth game, Frazier remarked that the team really hadn't gotten its thing together.

They started the pivotal contest in hapless fashion. The Lakers hit twelve of their first fifteen shots and Reed obviously could no longer overcome the pain in his knee, not getting a single rebound. With about four minutes left in the quarter and the Lakers leading by ten, Reed got the ball, feinted right, started to drive left, toward the basket, and collapsed, his leg giving out terribly and suddenly underneath him. Chamberlain scooped up the ball and flung it downcourt. The Knicks called a time-out and Reed hobbled to the bench. As the teams walked back on court to resume play, he limped to the locker room escorted by Danny Whelan, the team trainer, and the team doctor. Reed hadn't injured his knee, but pulled some muscles in his thigh. The doctor's diagnosis was that he couldn't aggravate the injured area if he played, but that he was feeling such intense pain he wouldn't be able to perform normally and would probably end up injuring something else. For that night, at least, he couldn't play again.

The Knicks heard this news at half time; until then they had hoped Reed would return to the game and had held off the Lakers using Bowman, Hosket, and finally DeBusschere against Chamberlain. "For four minutes at the end of the first half," DeBusschere wrote, "I didn't see the basketball game. I just saw Wilt's back. He didn't score a point in those four minutes. I don't know why, but he didn't." This success convinced Holzman to keep DeBusschere in the center position. Bradley suggested the team change its offense. Chamberlain had stationed himself around the basket during the first half, playing, in effect, a zone, where a man guards an area of the court, rather than another player. Bradley proposed the Knicks take advantage of their outside shooting accuracy and form a design of their own, a 1–3–1 pattern, Frazier at the top, Bradley, Barnett, and Russell in the middle, DeBusschere near the basket. If Chamberlain stayed around the hoop, they hoped to score from the outside; if he came out to guard them, they could then drive around him. The plan tried to use the strength of the Knicks, their speed and accuracy, to maximum effect, and minimize their weakness, the lack of a player who could match Chamberlain in size and strength.

Defense was the other factor in the Knick strategy, the weapon that had consistently won games for them throughout the season. Knowing they couldn't control the game off the boards, they tried to dominate the play on the court. From the start, the Lakers sought to get the ball to Chamberlain, who could easily shoot against the smaller DeBusschere. "The Lakers were too conscious of the mismatch," wrote DeBusschere. "They started forcing passes into Wilt. Some went over his head. Some were intercepted. Their whole offense stopped moving." At the same time, the Knicks hounded the Laker ball handlers, directing them to the corners, where they would double-team them and steal the ball.

They narrowed the Laker lead, and the shrinking advantage threatened and upset the Los Angeles team. Why couldn't they capitalize on the Knicks' weakness? Their players suffered miscues. Called for a charging foul, Keith Erikson compounded the damage by throwing the ball downcourt, away from the official, who hit him with a technical foul. "Now the Lakers were motionless, disorganized," the *Times* reporter wrote about the middle of the third period, "throwing the ball away as well as having it taken away." The Lakers began to believe they might lose and, more importantly, the Knicks started to think they could win. Their play became more inspired. Cazzie Russell guarded Baylor. Baylor was continuing his admirable performance of the previous game, but Russell matched him. "All year I've been getting my hands on rebounds and forgetting to hold on so other guys could grab them," Russell said. "Tonight I snatched one out of Baylor's hands and said, 'Hey, that should have been the other way around.' It was unreal." Stallworth replaced DeBusschere at center. Stallworth played in front of Chamberlain, picking off passes, staying away from the mammoth who was used to opposing centers leaning and pushing on him. When Chamberlain left the area around the basket to try to block Stallworth's outside shot, Stallworth easily drove around him. West was neutralized entirely. In the second half he tried only two shots and didn't score one field goal. "[He] was in a daze," DeBusschere reported, "a strange faraway look on his face." In the locker room, Willis Reed listened to the announcer proclaim the score. "It sounded like fantasy," Reed said.

When the score closed to 84–80, advantage Los Angeles,

Frazier became certain the Knicks would win. "They didn't know what to do. If they did get through [our] press they kept trying to go to Wilt and we kept picking off the passes. We stole the ball from them eight times in the fourth period. I stole it three times in the last twelve minutes." DeBusschere waited until the Knicks went ahead, 93–91, before believing they would triumph. "I knew we couldn't be stopped. I knew we had them. We were flying." Now Russell lifted his fist with every Knick basket and all the fans in the arena, as inspired in their cheering as the players were in their performances, rose as one body with him, their arms in the air. In the last minutes, Stallworth, Bradley, and Russell didn't miss any shots, Bradley hitting one last jumper with but two seconds left on the twenty-four-second clock to clinch the win, 107–100. "God dog," Russell shouted, "what a thrill." Stallworth explained that Bradley and Russell had set the pace—"how could I help but join in?" DeBusschere traded jokes with Stallworth about guarding Chamberlain. "We got the most out of everything on the floor," said Bradley, and singled out DeBusschere for special praise. "What a man that DeBusschere is! He's an all-star at every position." The Lakers had hit a higher percentage of their field goals than the Knicks, but had been held to just twenty-six shots the entire second half; they had outrebounded the Knicks, but lost the ball to them thirty times, nineteen in the last twenty-four minutes of play. "These guys," Holzman said about his team, "can do anything. There's nothing they can't do."

Reed accompanied the team on its trip back to the West Coast for the sixth game. He looked fine in a photo taken on his way to the doctor's the day after his fall, a large and smiling gent in a broad-rimmed hat, loudly checked pants, white shirt, and vest, but there was little chance he would play. John Warren, the rookie and Reed's roommate, accompanied the center to the doctor and told DeBusschere about the visit. "Will tried to jump and touch the ceiling. He got up all right, off his good leg, but when he landed he let out a scream. He nearly passed out from the pain." He didn't change for the game, sitting on the bench in his street clothes, and watched the Knicks lose badly to the Lakers, 135–113.

Chamberlain controlled the game. Holzman decided to start Bowman against him. "That sucker gonna need a hearse," Berger reports Barnett said when he heard the news. Frazier was to help Bowman. He had been guarding Dick Garrett, a rookie with whom Frazier had played in college. (Barnett was assigned to West: Barnett used his body more on defense than Frazier and it was hoped he would tire the Laker star.) In the fifth game, Frazier had ruined Garrett's game, and now he showed little respect for his shooting, figuring Garrett would pass the ball to Chamberlain and staying near the big man, hoping to make a steal. Instead Garrett shot and hit, seven tries in a row, and when Frazier left Chamberlain to cool down the rookie, the Los Angeles center with only the weaker and shorter Bowman guarding him started to score. "Lean on Wilt and put your elbow into him," Reed advised his substitute. "But when he gets the ball, back off him a little. Otherwise, he'll just put his arm back over your head and lay the ball in the hoop." But Reed's counsel didn't help Bowman and in the second period Holzman replaced him with De-Busschere. He fared no better. "You're playing Wilt all wrong," Reed told him at half time. DeBusschere answered that the only way he could play Wilt tonight was to grow five or six inches. The Knicks performed woefully; they got ten fouls in the first quarter, turned the ball over eight times in the first half, and hit only a third of their shots. Every time they drew close to the Lakers, Chamberlain spurted to put the lead out of reach. At the end, he had shot 20 for 27 and was credited with 27 rebounds. "All you have to do is give us one half Friday night," a frustrated De-Busschere told Reed in the Knick locker room after the defeat. "Just be out there one half of the game and keep that big guy off." To the press, he said: "Without Willis, we are an ordinary team."

The seventh game was to be held in New York on Friday. Three days had passed since the shooting at Kent State and there were demonstrations across the country protesting the murders and Nixon's policies. His administration was besieged. Fire bombings had occurred at the University of Nevada in Reno, the University of Alabama, Valparaiso University in Indiana, and Southern Illinois University, where Frazier had played college ball; across the country, eighty major schools were shut, including the entire state systems in California and Pennsylvania, and students battled police or National Guardsmen at state universities in Illinois, Kentucky, and New Mexico, where ten demonstrators were stabbed with bayonets. In New York, every college was closed down, the students on strike. The day before there had been a funeral for Jeffrey Miller, one of the victims at Kent State, and mourners had lined Amsterdam Avenue. The afternoon of the game, there was a march through downtown Manhattan and several hundred men wearing construction helmets charged the demonstrators, cornering them in the narrow streets and beating them up—in photos published the next day one pummels a kid behind the famous statue of George Washington that greets visitors to the Federal Hall National Memorial, and another holds a fellow by his long hair while two men in suits look on as they buy hotdogs and sodas at a Sabrett stand. "They're starting to treat their own children like they treat us, aren't they?" a black woman was quoted in that day's newpaper. "If they're turning against their own, then Lord help us." The next day there was to be a national rally in Washington, and Nixon ordered the White House to be surrounded by buses, the modern version of the circle wagon trains used to make when attacked by Indians. He was to speak that night, but in one of those calculated gestures he would periodically perform to demonstrate his grace and humanity, he announced that he was postponing his national address: He wouldn't give it until the seventh game was over.

In that morning's *Times*, Leonard Koppett announced Reed had a fifty-fifty chance of starting and described the game's importance. "For the Knicks, with or without Reed, this is the one victory that can seal their superseason. Whatever the explanations, or bad luck, a loss now would erase all the gloss from the last six months. It is unjust, but it's the rule of sports. Possession of the title 'champion' lends substance forever afterward to discussions about a team being 'one of the greatest ever.' Finishing second, even by one point, will quickly reduce the Knicks to just another distinguished entry in the record book . . . Game 101 should be something."

After two days of hot packs, massages, ultrasound, and whirlpool treatments, Reed dressed for the game and before a small group of reporters (and Wilt Chamberlain who looked on) tested his leg on the court, Donnie May tossing him the ball as the injured center shot from the foul line. He then returned to the locker room to show the doctor exactly where the pain was located and received three injections of 100 cc apiece of Carbocaine, a derivative of Novocain, a dosage so powerful that Pete Axthelm claims it would have disqualified a racing horse if found in his system. Years later, in remembering that evening, Reed was to tell a reporter that he had always *played* all the basketball in him, referring to the sport as though it were a part of his being that enjoyed a life of its own and had to be expressed, the way Eskimo sculptors say they merely free the shape inside the stone. Then he told Danny Whelan, the team's trainer: "This is it. There's nothing to save up for now." He heard an enormous cheer from the crowd. Cazzie Russell had walked out after the team, and the fans, desperate for Reed to appear, had mistaken the forward for the captain. Then, three minutes before the game was to begin, Reed trudged out. The cheers and applause increased as he emerged from the corridor that led to the court; they continued as he took several shots; when the announcer finally declared Reed would start, they reached a crescendo. "It was very inspirational for me too," wrote Frazier. "It wasn't for me, but I got chills. It was a great feeling."

Frazier had been undaunted by the defeat in Los Angeles. "I was glad they had beaten us," he wrote. ". . . if we had played them a close game and lost, it would have taken a lot out of us. By losing the way we did, what did it mean? Plus, I think they got overconfident. They were sure Willis wouldn't be back by Friday in one piece, so they figured they could wipe us out again." The night before the game, Frazier stayed awake in his hotel room in the New Yorker across from the Garden alternately imagining an easy, sweeping victory, and a humiliating, disastrous defeat. Then he slept a few hours, ate some lunch, wasted some time in the hotel lobby, and returned to his room to dress for the game. "I dressed casually in a Clyde outfit: dark-brown bell-bottom pants, beige coat pinched in tight at the waist, and beige boots. It was pretty cool, I thought." In the locker room, he passed Reed. "I just said, What's happening?—not really wanting him to answer the question." Holzman joked with Frazier, and DeBusschere told him not to let Garrett get his shots off—he didn't want the rookie to score from the outside as he had in L.A. Frazier assured him he wouldn't give Garrett any room tonight.

The game began with Los Angeles controlling the ball, Reed not even contesting the jump with Chamberlain. When New York got the ball back, Reed followed his team back to their basket, dragging his bad leg behind him. He had started, but no one knew whether he would be able to withstand the actual stress of playing. He halted at the foul line and received a pass. Chamberlain was under the basket. Reed lifted himself gently into the air and shot. The basket scored. "The Lakers moved downcourt," DeBusschere reports, "and passed the ball into Wilt. He moved to his left; Willy moved with him. Wilt stopped and passed the ball out." The Lakers scored and the Knicks took possession. Again Reed set himself at the foul line, received the pass, and scored. He ain't hurt, Frazier thought joyfully, seeing the captain make his shot. Then he corrected himself. "Of course I knew he was, but after the first few minutes it didn't matter." Reed's presence had fulfilled the mandatory requirements for a Knick win: Chamberlain would have to guard him away from the basket and the Los Angeles center wouldn't score any uncontested points against the New York team. "Just having him out there with us," Frazier said, "I got so turned on I couldn't stop."

Frazier proceeded to run the team. Garrett, the man guarding him, quickly got into foul trouble and started playing Frazier cautiously. Frazier began to shoot, making the first five attempts from the field and his first five free throws. "Each time I shot I was so confident I was on target that if the ball didn't drop through I was shocked." Then DeBusschere began to hit. By the end of the quarter, the two of them scored one more point than the entire Laker squad. "Don't let up," Barnett told DeBusschere. "Die out there if you have to." They entered the second quarter with a 14-point lead, and Frazier stole the ball from Chamberlain and passed downcourt to Bradley, who scored a lay-up. Frazier stalled, missing several shots in a row. ". . . [I] got mad at myself. That's when I stole the ball from West . . . I saw West feint toward the middle, then get up a full head of steam to try to go outside [Riordan]. He didn't notice me off to his left, so I moved away from my man, darted in front of West and swooped the ball away." He scored, hit the foul shot, and expanded the lead to twenty points. The Lakers got the ball and Riordan helped to force them into a twenty-four-second violation, returning it to the Knicks. "I knew we had them then. We killed their leader."

When the buzzer sounded at the half, they led by twenty-seven. The team ran into the locker room, shouted at each other, and immediately turned around and went back onto the court. "I have never seen a team so fired up," Holzman said. Bowman walked out to jump against Chamberlain. At the last moment, Reed appeared, replacing Bowman and repeating his surprise performance of the game's opening minutes. The Lakers attempted a small comeback, but the Knicks, who throughout the season had become famous for their third-quarter strength, throttled them. "I made a free throw," writes Frazier. "I stole the ball from [Garrett] and went all the way in for a lay-up. I hit a jump shot, and was fouled and made a free throw. A few seconds later Wilt missed two free throws . . . DeBusschere threw in one of his typical long jumpers and we had a twenty-seven-point lead again."

The Los Angeles team never challenged them again. The fourth quarter was simply a countdown. Barnett scored on lay-ups; later he said he could see dollar signs on the backboard. His wife saw the victory as revenge for the years he had suffered as a substitute in L.A. "[West] and [Baylor] always had to be the stars," she told Bradley after the game. "That's why they never won and that's why I'm glad we beat them tonight." Bradley hit for seventeen points and five assists. "[He] sprinted downcourt with both fists raised in the air," DeBusschere remembers, "he was glowing with victory." DeBusschere had eighteen points and seventeen rebounds. With ten seconds left in the game, Los Angeles scored, reducing the lead to fourteen. The crowd began to count. De-Busschere cradled the ball and when he heard "one" ran to the locker room clutching the ball to him. Frazier was there already. With four seconds left in the game, he had quit the bench, afraid of being mobbed by the crowd. He was exhausted and numb. In leading the team to victory, he had scored thirty-six points, missing but five of the seventeen shots he took from the field and hitting all twelve from the foul line, and was credited with seven rebounds and nineteen assists, altogether accounting for 74 of the Knicks' 113 points. His poise and concentration, the enormous grace and sensual intellect of his game had matched Reed's formidable fortitude and led his teammates to the celebrations and glories awarded the best basketball team in the world.

# 10

There is a song sung at Passover services that recounts the deeds of the Lord in leading the Hebrew people out of bondage in Egypt. Each verse celebrates one of the Lord's miracles and each chorus repeats one word, *D'ayenu*, it would have been sufficient. But people reserve such generosity only for the works of the Lord; they view the accomplishments of humanity more critically. Certainly sports fans do. Had the Knicks won eighteen games straight and not been divisional champions, it wouldn't have been sufficient; and had they won the divisional championship but not beaten the Bullets, it wouldn't have been sufficient; and even if they had won everything, but not played with the grace that marked them as a team, triumphing instead because of one player's exceptional effort or an opposing team's poor performance, it still wouldn't have been sufficient. To be champions, they had to fulfill all their promise.

You can still witness their progress on the game films from that year. The films are black and white, soundless, 16-millimeter reels, a sports team's movies. Everything on them appears old-fashioned: The Garden looks distant and antique, the crowd an audience watching a college double-header in the thirties. Even the game seems out of time. The action isn't continuous and it's hard to keep score: A player steps to the foul line, bounces the ball, preparing to shoot the free throw, and suddenly an opponent is dribbling upcourt. Occasionally a bulky silhouette crosses the screen, interrupting the film, the back of a husband returning to his seat after calling his wife, a businessman handing out beers to his friends, a kid who managed to sneak past the ushers and is looking for an empty seat. Other times, a bird flies across the screen, one of the pigeons or swallows that nest high in the Garden rafters. The court itself and the players appear shrunken, and the common television shots never fill the screen—a close-up of a player's face, a colorful or beautiful member of the audience, an athlete flying in slow motion through the air. These films are meant to be educational and the camera positioned high above the court presents a stark view of the sport: faceless players weaving a changing pattern on a brightly lit stage that is surrounded by the vague shadow of a crowd. Only by their numbers and gestures are the players recognizable. One shoots and his legs kick the air with a spasmodic defiance as the ball leaves his hand. It's Barnett. Another crouches deep at the foul line, then springs up and forward, popping the ball loose. It's Bradley. A big man runs downcourt, pushing himself to reach the basket before the other team, another hits a shot and runs backward, his hands fluttering with excitement like the wings of a bird, a third gets hit while taking a shot and lies still on the floor, knees bent, arms stretched by his side. It's Reed, Russell, Frazier. Moment by moment they prove themselves —DeBusschere stretching himself in the air, trying to block a shot, Riordan lifting his arm high above his head as he drives toward the hoop. Yet the film conveys no sense that in a short while these men will be remembered and revered for the deeds the film records. Even in the fifth game, when Reed crashes to the floor, the writers sitting at the press table on the court don't attend the calamity; as the huge man twists and grimaces in pain they follow the ball downcourt, turning their heads away from him. For them, life, the game, goes on. They are like the ploughman and the ship in W. H. Auden's description of Brueghel's painting *Icarus*:

> In Brueghel's *Icarus*, *for instance: how everything turns away*

*Quite leisurely from the disaster; the ploughman may*
*Have heard the splash, the forsaken cry,*
*But for him it was not an important failure; the sun shone*
*As it had to on the white legs disappearing into the green*
*Water; and the expensive delicate ship that must have seen*
*Something amazing, a boy falling out of the sky,*
*Had somewhere to get to and sailed calmly on.*

Unawares, they witness the creation of a myth even as its protagonists attain their great moment of collective fulfillment and, Icarus-like, start the plunge into their imperfect, individual lives. The dream team is born.

# 1979

# 1

The team didn't last the year. A week after the championship, the league held an expansion draft and several Knicks were selected by new franchises. After that, players left because of trades, injuries, and age. When New York won the title again in '72–'73, only half the squad had played in the first championship three years before; and by 1977 all of the original victors had disappeared from the roster. At the same time, the team grew in stature, its achievement enhanced, rather than diminished, by the passage of years.

This was partly the result of basketball's hectic development after 1970. The Knicks' triumph symbolized and spurred a boom of popular enthusiasm that turned the sport of pro basketball into a profitable national enterprise. Ten years after the 1970 championship, the value of franchises had increased more than 600 percent, and the average yearly salary of players had risen from $35,000 to $180,000. The Seattle Super-Sonics, an expansion team in 1969, were champions playing regularly to audiences of forty thousand, while the Portland Trail Blazers, one of the teams created by the league at the end of the '69–'70 season, not only sold out their arena but also a theater where they televised a closed-circuit live broadcast of the game. The exorbitant figures in the rookie contracts signed by Bradley and Russell were now common sums. Prize rookies were sometimes paid over $500,000 a year, their first contracts turning the college graduates into instant millionaires. They found immediate employment in television commercials, the land of opportunity the Knicks had explored with their famed approval of Vitalis, and were also the subject of endless newspaper and television stories. The sort of journalistic investigation first awarded the Knicks had become a regular feature of sports news, the stories ranging from the announcement that several businessmen were planning to invest some $12 million to start the Dallas Mavericks, the NBA's newest franchise, to the gossip that one of the game's sharpshooters was addicted to popcorn, the treat threatening to shorten his career by expanding his waistline. Faced with this demanding interest, one star announced he would speak only to a few reporters and answer only particular questions. But this pronunciamento didn't save him from the mob of reporters whom he wanted to avoid: His reticence became the subject of articles about him, receiving approximately the same attention as Jimmy Carter's lust. And in these and other similarly significant ways, the game announced that it had established itself as part of the national culture.

This flood of success produced a tangle of stars, lawsuits, leagues, and franchises. In the past, owners had controlled players through regulations and agreements that allowed the proprietors a virtual monopoly over the professional game. The players, although rarely rich, enjoyed the privileged status of genuine heroes among the general population—men whose deeds on the field excused any unseemly behavior off of it. The new money pouring into the game swept aside these traditions and loyalties. In 1967, the ABA, the American Basketball Association, was founded. The new league bid with the NBA for players and markets, and the competition resulted in skyrocketing players' salaries and a lawsuit that challenged the NBA's control of the game. An anarchic capitalism prevailed as owners even within the same league betrayed one another for their own gain. Players received increasingly big money contracts, changing the public's perception of the athletes. Their feats still thrilled fans, but the performers were no longer viewed solely as objects for admiration and sympathy. They became targets for popular resentment: Every time an increase in the average NBA salary was announced fans complained that the players performed lazily, shiftlessly, stupidly. The game featured great individual stars, the popular argument went, especially high-flying forwards such as Julius Erving, George McGinnis, Spencer Haywood, and Connie Hawkins, lithesome, quick scorers cut from the Elgin Baylor mode who dominated the game and performed acts of imcomparable athletic daring and imagination. But the game suffered. Teams were haphazard creations, lacking the strong features of a collective personality that emerge when players work together for a period of years. Expansion squads often relied on only one performer or were merely bland, faceless creations. Units performed erratically, expanded schedules and increased traveling placing new demands on the physical and emotional resources of players, and winners for one season promptly became losers the next when key players were injured or suffered a bad slump. The league didn't enjoy the presence of a truly superior club. The one team that qualified for every play-off during the decade ended this glorious episode of its history with only one championship. Indeed, in the decade after the Knicks won the crown, no team won the title in consecutive seasons. For all the individual theatrics of the players, the game as a whole often seemed a botched and thoughtless entertainment.

In this period of newfangled change, the '69–'70 Knicks became an instant tradition, the essential moment of the sport's golden age. The incidents, men, and tactics that had contributed to the team's success were turned into legends. Promoters of the sport and team tried to revive the myths, hoping to bring some order and glory to a frustrating, nasty period. Even members of the championship team participated in these rituals. But each attempt to bring the past back to life failed; the veterans of the old team or their new reincarnations would momentarily promise triumph, then falter rapidly, ancient artifacts revealing their unearthed beauty for a second before decomposing in the air.

In the midst of this chaos and veneration, the men who had made up the team pursued their lives. Ten years after their triumph, I interviewed them. Their stories appear in the following pages, though the collection is not complete: One of them didn't wish to speak to me, and I have omitted some because they repeated themes and experiences presented more dramatically in the tales of other players. I had several general impressions of the players. They were unfailingly charming, a genial and intelligent group of men. Without any snobbishness, they were also all clearly members of an elite. Within the different confines of their successes, they had all reached the top of their stations—if you were going to be a twelfth man on the bench, there was no better bench to sit on than the '69–'70 Knicks', and if you were going to be a star then you could want no more popularity and acclaim than that accorded the key members of the championship team. All had changed physically, except for their hands. Hands are an almost magical property of a good ballplayer—"good hands" is the inexplicable gift of hanging onto the ball while rebounding, dribbling, or passing—and while their bellies, hair, or legs showed the coming of age, their hands had remained youthful and athletic: large palms, long and lean fingers, solid grips. Mottled or manicured, their hands were the healthiest, firmest, hardiest hands I'd ever shaken. They all spoke with a pleasing honesty, a kind of fearlessness toward the world's judgment of them, sometimes even expressing their confusion about intimate matters: "Why is everybody into oral sex?" one asked me, displeased and baffled by the new fashion. "Man, when I was in college, you screwed." None were surprisingly different from the public selves they had presented—or in which they had been framed—during the championship year. Rather, the extent to which they remained true to these portraits was startling, and also the drama of their experience: Their lives possessed the logic and suspense of stories, not random existences. The experience of playing in the championship dominated all of their lives, its brilliance casting into shadow and light everything that followed; but their relationships to the team and the game were as wide-ranging as the talents and backgrounds which each had brought to their collective triumph ten years before.

# 2

The subs were the first to go. Toward the end of the season, the league created teams in Cleveland, Buffalo, and Portland, the players for the new franchises taken from a pool of talent stocked with the most expendable members of the already established clubs. There was some fear that the draft would break up the team's first eight players, but only the four rarely used bench warmers left: May, Hosket, Bowman, and John Warren.

For them the change was a mixed blessing. Expansion teams are the opposites of champions. Their seasons are losing streaks interrupted by occasional wins. They attract scant attention from fans on the road, and at home they perform before audiences more interested in visiting stars than local heroes. No one expects much of them and they play in a haphazard, unrewarding style—jokes, not exemplars. At the same time, they provide players a chance to display their talents. None of the Knick bench warmers were going to get a substantial increase in playing time if they stayed in New York: two and sometimes three players stood between them and starting. On their new squads, they all enjoyed a good chance of instant promotion, and though they regretted leaving the champion, they had known well in advance that they wouldn't be playing for New York in the coming season. In exchange for the glamor of membership on the Knicks, they received a chance to test their talents and establish themselves as stars.

John Warren, the rookie who roomed with Willis Reed and dreamed of stuffing Jerry West, went to Cleveland. A man of modest and precise ambitions, he planned to play seven years in the NBA, until he was twenty-nine, then begin a new career as an accountant. He never expected substantial success at the game. "Ten years," he told me, explaining the calculations that determined his professional career. "Okay, then I would have been thirty-two and I wasn't going to be that rich and would still have had to get a job somewhere—and this way, stopping at twenty-nine, I would have three more years to work at it." Instead, he played for five, and the last three were frustrating, bewildering seasons that betrayed the calm and satisfying exit he had expected to make from the game. Warren is an articulate and cautious man—he expresses his deepest thoughts and feelings by repeating words and phrases, adding "really" or "very" for special emphasis. Unlike many players who have never achieved the recognition they believe they deserved, he leads a rewarding and orderly life: The winter commemorating the Knicks win, the tenth season he never made, he was studying for the difficult C.P.A. exam. He doesn't spin complicated conspiracy theories about people out to get him, or blame his fate on accidents; he is remarkably level-headed in his evaluation of his failed basketball career. But his diffidence founders on a hard truth about his experience: He will never again be able to prove that, like his teammates in '69–'70, he is a master of the game.

His early basketball history was inauspicious. Caution marked his adolescence. He could "throw the football," but his mother forbade him to play the game; later the Army rejected him because of a heart murmur and he feared any strenuous physical exercise until a trainer assured him that playing was harmless. He lived in Far Rockaway—his father, a dredgeman, helped reclaim the marshes of Jamaica Bay—and played ball at the local high school, his team winning four games in two years. Warren remembers shining in a contest against one particularly good team; afterward, the coach of the opposing squad told Lou Carnesecca, the nationally respected coach of St. John's, about Warren's talent. Carnesecca attended a few games and "liked the way I played." Warren wanted to go to Columbia, but didn't score high enough on the college entrance exams for the Ivy League school. He wasn't impressed by the other colleges that wanted him—"I could have gone to The Citadel," he told me with a laugh, dismissing a southern school known only for its peculiar name and occasionally excellent basketball teams—and St. John's had just enjoyed a good year and was near to home. There he starred on a winning, but unexceptional, team. "I had two good years there. I was the second leading scorer and rebounder when I was a junior and I was the leading scorer and rebounder in my senior year. I just wanted to win in college. I wanted to get my points like everyone else, but I also passed the ball around and rebounded. I played to win; I did a lot of things to win."

Throughout his first three years at the school, he didn't imagine he would become a professional ballplayer, and apparently didn't think he would miss playing the game. "I never really thought about it; I just wanted my degree." One practice, early during Warren's senior year, Carnesecca talked to him about the future. "He told me—we were just sitting around—and he said, John, you don't have to score thirty points. You're going to be a pro just for your defense. You just play your game. And that was the first time it really hit me: I got a chance, hey." The prediction didn't change the way he played—"I still got my fourteen or fifteen shots a game"—and he didn't dream about a golden future. "It wasn't that I didn't care about making it—you wanted to make it—but I didn't think about it all the time because then I would get too tight. So I just played my game. My main concern was just playing the game and winning, and wanting to win made me play well."

He suffered little as a rookie. He fetched beer for the locker room, but didn't act as any player's porter, the Knicks eschewing any behavior that would tarnish their reputation as professionals; and he was robbed of his first two professional points. "It was my first game. I can remember I was nervous —ah man, very nervous." Warren went in for a lay-up and, as he put the ball in over the rim, the opposing player—Warren is pretty sure he recalls the culprit—knocked the ball away from the basket, a prohibited kind of interference that results, when the referees call it, in counting the hoop. This time, the refs looked the other way. "It was my rookie year, right?" Warren explained, accepting the injury.

The team itself simply awed him. "You had better individuals in the league," he told me, referring to both the Baltimore and Los Angeles squads, "but you couldn't find a better team than the Knicks. It was amazing to see them play." In practice, Warren played on the second team, the squad composed of the substitutes, which was matched against the starters. "We knew what they were going to run, and still they would score on us, every time. They would read the defense and move the ball where we weren't. It was amazing. We knew what they were going to do and we still couldn't stop them, and we were good players on that second team—Cazzie Russell, Dave Stallworth, Nate Bowman, Bill Hosket, Donnie May, we had a very good second team." To him, the starters were invincible. "That first team, really the first eight guys, didn't lose too much," he joked. "I was sitting on the bench [during games] and it was amazing to me. I knew we were going to win the games; I didn't care whether we were down twenty points, I knew we were going to win. The only thing that really crossed my mind was whether or not I'd get into the game. I knew that once we had a fifteen-point or twenty-point lead that I would get in. But I never thought about losing. I was just happy to be part of the team."

When the league held its expansion draft, Warren became a founding member of the Cleveland Cavaliers. The team was coached by Bill Fitch, the same man who had trained Phil Jackson as an undergraduate in North Dakota, and played in a dank downtown arena to sparse crowds. It lost its debut and the next fourteen contests, and went on to win but one out of almost every six games it played for the entire season, compiling the then worst record of any new team in the league's history. Warren was a starter and starred, playing more minutes than any of his teammates, contributing a modestly respectable 11.5 points per game, fifth best on the team, and leading the squad in assists. For him the season that disgraced the town's pride was an unqualified success and he anticipated his good fortune to continue. "I think after my first year in Cleveland, after that year of experience, if then I would have come back to the Knicks I would have made a very good Knickerbocker. I would have loved to play with Frazier in the backcourt—the two of us used to play against each other in scrimmages. But after that year in Cleveland, that would have been the turning point."

But the season he imagined to be the prelude of an excellent career became its climax instead. The next year, Cleveland acquired some new and younger guards, including one All-American, and Warren lost the competition for a starting assignment and resumed his old role as a substitute. His playing time was cut by more than half, and his scoring and assist totals decreased dramatically. The never extremely promising opportunity of returning to New York disappeared altogether. "I heard reports that the Knicks tried to get me back, and I ran into Holzman over the summer and he said they were trying, but Cleveland wouldn't trade me. I couldn't imagine why they wouldn't because they weren't using me at all —they just sat me there. The next year, the Knicks drafted some guards and that ended the chance."

In the following two seasons, Warren's p.t. diminished to a fraction: He played but eighteen of the more than one hundred thirty hours his team performed before audiences. The loss of playing time hurt Warren's ability and ruined any value he might have commanded as a player on the market. Warren bore little malice toward his competitors on the team, but Fitch's behavior bedeviled him. "He claimed I couldn't play defense. But when it came around to the last minute of a game and he wanted someone to guard Jerry West to stop him from scoring he would send me in. It just didn't make any sense." The frustrating tactics of the coach spoiled even promising moments. During one road trip, Warren replaced an injured starter, teaming up with Lenny Wilkens, a veteran whom Warren claims liked his style of play, and whose confidence encouraged Warren to perform well. "I hadn't played in ten days, but I shot almost sixty percent and led the team in scoring." The next day, the team traveled to Houston. Warren had heard a scout from another team would be watching the Houston game; he hoped to play and whet the scout's interest in his talents. But Fitch never called him off the bench. "We went back to Cleveland and the next day in practice Lenny told me to calm down no matter how I felt. But it was hard, very hard." Warren believes the slight was unjustifiable. "I think every guy on that team would say I belonged there and that I should have been playing—ninety-nine percent of the guys would be saying that and that I should have played. There were good players on that team, but a lot of them were good because they had a chance to play. There's one guy who's playing now and there's no way he deserves the reputation he has. I really think that Fitch made everyone in the league think this guy could play." But Warren remained uncomplaining. He felt slighted by his agent, a man named Arthur Morse, who represented Cazzie Russell—"I'm not sure he was looking out for me as he was looking out for the bigger names"—and he was afraid that if he started arguing with Fitch he would develop a tainted reputation as a whiner. "I guess after the first couple of years of not playing I just didn't know who would pick me up if I became very vocal—maybe I wouldn't have a contract at all." As a result, he kept his miseries to himself, letting his anger rage unexpressed.

Each summer, he returned to New York to study—"I always wanted to do other things"—and in late August prepared to compete again for a job on the team. "You would not believe how much I hated packing and going back to Cleveland to try and make that team. By that time all my enjoyment of the game had gone. I was going back for the few dollars I could make. I didn't enjoy the game at all."

Still, the '74 training camp went well for him. After its first seasons of humiliation and defeat, the team had begun to evolve some recognizable style, playing a consistent, patterned offense. The roster was settled, no longer a long list of asterisked names indicating players who came and went before the season ended, and the team was about to make a quantum jump into respectability. In his view, Warren shared in the success. "I was playing the best ball I ever played. I really felt that I was better than I had ever been. I felt I could shoot the jumper on anybody. I feel I had only one weakness—ball handling. But that was a function of confidence and experience: I don't think anybody can just play for two or three minutes a game and learn to handle the ball and not have fear. But I could shoot the ball with anybody and I could jump with anybody."

Then, before the regular season started, Fitch cut him from the team. "Nothing really happened. Fitch offered me an assistant coaching job. I'm not going to tell you the money he offered because it was so small. He said I knew the system." Warren was relieved to be cut—he couldn't have taken another year in Cleveland anyway—and the news pleased his wife. "She saw what was happening to me without playing." Fitch's decision didn't necessarily end Warren's career; he was on waivers, and any team could have added him to their roster for only a small sum. Warren had played five seasons, two less than he had planned years before, when he had never seriously thought about becoming a professional. "I was twenty-seven.

Deep down in my mind I felt that somebody out there must know I could play. Nobody did."

He returned to accounting, the profession which he had always intended to pursue when he could no longer play ball, and the New York neighborhood of his youth, Far Rockaway. "When I was first waived I guess that somewhere in my head I figured I could try out somewhere. But then the years and the seasons start going by and I started to realize that without a contract you have to be some sort of superman to get a job, and I didn't want to waste any more time. You know I got a wife and two kids and I couldn't afford that and I didn't want to play ball in Europe."

He worked steadily for a large business firm and resumed his studies to get a C.P.A.'s license. He saw his teammates from the Knicks only occasionally, including Willis Reed, his old roommate, and rarely attended professional games. Living in New York, he was frequently reminded of his failed promise as a player, and his sense of having disappointed people's hopes. "A lot of people felt that I was going to be a very, very good player in the NBA and I felt I could have been also. And that hurts, you know? Sometimes your friends say—hey! Johnny's going to do it! Johnny's going to do it! And I know I could have done it and I never got the chance." Particularly annoying were newspaper articles that included his name among lists of bad Knick draft choices, a judgment that Warren feels is unfair since he had only one year—"one year in New York," he says, "one year"—to prove himself. At the start of the '79–'80 season, he was invited by the management to participate in an old-timers' night and stood with several other players waving to a good-natured crowd that cheered each performer, though many of the kids shouting the loudest didn't know whom they were honoring. But once the game started, Warren left his seat, retiring to a private room away from the court. "I couldn't take watching them play. I start to sulk."

One late afternoon, coming from work, he joked about his

fate. He stood on the steps in front of a modern Park Avenue office building dressed conservatively in a raincoat, black shoes, brown checked shirt and matching brown tie, a nattily attired accountant. He has kept the mustache he wore as a rookie, but his hairline has receded and he wears glasses, a concession to checking figures, rather than players, all day. His face is long, with high cheekbones, and his broad shoulders taper down to a narrow waist. "I have a young man's body," he boasts. His long fingers were without the thick gold band of the championship ring. Warren wears the ring at home—he treasures it more as his playing years recede and only that morning had put it on—but he takes the subway to work every day and is afraid someone will grab it from him. He cracked his knuckles and yawned. "Oh man," he sighed, "I'm beat. I knew I should have shot those jumpers more often."

For several hours he discussed his career over dinner. He exhibited no mean spirit toward his colleagues or bosses. He exonerated Holzman for letting him go in the draft, and, at worst, accused Fitch of refusing to admit bad judgments. Still, he viewed himself as a victim. First, his talent was ignored; now he can't display it. Again and again, he returned to this theme. At the start he was tentative. "I was happy about being drafted by the Knicks, very happy. It was like a dream come true, really. I look back at it now and I think I sort of took for granted that I was going to sit on the bench. I think if I had played my cards right—who knows? I could have started on that team. It would have been hard, but at least I could have been third guard." Then he was accusatory. "I really feel I deserved to play much more. I really feel that my job was taken away from me unjustly. With hindsight, if I had to do it all over again, I would have done it differently. I know I would have because I've played against most of the guards in the league and there's no doubt in my mind that I can play with anybody in the league . . . I should have played. If I had to do it over I would have bitched like crazy. I really would have." Finally, he asserted his own excellence. "I am some-what bitter, but I feel I had to do something else anyway. I feel I could have been one of the big money-makers like Walt Frazier or Willis Reed. Frazier—what can he do that I can't? You give me a Willis Reed and a Dave DeBusschere and a Dick Barnett and a Bill Bradley and me and a couple of years' experience and you'll end up with the same team. I really feel that way."

He had only one more thing to say about the game. We left the restaurant and I drove him to the subway. The air was a little chill, the start of fall and the basketball season. Warren still plays regularly in an amateur league, though he figured he would be out a lot that winter while studying for the C.P.A. exam. We discussed professional players, noting their special qualities, and Warren displayed an admirable generosity. I mentioned a guard, a deadly shooter. "Yeah, he can shoot," Warren agreed as I stopped for a red light. Wistfully, his hands made the motion of releasing the ball, the wrist spring-ing forward, the fingers spread wide. "Shooting," he sighed, as the light changed and we approached the subway station where he would catch the train back home to Far Rockaway. "Ahh—I love that."

# 3

Nate Bowman and Donnie May were picked by Buffalo. The two are opposites. Bowman comes from Fort Worth, Texas—"cow town, U.S.A."—and is a figure of excess. Tall and wiry—John Warren calls him "long"—he wears designer western shirts with snaps, fancily stitched boots, and a Stetson hat, his boots and headgear a redundant addition to his height:

Even unadorned, he towers and sways over every person he passes on the street. His opinions are strong but instantly changeable, and he uses his drawl to express every shade of emotion—long vowels that charm one minute, threaten the next. He appears to have lived in perpetual antagonism with his environment, an outsider or outlaw. Black, an only child whose parents separated when he was a baby—he must remind himself of his father's occupation as though it were a fact he learned in school—he grew up scrapping. "You had to have a gun in Fort Worth. Everybody packed. When I was a kid I used to walk around with two pistols and I had a shotgun in the trunk." To further his difficulties, he sprouted to his current height of six feet ten at fourteen. "I almost had a heart attack. I didn't know what the hell was going on. I went into a slight little depression. I couldn't really relate to kids my own age because I was so much bigger than they were and they didn't want to relate to me because they'd say, Hey, you're too big to play with us, and I'd say, Hey, I'm the same age."

A native of Dayton, Ohio—"the factory worker used to be the bulwark of Dayton, but it's becoming more of a professional town now"—May is blond, blue-eyed, modestly good-looking, his body a sturdy, almost bulky, six-feet-four frame. He speaks in a neutral twang, an accent as mild as the carefully considered opinions he offers. He dresses in neat, fashionably nondescript clothes. He accepts his fortune calmly. His father worked in a local mill and was an alcoholic; May claims his mother never even considered leaving him. "My mother influenced me. She was: Make the best of a situation, don't hurt anybody, turn the other cheek. If somebody's had a sad story, she always had something worse. It's almost a stoic-type thing. She had to put up with a lot, living with my dad, because there were a lot of problems, a lot of embarrassments. Perhaps she more deeply developed that attitude because of that—like it's not even there, make do. So I'm sure I'm a product of that. Though I see what ambition can get you. If you want to do something, it's there, all you have to do is go for it."

Neither Bowman nor May enjoyed much success on the championship team. May's most famous moment was his appearance as the greasy-haired rookie in the Vitalis commercial. Bowman played an unwitting figure of fun; as the backup man for Reed, the team's most formidable force, Bowman's occasional ineptitude on the court made the crowds more fully appreciate Reed's strength and grace. Yet, in the end, basketball served both as a means of survival and advancement in the social world.

Bowman arrived at the Knicks with a spotty career. After his sudden spurt of growth, he was dragooned into playing high-school ball. Scoring twenty-nine points his first game, he imagined he would be a star, but promptly fell ill. "My mother took me to the doctor and he said I was growing too fast for my heart and he advised me not to play any more because I could have a heart attack." Later he resumed high-school competition—"I averaged about thirty-one points a game, first all-stater in my high school"—and attended Wichita State with Dave Stallworth, playing on a nationally top-ranked team. "My first love in the game was to win and be outstanding and that's what I was. I liked blocking shots and rebounding. I let other players think they had me and then I'd do a Bill Russell on them." He was drafted in the first round, but moved from team to team, a big man who disappointed the general managers and coaches who hoped he'd prove to be a starter.

New York bought him from the Philadelphia 76ers to substitute for Walt Bellamy—the reorganization of the team that resulted in the championship had yet to begin—and Bowman contributed to the chaos that attended both practices and games during his freshman year. "Dick McGuire [then the coach] would throw out the ball and say go ten hoops and we'd go ten hoops, and he'd say go ten more. No patterns, no organization, no nothing. I used to go and buy my own hotdogs in my uniform! I'd walk right to the concession stand!

I'd go out, get two hotdogs, talk to people, and McGuire wouldn't say anything. If we'd come to the locker room and there were no hotdogs we'd get mad. It was hilarious."

But Bowman was also contemptuous of the team's spiritless attitude. For all of his apparent cynicism, Bowman has a strong, almost innocent sense of the fundamental virtues of athletics—loyalty, sacrifice, companionship—and welcomed Red Holzman's appointment as coach. "Red gave us organization, patterns, had us playing defense, playing together, and he didn't take no shit off anybody, and this started some team spirit and everybody started doing what they had to."

His job now was to back up Reed. Bowman fulfilled his responsibility vigorously, including one night when Reed got into a fight in Atlanta. "New York and Atlanta would always have some grudge game. This particular night, they had Joe Caldwell, Paul Silas, Lou Hudson, Jim Davis, all these big guys, and we were just kind of knocking each other around all night. I was sitting on the bench and Willis got into a minor altercation with Lou Hudson. They squared off to fight and Jim Davis ran up and Willis knocked Davis down, bam! and he landed on the floor. Bill Bridges was approaching Willis from behind. So I went up behind him and grabbed him around the neck. Not hard, just to say, Hey, Bill, stay out of it, let them fight. He started trying to elbow me in my face. So I tightened my grip around his neck and I hit him blind side, getting in as many punches as I can, while I can, because when he gets loose he's going to kill me—he's six-eight and two hundred and sixty pounds. Atlanta had a college-type arena then with a rail all around the court and the fans sat right there. Bridges backed me up against the rail and a fan hit me on the back of the head with a chair, as hard as he could. I saw stars, and stripes too, but before I hit the floor, I was still thinking and I flung Bridges away from me, about twenty yards. Now I see Bill walking toward me, and at the same time, Richie Guerin, who was their coach, is acting like he's trying to help me, like, C'mon Nate, let me help you up, picking me up. He's got my arms behind me, and he's holding me up and I see Bridges coming at me. I act like I'm unconscious. Bridges gets about a foot away and takes a stand and throws a punch as hard as he can, and when he does I duck and he throws himself off balance. I grabbed Richie and punched him and threw him into Bridges. By this time, everybody had come off the bench saying, Come on, let's break this thing up, and they threw Willis and me out of the game. After the game, we were in the dressing room and Bridges comes in and looks at me like he still wants me and he sits on the bench—we were dressing—and he says, Man, you shouldn't have done me like that. I said, Man, I told you to stay out of the fight. You started that shit yourself and if you ever swing in my face like that again I'm going to kill you. He said, Yeah, okay, and he walked out and that was the end."

At the time, May was a rookie, beginning a process of adjustment and accommodation that marks his professional career as distinctly as conflict denotes Bowman's. May's college speciality had been an inside game, taking his man down low, near the hoop, and using his strength—he weighed 225, or 20 more pounds than he carries now—to "bounce him around." With this tactic, he had averaged over twenty-six points a game in the previous year's NIT, the peak of his college career.

But in the pros, his weight was a liability, making him slow and cumbersome, and he was unprepared to develop new skills, especially ball handling, a prerequisite for time on the court. "I wasn't sure what to anticipate in the pros. I knew it would be a different game. I probably didn't give it enough thought. I knew what I could do and they drafted me on that basis, on the way I played in college, so I just figured I'll do what I know best." During his rookie year, he played 560 minutes, and failed to perform well. "I got as much time as he [Holzman] could afford. I mean, he just had just a wealth of talent on that team. I would have liked more. There were spurts when people got hurt and I played, and maybe I wasn't ready. After a while when you get so little playing time if you are called on to go a whole quarter—which isn't much, but it's a lot when you're not playing—it's difficult. You have to be able to do it over an extended period of time."

There were other difficulties. To him the players were monuments, not colleagues. "I knew when I saw DeBusschere or Bradley or Clyde or Willis that there was no way I could approach what they were doing together. They just had too much ability; I wasn't in their class." And Holzman was threatening and distant. "Red was not a very personable guy; he was very businesslike. Maybe he was under a lot of strain and tension and didn't know how to react to certain things. I didn't have that much of a relationship with him. We didn't talk that much: How's Dayton? How's the wife? Dayton. That was it. He was a hard man. He didn't smile much. He didn't go in for trivialities. He was my first coach in the pros, so it was a learning experience trying to deal with him."

Finally, there was the problem of working and living with blacks. "My high school was all white and at Dayton we had just a few blacks and there was trouble there, the whole thing culminating in the 1968 NITs when they didn't even let two black guys play because they had problems and were causing trouble—not unjustifiable: We were basically racists. I look at it now and I realize it, but at the same time that's the way I was—I was a product of my environment. My father was a very bigoted factory worker and I was raised thinking a certain way and I didn't know anything else. It's painful to me [to recall his role in the NIT incident] because I realize that I did things and said things and just had a mindset—I was just prejudiced without knowing. It was just something that was fed in and I was ignorant of what was the case. It was worse than calling a guy a nigger. We would never really confront them; it would just be like snide things and avoidance. It was bad, and I really feel bad about the whole thing. I've never seen the guys since then. I feel regretful about that.

"It was a real education to come here [to New York] and

play with the Knicks. One experience didn't make me change; it was a gradual realization. When I first came to sign, Frazier was here. He was the last year's MVP. It was the first time I met him and I got the impression that this guy is a pretty straight person and it made no big deal how he was different. Then Willis, who was just a superfine person. So it just dawned on me that you've got to take people on an individual basis. It took me a while. But you don't eliminate a whole lifetime of pollution overnight. Even though there were times when I would say, Goddamnit! I just can't stand this! Like Nate would have his loud music on and be yelling and Cazzie would be mouthing, but I wouldn't look at them as niggers, just as guys who are doing things that happen to bug me right now. My defense was withdrawal. But it wasn't a black-white thing anymore, and I think that kept me in good stead."

Bowman was one teammate who tested May's new equanimity. "Nate was very gregarious and outgoing a lot of the time. But he had a very dark side also. He was just strange. Other guys, like Willis, I never got that feeling. They were very level."

Bowman didn't share this attitude toward Willis. Bowman's feelings toward the man he subbed for in games and played against in practice were complex, troubled, and remain at the very center of his associations with Knicks. He respected Reed's strength and skill as a player—"Willis was a hell of a force on that team; I've never seen anybody as strong as Willis out there"—but he felt betrayed by Reed. Reed acted wrongly by Bowman's standards and he speaks of the team captain with a still vibrant frustration and anger, the disappointment of a follower whose leader has betrayed him.

His original unhappiness occurred while Reed still played forward, before Bellamy had been traded. At the time, the players held clinics around the city during the summer, leading kids through exercises in neighborhood playgrounds, a community-minded form of publicity for the team. "We weren't getting paid that much money—we were just drumming up business for the Knicks." One day Bowman and a teammate discussed running their own clinics. "This was before Walt [Frazier] had his camp, or Willis—this was '67, and nobody had any camps going. So we said, why can't we do this? So I said, The main reason is that we don't have a big name." They proposed the idea to Willis. "He says, Yeah, sounds like a pretty good idea. The next thing we know, we look around and see the Willis Reed All-Star Camp. He just never invited us up there."

Bowman's disapproval extended to the center's behavior on court. "They [Knick management] used to almost run Willis to death. We would be up thirty-nine points in Los Angeles, have a game in Chicago the next night, there'd be seven minutes to go, and Willis would still be out there playing. How could we have lost? I could just see Willis killing himself out there with his bad knee and stuff and I'd go up to him and say, Like Willis, why don't you ask Red to take you out for three or four minutes and I'll give you a blow, we're up thirty-nine points, we can't lose. He'd say something dumb to me, like, I'm not going to tell the man to take me out just because you want to play. I'd look at him kind of strange. This happened once and I never asked him again. Guys like Bradley or De-Busschere, they were smart enough to see if the team couldn't lose to ask Red to give them a blow. Hey, we got a game tomorrow night, I've got to rest. And Red would take them out. But Willis! I don't know what his problem was, but he would just stay there. He told me something. He said, The man give me good money to play ball and I'm going to play. I said, Willis, they're trying to kill you, can't you see it? You're going to die, you can't keep going on like this, they're trying to kill you. Guys in the league were calling Willis slave—calling him slave because he just be out there playing. They felt like he was a Tom because he never talked up and he never did anything to help the brothers. He just helped himself. If

Wilt Chamberlain was up twenty points with five minutes to go, he was smart enough to tell the man to take him out, or Bill Russell, or anybody."

Several months after the fight in Atlanta, an incident occurred in which Bowman felt Reed acted unforgivably. The Knicks were playing the Bullets in a weekend series, hosting them at the Garden on Saturday, guests at their arena the next afternoon. After the first game, Bowman went to Harry M. Stevens, the glass-sided bar at the Garden street level where the players congregated before taking the bus down to Maryland. Bowman spotted Willis, Cazzie, and some other players socializing at the bar as he entered, but stopped to speak to a friendly reporter. "This writer and I are standing there, talking about the game and whatnot, and these two Italian guys walk up and push him aside and say, Come on Nate, we want you to meet our family. One guy grabs my one arm and the other guy the other, and they're just going to haul me over to a table in the dining section. Willis, Cazzie, and all of them are at the bar. I got raging mad and I started fighting, punching them and everything, right there in the door. I was fighting these guys like hell and they're tearing my shirt all up and carrying on and Willis is still standing there, watching—not that I needed his help because I could have destroyed them right there. The guys are still woofing me, Come on Nate, we want you to meet our family, and I say, Man, don't put your hands on me! I'm almost crying I'm so mad! Then this Italian boy who works the door comes over to help me out, and the same people who are standing there and drinking and talking with Willis start calling this boy nigger lover—nigger lover, nigger lover. Some of the same people who are standing there talking to Willis! I said, What! I don't believe this! I don't believe this shit is going on! Then a cop came in and took the guys outside and calmed everything down and Willis comes over carrying his glass. What happened? I said, Hey, Willis, just get away from me, man! I was mad. I said, Willis, don't say nothing to me! You saw what was going on here! You stood there with your drink! You didn't come around and help or nothing! Not that I needed your help but you should have come over to see what was going on. He probably felt that I was doing something wrong and that he didn't want to get involved. They [members of the team] all walked up to me afterward, asking me what happened. I said, Don't any of you motherfuckers say nothing to me! I got on the bus, went to the back. I was damn near crying I was so mad. A couple of guys who weren't even in the bar came up and asked me what happened. I said, Man, get away from me. I didn't talk to nobody. Red Holzman, he came up and spoke to me. Nate, what happened? I said, Red, leave me alone. I never mentioned the whole thing to anybody. This is the first time I talked about it, but it changed the complexion of the way I felt about Willis."

May has similarly hostile feeling toward Bradley. Bradley was May's model of excellence among the starters—May constantly refers to Bradley while discussing his own accomplishment and failures as a player—and the two shared midwestern boyhoods and college celebrity, though their class backgrounds differed sharply: In the heat of the Missouri summer, Bradley's bank president father ate breakfast in a tie and jacket, a model of domestic decorum compared to May's ne'er-do-well old man. May didn't trust Bradley. He believed Bradley's political ambitions made him act with a self-serving duplicity, national politics, in May's view, shaping Bradley's behavior as white society, in Bowman's understanding, controlled Reed's. "His basketball to me was all just part of his step-by-step program to the White House. Everything he does is calculated and basketball was part of it. He was so calculated. The strangest thing about him was when the team was in Phoenix laying over there for two or three days during the All-Star break. He asked Red for permission to go away for a couple of days to Florida—I was told about this; I wasn't with the team then—and flew off and got married. He came back and hadn't told anybody, even his closest friend, DeBusschere.

To me, that was really strange. To not be able to share something like that with your friends makes you wonder how close he was to anybody, at least on the basketball level. The Washington thing was always where his heart was. He played for the love of the game, but I don't think anybody else had the higher goals he did and basketball was just a step in that, and that manifested itself in strange ways. Everybody just thought he was a weird bird. You never really knew where he was coming from. His political aspirations weren't any big secret: We used to call him Mr. President and all this stuff. He tried to be one of the boys, but at the same time, he wasn't. He was thinking that he really had to watch himself because somewhere along the line something would come back to haunt him."

Unlike Bowman, May didn't show these feelings; he followed a policy of studied ingratiation, hoping to secure more playing time. But his role on the team became increasingly marginal as the championship year progressed. "Here in New York, my main satisfaction as a player was having a good practice. Even though the starters weren't going all out, if I had a good workout I felt something good about that, being able to demonstrate a little bit that I could play, having the team win, and being part of it."

Indeed, the Vitalis commercial was the high point of his regular season. "I gained prominence through that commercial. It wasn't until after that I began to get a little attention. It was on network television, and that was the most exposure I had gotten in two years of playing ball. It was a nice kiss. The commercial was set up in such a way that this was my first start. I was nervous on the sideline, rubbing my hair and getting the grease on my fingers, and then going out and slapping hands with the other starters. They call time-out and tell me I'll get the ball all greasy and stuff like this. Substitute, Riordan in for May, and I walk off and Red's giving me hell as I walk off with a dejected look. I used to catch hell from kids about it—they thought I had sold out making a commercial

DREAM TEAM / 155

like that. It was kind of weird; I hadn't thought about the commercial that way. They would say, How could you do that, Donnie? What did you do that for? Maybe the kids thought—I don't know. I was just having a good time."

He contributed little during the play-offs—"I wasn't a factor anywhere along the line"—and he never appeared on court during the final round against the Lakers. "This was probably my worst moment as a professional player. It was the sixth game of the play-offs against the Lakers. We got beat by forty and I didn't get to play that game. On the plane at the airport going back, Red walked up and said, Sorry I didn't play you, I just forgot you were there. That really hit hard. It had to be the low point of my life, basketballwise, the coach forgetting I was down there. As I found out, it's not unusual: Coaches do it all the time, they get caught up. But not a forty-five-point loss or whatever it was. I don't think he had anything out for me: Not even Red was mean enough to do something like that. It took me the flight to recover, I was so stunned. And the comment took some of the edge off my enthusiasm for the win the next night."

But he didn't lose his sense of history. The night of the seventh game, he secretly recorded Holzman's pregame locker-room talk. May imagined the speech would be an inspiring one; instead, Holzman delivered his standard, gray address. "I listened to [the speech] afterward and it was so similar to other games that there just wasn't much difference. Unless you were there and knew what was going on, I don't think you could appreciate it." Later, at the end of the game, May made his last attempt to become part of the team. "There was a minute to go, and we were twelve or fourteen points up and everybody was standing up, jumping up and excited. I ran up to Red and said, Red, put me in, just for a minute. He didn't react. He didn't know what to do, he was so excited himself. Then the Lakers made a couple of baskets so I didn't get in —I just wanted to get in for a second anyway."

For the aggressively self-assertive Bowman, the year provided considerably more satisfaction. He remembers several moments of personal triumph including a game against Alcindor when Bowman blocked some of the young center's shots while making a few of his own, and a match against Chamberlain when he challenged and quieted the giant. "Wilt was the kind of guy where you'd get a position before him on the court and he'd just walk up and push you out of the way. In one game—I don't know if it was that championship game or what, but it was during that time when we beat the Lakers—I got position on Wilt but he just walks up and pushes me. Mendy Rudolph [an NBA official who died several years ago] was officiating and he's standing right there. I said, Mendy, Wilt just pushed me out of the way, how are you going to let him do that, that's a foul, Mendy! So Mendy said, Play the game—you know Mendy, God bless him. So I said, Wilt, don't push me anymore. If you do, I'm going to wrap one of these chairs around your head. I wasn't scared of him. You just had to show Wilt you weren't scared of him and he'd stay back and start respecting you. He said something like, Well, I'm going to be me, I'm going to be Wilt. I said, Yeah, well, don't push me again. So he didn't. I respected Wilt and I liked him, but I had played with him in Philly and I knew he was a pretty arrogant person with players unless he respected them, and you had to make him respect you, you couldn't just say, Wilt, respect me, okay? I wasn't afraid of getting into a fight with him. Either he would beat my ass or I would beat his. The odds weren't all on his side. He wouldn't necessarily have won—not if I had gotten to that chair fast enough."

Bowman did play during the championship series, and during the seventh game watched Reed with both admiration and contempt. "I thought Willis was very brave to play that game. It was his presence that really stimulated us and gave us the inspiration to get out there. I didn't even know he was coming out. No one did but him. He was sitting back there and no one knew—we had arranged to do without him, and then everyone knew what was happening when he appeared. That night Willis went the first two quarters and after half time he came out and played maybe two or three minutes. Then he dragged himself, literally *dragged* himself over to the sidelines and looked at Red and said, Red, Red, take me out, I'm hurt, I can't go no more. And Red said, Aww, stay in there a couple of more minutes. And Dave Stallworth and I literally leaped up off the bench and told Red to take him out of the game. We said, Man, take the man out of the fucking game, you see that he's hurt. So Red called a time-out and Willis came out and I went in and I played the rest of the third and fourth quarters because he was so hurt. Stuff like that messed up my mind as far as Willis was concerned. I felt they were trying to kill him and he was letting them do it. Holzman, the Knicks, all of them, ain't none of them shit, none of them. I have no respect for them or for Willis because he let it be done."

Two weeks later, both Bowman and May were selected by the Buffalo team. Bowman thinks his selection was part of a political vendetta. "I had a friend. His name was H. Rap Brown. He was a real good friend of mine, though we haven't been in touch in years. I met him when I played ball at the Rucker tournament. He was kind of revolutionary at the time, but not as revolutionary as he got later on. We hung out together, and I'd leave him tickets for games and he'd come down and no one would recognize him—just watch the game and go home, never letting anyone know who he was. One game, I left him a ticket for the front row and Jim Wergeles [one of the Knick publicity men] found out that Rap was sitting in my seat. I don't know how. Wergeles went to Red and said, Red, Nate is becoming a little controversial. Red said, Naw, he's all right, he's enthusiastic, and he's good for the morale of the team and fans like him, he does his job, what do you mean? So Wergeles says, He has Rap Brown sitting in his seat. So Red says, Who the hell is Rap Brown? Wergeles says, Rap is one of those guys talking about burning down America. So Red says, Well, I guess Nate is a little controversial, and off to Buffalo I went. At the time, I knew nothing about this, but two or three years later I met a reporter friend and was talking to him and he said he was in Red's office when the conversation went down." Brown went underground that spring and Bowman met him a few times. "I ran into him on the street. He was just walking around. Sometimes he walked around in a priest's suit and nobody knew who he was." But Bowman claims the FBI bothered him about Brown in Buffalo. "After I went to Buffalo, I bought a little pad out there in the suburbs and every now and then an FBI guy would come to the house and question me about Rap and I'd wonder how the hell he found out I knew Rap. They came by twice, but they had my phone tapped—I'd always hear something—and I'm sure they had to go through the Braves to find out all this info on me and I'm sure that cut short my career. The expansion thing was a lot of bullshit. All the guys in Buffalo were the black sheep of all the teams."

He lasted a year in Buffalo, playing in only forty-four games, less p.t. than he had received in New York. A back injury hampered him and he fought with the team's coach, Dolph Schayes, a pioneer NBA player who had been the main attraction of the league's old Syracuse franchise. "Schayes was a real ding-a-lingey. He was a hell of a player, but he knew nothing about basketball. I never liked him or his attitude. The way he treated people or spoke to them, he just didn't have any respect for anybody. One time I brought my gun to practice. The day before, he had called me some names and I wanted to get him there then, but I was restrained by some guys and Schayes told me to go home. I was so freaking mad that I said, If he says anything I'm going to kill him, and I put my gun in my bag. I was going to fire his ass, but he didn't say anything." Finally the general manager let him go. "He wouldn't tell me a thing, he just waited until the last minute to tell me I was on waivers for what reason I don't know. I felt I could play—I just needed the time."

He joined the ABA Pittsburgh Condors. "I go to Pittsburgh

and Buffalo fires Dolph Schayes and then guess what? He shows up in Pittsburgh looking for a job." Bowman had earned thirty-two thousand dollars in New York—"that's no money at all, compared to now"—and a little over fifty thousand in Buffalo, but his investments went bad. "I went into business and out of business. I was trying to prepare myself for leaving basketball, but I came up short with money, had no finances to do anything." When he arrived in Pittsburgh he contemplated selling his championship ring. "I had no money, but I had this big diamond ring on my finger, so I tried to take that damn diamond out and hock it. I went to a jeweler and asked him what it was worth and he said about three or four hundred, and I told him no." After his one year of duty with the Condors, he was finished with the game. "I didn't try to stay in basketball. When I left, I felt I had been screwed. I didn't want to have anything to do with it. I didn't want to play or nothing. My first year out of the game was sort of traumatic for me. I felt adrift—anybody would have after spending your whole damn life playing and using that as a means of support and then not having nothing."

May fared better at Buffalo, once again adjusting to survive. He lost weight, gained some proficiency at ball handling, and developed an accurate outside shot. "I became more of a player like Bradley, moving all the time." He was promoted to starter, and finished the year averaging twenty points, second best on the squad, and receiving credit for over five hundred rebounds, third best for the team. He also adjusted socially. He concurs with Bowman's judgment on Schayes, saying the same thing about him that he did about Bradley: Dolph was a strange bird. But, unlike Holzman, Schayes neither frightened nor awed him.

Most important of all, May became comfortable keeping company with blacks. In his view, his ease with black players kept him working in the NBA for the next several years. One college coach has remarked that basketball is the only thing in America blacks enjoy a monopoly on besides poverty, and especially in the past ten years blacks have become a dominant force in the league, making up 70 percent of all active players, and the majority of established stars and aspiring rookies. Because of this a white player with average talent has a better chance of staying in the league than his black counterpart, especially if he is a companionable fellow. May frankly attributes his success as a player to fitting this mold. "Every year I learned to associate with blacks better and that kept me going. I was able to be a good influence on teams. There were racial feelings on every team I went to and I could be a buffer-type player—I could relate to everybody."

Atlanta was the first team to employ him in this role. After his successful year in Buffalo, May had problems negotiating a new contract. Some friends knew the owners of the Atlanta franchise. The season before, the Hawks had signed Pete Maravich, a great college star from Louisiana State University, and May's friends suggested the ex-Knick would help the team "not only basketballwise, but also with Maravich." A trade was arranged, and Atlanta promptly extended May's contract for another three years. "My stock had risen appreciably when I was traded to Atlanta: I had some value other than as a bench warmer and unknown. They knew I could score and that I could do some things on the court, and that I could be a good influence on Maravich. At the time, Atlanta had a serious black-white problem and Maravich was in the middle of the whole thing. They had mostly black players, and then Maravich, and he's coming from a southern school, and the South being what it was ten years ago, and they thought I could help settle Pete down a little bit. I was just going to be like a buffer. He had been really wild; he just didn't know how to handle the whole thing. He was having so much trouble relating to the players. So I went down there to the training camp and the first few days I was rooming with Maravich he got mono and I never roomed with him again."

May liked Atlanta, but he saw less p.t. there than in Buffalo and, halfway through his second season, was traded to Philadelphia. "After a while, you might say I became a token or a journeyman." He stayed with the 76ers for a year and a half, finishing his contract there on a desperate squad that managed but thirty-four wins during the two seasons he spent with them, one of the worst records in the league's history.

Unprepared for a return to civilian life, May thought his career was over and went home to Dayton, where he received a call from the Kansas City-Omaha Kings. "They were down to the final cut and they had two guys they were trying to choose, both black, and the general manager I guess remembered me and they wanted a white veteran who would be a team man and I fit the bill. He asked me if I wanted to come out and I said I'd be out tomorrow. Three days before the season began I went out and the first game of the year I get in during the last quarter and hit five for six for twelve points, bringing the team back from like fifteen or twenty points down, and we win the game, and I thought, What is this? Two days ago I was sitting in Dayton wondering what I was going to do with myself and here I am after the game, star of the game type thing, oh man, this is far out! But it went downhill from there. I didn't play much; I was just part of the team."

Trying to keep a good spirit on the team—"I thought that was my contribution"—May looked to the future. "I wasn't a guy who always had my eye on something, like John Warren on his C.P.A. I knew something would happen; I knew I'd get a job somewhere there, in Dayton, or Atlanta." During the year, he met the representative from Converse sneakers, and after "talking back and forth—they're always looking for guys," he was awarded the right to represent the line in the Dayton area. "It was a real nice transition job because it was still basketball. I called on sporting-goods stores and Ohio colleges and the Cavaliers, and at the same time the job gave me exposure to the business world and selling and so in another year a local television station who's involved in UD [University of Dayton] basketball—the whole community's involved in it—called to see if I were interested in selling time for them. And I talked to them and it seemed a good opportunity."

The duties excited him—"I got into it; I had to; there was a lot to learn"—and he capitalized on his local reputation. "I had a lot of residuals from playing ball—it covers up a lot of things. Coming in clients want to do business with you: They just look for a reason. I hated the thought of trying to take advantage of somebody just because they were a fan. You still have to be fair with the guy: So you end up trying to have an honest relationship. I try to be a good representative of the station just as I tried to be a good member of the team. If a guy has a son he wants you to meet, then fine, but to try to take advantage of it just doesn't work out. I feel self-conscious when guys talk about the past because it is history, but at the same time I'm not stupid enough to turn it down. It's a selling tool that I have and I'm in the business of selling, so if it happens, okay." The station is the dominant one in the area— "our Sunday night line-up with Archie Bunker is strong, and our Monday night with *M\*A\*S\*H* is all strong, and Friday night is extremely strong with *The Incredible Hulk* and *The Dukes of Hazzard*"—and May's accounts include the local Coca-Cola bottling plant, Blue Cross-Blue Shield, a carpet store, and some auto dealers. Now much of the original satisfaction has left the job, and, although May is still grateful for the position, he is preparing to change his career. "I have a brother who's an attorney who works for savings and loans and I have another brother who works for a home builder and we're forming a partnership to get into real estate. This summer I got my license and that looks to be my future. Over the past year we've been trying to find what is the best thing to do. When we make a move it's got to be whole hog and we're finding it's not so cut and dried to go out and buy fifty acres and build forty houses and sell them as subdivisions or to buy a twenty-unit apartment building and operate it or to build an office building or buy new land—we're still trying to find the one thing we can all contribute to. I'll be the marketing guy and I have the capital. I saved some money from basketball; it's enough to make me fairly secure—but not enough to do anything big: just one year's salary for some guys."

He is grateful for the way his life has worked out. "I never set my sights on being a star. That wasn't part of my upbringing. I hate to use the word contentment because it connotes not ambitious, but I can adjust to most situations. It's my personality. I can be content with a lot or a little. I was just fortunate to go through this basketball thing that set me up. If I had had to go out and work for a living right out of high school I don't know what would have happened. I was much more competitive then, but I might have had a whole different life and become a factory worker like my dad was, so I'm just appreciative of what happened to me." Playing on the Knicks remains his great satisfaction in basketball. "Being part of the '69–'70 team was thrilling. I felt that I was part of it and I didn't feel sensitive about the fact that I didn't contribute to it. I was part of the team and they can never take that away. I tried to wear the ring for a while, but the damn thing was so big and bulky, and I'm not one to be gaudy with a lot of stuff, so I just put it away. But winning the championship was like a dream come true. Guys play their whole career—Wilt Chamberlain played his whole career before he got one. Even in Buffalo when I was self-gratified by being able to play and prove my talents to myself, it wasn't the same as a team championship, which is what you're all working for. It just happened that it occurred at the start of my career and not at the end when it could have been a real climax."

Living in an all-white community in Dayton, he occasionally encounters his past in unhappy ways. "I talk to people now in Dayton who knew me in college and they still think I'm a racist, hate-the-blacks-type guy. It's real hard to change that image. Still, today, I live in Dayton, I'm close to the basketball people down at UD, and they say things and I just think—well, I don't have any defense because that's the way I was. So that's the past that probably bothers me more than anything, but there is nothing I can do about it." And the benefits more than compensate for this discomfort. "I look on Dayton as a haven because I grew up here and played ball and I'm still a special person to some people here and I need that: My ego needs that. I come to New York and I say, Damn! people don't realize that there are places where it's nice to live! Maybe I'm sinking into a comfortable little niche, but I like it. Why should I go out and aggravate myself? For what? Maybe I'm not ambitious in the same way other people are. My ambition is to be happy."

The game also aided Bowman off the court. "I got a job with a corporation called Executron for a while. They made telephones for conference calls and I was a salesman. I got a little weekly salary, plus a commission for all the phones I sold. I'd go around to guys like executives, guys like Dustin Hoffman—I knew a lot of people who came to the games, and I met a lot of stars and actors—and I'd go to them and kind of play on who I was, say, I'm Nate Bowman, you remember me, from the Knicks? Hook up your business with these phones. And most of them would do it because it was a good operation. I see some of these guys now—I see Dustin, and he says, Hey man, that was a hell of an idea you brought into my office, we're still using it."

He soon quit Executron—"I just didn't get along with the guys I worked with"—and started modeling. "I got a couple of good commercials where I was the main principal and they sustained me where I didn't have to get a regular nine-to-five job, which I didn't want anyway. The first ran three and a half, four years. It was very, very successful. It was a Pabst's commercial, Pabst's Blue Ribbon. I played a player-coach in it. In the first sequence I was coaching these guys; the next we were playing the actual game; and the third we were in a bar, drinking. It was one of the best commercials I've ever seen. Then I did a Vitalis commercial. It didn't run that long, only about a year. Those were the only two that were successful. Then I did print work for magazines. Seagram's V-O, stuff for *Oui* magazine. There you just get a flat fee, not residuals or anything like that—just five or six hundred bucks." When work ran out, he hustled other jobs—"anything I could do to survive I was doing"—including a brief stint as a "doorman at a neighborhood club who would charge admission and collect the money."

Finally he signed with one agency, working for them both as a client and a salesman. "I've done three commercials in the last year. Two are 7-Up. I haven't seen either one of them yet, but I've gotten a couple of checks and they're not sending me that money just for the hell if it. And I did an Olympia Gold Light Beer commercial about two months ago. It's not national, it just runs out West—Utah, Texas, California, places like that, where they mostly sell that kind of beer. I also recruit athletes for the company. Most of the time when they get actors to be athletes in commercials, they don't know how to be actors, so I'm trying to get more of the ballplayers to learn how to act a little bit, and it's better for me to speak to other athletes rather than somebody else, because basically I've been into that field myself and I'm an ex-ballplayer and I can show them where it can be beneficial." Once his present occupation recalled his former days. "It was a funny thing. Last winter a fast-food chain wanted to do a promotional campaign with Willis Reed. The whole thing was set, but at the last minute he couldn't do it. So they called me. Ten years after the championship, I was still being his backup."

Presently he lives in a sunlit apartment on the West Side of Manhattan; thirty-six stories high, the view from his living room flattens the steep cliffs that line the Hudson River, making New Jersey a wide tableland stretching west. He is married—his wife is a stewardess—the father of a ten-year-old daughter and the master of the family dog, Munch, short for Munchkin, a noisy, nervous, tiny pet who barely reaches Bowman's ankles and runs around his feet, yapping shrilly while the ex-center tries to shush him, crying, "Munch! Be quiet!" He is as settled and content as May, and, like his white counterpart, he still has ties to the past. Recently he got a part-time job as a bodyguard for a young black woman rock star. "I travel all over the country with her. Six or seven months ago, her ex-road manager called me and asked if I'd be interested in doing that, and I thought about it for twenty minutes and said, Yeah, sure, great! I like the work. When we don't fly, we travel on a customized bus. It's got a front compartment in a little lounge where we can listen to tapes and watch TV or the Betamax, and in the back she has her own apartment. Right between they got a room with sixteen bunks. It's all right, even for me because they made an especially long bed just for me. I get to be back on the road and do a lot of traveling, and I love that, I miss it. There are going to be some tours pretty soon in Europe—we'll go to France, Sweden, Tokyo, places like that. I've never ever been there, so I think I'll hang out with her a little longer."

# 4

In Buffalo, Bowman and May worked for Eddie Donovan, the ex-general manager of the Knicks. Since 1965 he had tried to put together a champion. But in the middle of the '69–'70 season, as the team began to realize his hopes, he accepted an offer to run and own part of the Buffalo franchise. "I went to Buffalo because it offered me part ownership, which would have never happened in New York," he explained to me, "and I thought that would give security to Marge, my wife, and education for our kids. And, to make a long story short, I'm glad the five percent I had of the team wasn't ten percent because the IRS came along and said, Is that so? and the money had to be paid and whatever I gained I lost. I regret that it didn't work out. I think Buffalo's a great city. They're blue-collar people up there, hard workers who enjoy sports, and they're very knowledgeable fans—like fans in New York, Chicago, or Philadelphia. The fans gave us some heat at first because we didn't move a lot of guys in and out. We stayed with what we had until we got into a position where moves were available to us. I think sometimes there's an unnecessary pressure—let's get another guy, got to get another guy. But you see—you can't get to the end of the tunnel until you see the light. To change for change's sake doesn't make sense to me. To me the only way to build is through the draft and you build a team through the draft by getting to know the kid before you draft him, by putting in a lot of homework—who they played for, their families, their schooling. I mean you can't build a team of character with a lot of characters. It's got to be there. Like with the '69 Knicks—you go to them and you'll see: They were all outstanding people."

Presently, Donovan again makes his professional residence at Madison Square Garden. He returned to the Knicks in 1975 when his Buffalo contract ended. The Knicks were eager to take him back. The greatest general manager in basketball is Red Auerbach; he has run the Boston Celtics for thirty seasons and the team has missed only two play-off appearances during that time, a peerless record for any sport. But among mortal general managers, Donovan ranks at the top. The collaborative construction with Holzman of the championship team was only his first accomplishment in the professional game. After that, he designed from scratch a Buffalo team that qualified for the play-offs within four years, the quickest success of any expansion squad (excepting Milwaukee which, once it got Abdul-Jabbar, was an immediate contender for the crown); and upon returning to New York, he helped give purpose and strength to a weak and floundering unit. He has sometimes picked clunks—no selector of basketball talent displays an unblemished record, Auerbach included—but he has consistently made surprisingly acute trades or draft picks, receiving true value out of even unpromising situations.

Still, the rewards for his excellence have not been great. After thirty years in the business, he lacks significant financial security or public recognition. He remains an essentially behind-the-scenes character. He lives in the business world of basketball, a maddeningly small and cloistered community of deals, gossip, old friendships, and new betrayals. Appropriately, his office is a windowless chamber off a dead-end corridor in the innermost sanctums of Madison Square Garden; unless he leaves the building altogether, he can easily pass a day without even seeing the street outside and unless he leaves his office he is surrounded entirely by people whose sole concerns are points, tickets, and injury reports. When he does wander from his room, he usually is going someplace in the Garden itself, navigating his way down mazes of cinder-block passageways and past acres of empty warehouse space that serve as barns for elephants when the circus is in town or communications center for television networks during the Democratic National Convention.

Several reasons explain this lack of renown. One is that Donovan quit New York just as the team triumphed. Ambition prompted the move: If the Buffalo franchise had succeeded and Donovan owned 5 percent of it he would have been a well-rewarded man. Still, the change defies the logic of his job. The aim of a general manager is to build a good team quickly; the task completed—and if you haven't hit gold the first couple of years you're in trouble—you tinker with your invention as it chalks up wins, these essentially trouble-free years compensating for the ones in which you scrambled to assemble a unit. By leaving New York, Donovan denied himself this leisure, and instead took on the hardest task in the field—creating a team in a city new to the professional sport. And in Buffalo too, he was denied the satisfaction of resting on his laurels—though this time the cause was the ownership, not him. Consequently, though his views decisively stamped the

Knicks, he never was fully associated with the team, a pioneer who left the homestead just when the first harvest was coming in.

Donovan also has personal quirks that kept him from enjoying the limelight. The Knicks were one of the most public teams in sports history, but Donovan is essentially a private man, retiring, modest, at times almost unfashionably diffident. When he left New York, Leonard Koppett, the *New York Times* writer, suggested that Donovan was never entirely comfortable in the city. He still doesn't seem quite at home in it. Born in Elizabeth, New Jersey, and a longtime resident of the upstate area around Buffalo, he often recalls those smaller and grittier places with a fondness missing from his voice when he speaks of New York. There is no show in him, no flamboyance whatsoever. Donovan so sincerely dislikes being in the public eye that he is ill at ease even in press conferences; standing before the crew of friendly reporters whom he sees practically every night during the season, he sets his normally genial face into a hard, determined look, appearing more like a general briefing the press on an invasion than a general manager announcing the acquisition of a new player.

Donovan's shyness accompanies other traditional virtues. He believes in piety and ritual. He can't mention a dead person without immediately muttering, "God rest his soul in peace." His main criticism of the modern professional game is that there are too many teams and not enough match-ups between players: "Bradley against Havlicek, DeBusschere against Johnson, Frazier against Monroe, that's what people pay to see." He is a family man, and his conversation refers constantly to kids, his domestic concern drawing, with basketball, the full circle of his world: He is proud all his children will complete college and when asked what was the most satisfying event in his basketball career he told me that when he coached St. Bonaventure's "all the kids who went into their junior year graduated, and that was satisfying because there you are talking about human lives." He is genuinely friendly, interested in people and politics, and exudes a kind of general cheeriness: As Donnie May said about his mother, Donovan can always find something good to say about the disaster you've just told him or a worse story about someone else, and in the midst of catastrophe answers his phone with the same high, ringing happy voice with which he greets people when everything is going well. Indeed, only his eyes indicate any emotion other than good-spiritedness; brilliant points of light in his otherwise familiar, slightly puffy face, they express fatigue, anger, puzzlement.

But Donovan's cheeriness isn't optimism. His universe revolves around basketball; the game—both sport and business —has been his public life and informs his views on all experience. He is both modest and generous with this store of knowledge. Donovan was one of the first professionals I met in basketball. In our talks he would occasionally refer so casually to some bit of arcane lore that I would find myself nodding stupidly, as though he were speaking a foreign language and I were listening for the telltale word or phrase that would clue me into his meaning: "Oh, into the *pivot*," I would exclaim, desperately grateful that I had finally caught his drift. This lifelong association with the game has made him a realist; his hearty, encouraging manner is really a guiltless, cynical, Irish fatalism. "I never speak badly about anybody in this business," he once explained to me, "because you never know where they'll be two years from now." Another time, I asked if a general manager were looking to change jobs. "Hey, the only time to look for work is when you've got it." The job's demands force him to dismiss even treasured players. Two years ago, he recruited Hollis Copeland. A speedy, jumping-jack small forward, Copeland had suffered a disappointing freshman season in the pros with another team and was scouted by Donovan the following summer in a semi-pro league. Donovan invited Copeland to the Knicks' training camp and liked what he saw. "I'll tell you what impressed me about Hollis. The first morning we're there, we're all sitting around the table to eat breakfast and the food comes and the guys start to eat and Hollis crosses himself, and hey: That took guts in front of all those guys, I respected that." Copeland became a regular substitute on the team and a Garden favorite, but the next year financial considerations worked against him and he was cut, personal integrity and all.

Because of any number of situations like this, players sometimes express bitter feelings toward Donovan. "I hope he's having a hard time," one remarked to me about him, "because he's owed it for all the hard times he gave others." Reporters also occasionally complain about him. One once remarked that when talking to Donovan you feel you're getting the unvarnished truth about the team; after you walk away, you realize he hasn't told you one hard fact. There is some truth to these criticisms. Donovan likes to think that everything he does is for the well-being of players and often his decisions necessarily disadvantage athletes, and he will often promise more than he can deliver: He doesn't like saying no. The exigencies of his trade have also left him cautious in judgment and calculating in strategy; he would not have survived in professional basketball without these two qualities. But his fundamental views about the philosophy and practice of building a team are relentlessly practical and simple.

For him, Willis was the core of the squad. "We looked for good people: good people off the court as well as on. You get good people with talent. Once we had Willis we knew we had a special person." Willis also determined the future composition of the team. "Center is the position you have to key in on and then you go from there—it dictates what you're going to do. That's why the trade for DeBusschere was so important. Before the trade we were a team with two centers, Willis and Bellamy, and if you were going to get a shot at the marbles, you had to break them up. With the two of them you would overpower people. It wasn't a team that had great continuity. If Bellamy and Reed are together in a situation you can't have Bellamy come out and set a pick for Reed—you're going to have a collision. And there were leadership problems too. When Willis wanted to go inside, he just went in and Bellamy went out. There were times I said, Bells, you've got to move him out and be more aggressive. But Walter very seldom did that. He wouldn't chase Willis out."

Donovan speaks modestly about his own role in the trade. He had pursued the deal for some time. "Donnie Butcher was the coach of Detroit and we had been talking trade quite a while. He didn't want to do it and then Coyle came in and I don't think he wanted to do it, but then Donnie was fired and Paul Seymour took the job. Paul had had Bellamy in Baltimore originally and he won with him, and he loved Komives because Komives was a scrapper like Seymour was—I think they even went to the same high school together. And they weren't playing that good and we were. We were sure that Bellamy and Reed wouldn't work out—but how sure are you? We were sure, but you're never altogether sure—you think this will come out right, you never know.

"The trade was almost a change in philosophy because we went from two centers, two guards, and one forward to one center and four guards. It gave us a team of motion.

"We started playing pretty good. There was a confidence they took into every arena. A good feeling. They were respected, and I think that gave them an edge. The teams they knew they should beat, they beat ninety percent of the time. They were outstanding against the expansion teams. There was no jerking around. They just beat you nice and easy with basketball. They had a lot of mental toughness—a lot of mental toughness. A losing team or a team that's unsure of itself can be up by eight or ten in the fourth quarter and there's a feeling: Okay, now we'll play the clock, the clock's our friend. They forget how they got the lead and the whole team almost gets the feeling: Okay, now who's going to screw up tonight? But when you're positive, like the '69 team, the feeling is different. It's who's going to bail us out? You can be ten down and you're playing with such confidence that when you lose the game, it's like, Hey, we must have another quarter. They were a tough club to cheat on. You could have them 32–19 and you never had a good feeling. You had to shoot fifty-five percent to get ahead of them by half time and it was hard to keep up because they were a good defensive ball club. The ball was always in good hands, and they were a great perimeter shooting team. So you had to play them one-on-one because if you left the guy you were supposed to be guarding, they'd just burn you. They went to their strength."

He credits Holzman for disciplining the team and making it work as a unit. "Red's a knowledgeable basketball man. You don't know anything unless you've sat on the bench and I have sat there. It's easy to say, Why the hell did he put that guy in? Hey, go sit there for a season and you'll find out why. Did he put him in to lose the game? You put a guy in because something happened in Kansas City two months ago when you played this guy against so-and-so and so-and-so went whacky, he didn't know what was going on. But the coach remembers and makes the move. One of the things about a coach is to know your players. A guy isn't a great passer. He's just not. All the greats had weaknesses. So you don't make him the passer. Let him shoot because he's a great shooter. You've got to let them know their role, every guy from the first to the tenth, and Red did that. Like Nate Bowman. His role was to get Willis ready to play. He used to drive Willis up a wall in practice and Red would have Nate hollering at Willis, Face the ball! Face the ball! and Willis would say, Shut up! But that was Nate's role and it worked. Another example was Mike Riordan. At first his job was just to give a foul and this was important to winning the game. He understood that. So he didn't throw his jacket on the floor and make a scene: What am I, nothing? He made a science of it."

But he believes the team's most exceptional quality—besides Reed's intimidating presence—was that so many of its members could handle the ball. "I don't think you'll ever get a collection of talent like that again. It was deep. People forget. Barnett. Very important factor. We got him from L.A. for Willie Naulls. His reputation was that he was a shooter. We knew he could shoot, but he was a hell of a defensive player—he used to give guys fits. He was pretty complete. Frazier. He was pretty complete. When we first had him at camp, when Dick [McGuire] was coaching, we knew we had something special. Then he hurt himself, a bad sprain, and missed a lot of games, and we couldn't start him then right off, so he had to play himself onto the team, but he was always going to be there. Dave. Bradley. Everyone forgets what they thought of Bradley at first. Dave Gavitt said it and I never heard it before: Bradley was the greatest ballplayer I ever saw from the shoulders up and the wrists down. He didn't catch the ball really: He just steered it. He moved constantly and if he had the shot, he caught the ball and it was gone, and if he didn't, he caught the ball and it was gone. He didn't catch it and start looking. Everything was quick and precise with him. And he was moving constantly. He would go down through the middle and even if he didn't receive the ball he would do the same thing again the next night and sooner or later the move would work because the defense would close up and the perimeter would open and one of the team would either get an open jumper or Bradley would get a cheap lay-up. Stallworth—he was so good with the ball that we used to play him against Hal Greer at guard. All of them really. Once you saw them play, you just knew: They were there."

Donovan felt this first during the season preceding the championship. "It was exciting to me when they got into the play-offs that year. I think it was then that Gene Shue [the coach of the Bullets] decided he was going to bust Willis. He had Unseld [the Bullet center] bring the ball down. So Red calls a time-out. Okay, this is Gene's secret weapon. He's going to make Willis tired by having him chase Unseld. But why should Willis chase Unseld? Red puts DeBusschere on Unseld and Unseld kept bringing it down and when he crossed over at half court, then Willis picked him up. Big secret weapon!"

Then they played Boston and lost. "I remember Riordan had a great game. He played forty-eight minutes, got twenty-six points, challenged Russell, going over, under, and around him. His contract was up that year and when we got on the plane back to New York after the game, I saw him and said, You know Mike, if you're ever going to have a good one this is the time. I'll see you in September, I don't want to talk to you for a while."

By the time the team was fighting for the championship, Donovan had already settled in Buffalo. "I left before the season ended. I came down only for the final game. In fact, Sean, who is now a sophomore, was sitting between Marge and me and he starts to cry. I said, What's the matter? He said, I'll never see the Knicks win. Everyone was saying that L.A. was going to kill them. They kept talking about Bradley and Counts. They said Bradley couldn't play Counts. Counts was too big for him. Hey, Bradley wasn't going to play Counts and if the world championship is going to be determined by Bradley playing Counts then you'd better bet on Bradley."

Donovan's long experience as a college coach of St. Bonaventure's in Buffalo, part ownership of the team, and familiarity with the area seems to have inspired him to his best efforts on his new job. He talks about the time there as a sort of pleasurable adventure. "It was just me and Carl Scheer [the present general manager of the Denver Nuggets] and we worked day and night the first year. We had players but no money, and it wasn't a good time to buy a team because the market was going down. Once a theater guy came up to see if he wanted to buy it. I remember he was sitting at the desk and the phone would ring and he'd say, God! What! Another million! He was getting sicker and sicker. A couple of years later, we got into the play-offs and the building was rocking with fans and I thought of him—he's dead now, God rest his soul—and I thought he would have loved that sight.

"I enjoyed putting that team together and I think we accomplished a lot: We were the first expansion team of that group to make the play-offs and we were an exciting team. I didn't change the way I operated as a general manager because I was a part owner. It's like defense. Defense is closing lanes going to the basket, offense is opening them. You teach it playing with your left foot out; I teach it using the right. You take American to California, I take TWA. But we're all teaching defense and we're all going to California. We built through the draft. You look for good kids, kids who've been coached under guys you respect. Dean Smith, Dave Gavitt, Joe Mullaney, Ray Meyers—if they say someone is good, he's solid. Or Newton down in Alabama—any of his kids in the league are great, and you look to a guy like that. All the successful coaches are close to their kids and when they recruit they want to know the same things we do: Are the kids willing to pay the price? Character instead of characters. I'll never forget Don Adams. He had a rotten reputation, but he was a pro. He'd come into the locker room. Turn off that music, he'd say, we've got a game to get ready for. *That's* the guy you're looking out for." One of the team's best players was a guard named Randy Smith, a seventh-round draft pick who later became an all-star. Donovan ironically comments on all the praise he received for making the selection. "Everybody says, Randy Smith, sensational pick. But if we were so smart then why didn't we pick him earlier? We picked him because he was a local kid and would make good copy and maybe sell some tickets."

For its first three years the team lost, winning only five games more than the Knicks had in their one championship season. The failure made Donovan's job more demanding. "To do this job right, you can't turn it on and off. It's the only job where you either win or lose. You don't go to work and have a good day and come home. You either win or lose and everybody knows it, and if you're on the down side it has a tremendous effect on you, your family, and everything. In Buffalo we were very involved. We would have the wives and kids over because we knew what it was to move and we were conscious of that. And it was also difficult on my family because I was on the road. Things happen, personal things, and getting a big guy in the middle doesn't matter so much."

The ownership of the team didn't make things easier. Donovan is critical of the league's unchecked expansion and the new money that controls the game. He believes that team owners should know the game and have a financial stake in their team's success; instead many owners are successful businessmen who are untutored in the sport and have only their egos at stake in the team's won-lost record. "Years ago, you could make a deal with Biasone, Eddie Gottlieb, Ed Coil, Ben Kerner. You say, February one you make a deal, February one the deal is made. Now you've got to have attorneys, conference calls, accountants, and contracts, and there are twenty-two teams, which is great, but you've lost that closeness between managements. And hey, you wanted to beat each other's brains out, but it wasn't on that level of business. There was more loyalty because these were all the guys who used to have dancing at half time: Basketball was their only business. Today it isn't. I remember Ben Kerner [the owner of the St. Louis Hawks] in one meeting saying, Look, I don't care if we're here until June—this is in May—we've got to get this thing settled and don't be looking at your watches because it's four o'clock and you've got a plane to catch. This is my business, and I don't have to call a board meeting or go to a bank to vote yes or no: This is it, this is what I do for a living."

The owner of the Buffalo franchise was one of the new breed, and Donovan hints at the discomfort of working for him. "It can be tough to be a general manager. You get a guy who owns a milk company, say, for fifty million dollars and he buys a team and it's a new toy, and ego gets into it. And it's tough losing because most successful people have stepped on a few guys along the way and then they're out at the local country club and someone says to them, Hey, how'd you bomb out last night? It's a kind of retaliation. And then the owner says, Get the general manager on the phone, and he's saying, We've got to get this guy and that guy. But if they would run it as they run their own business they'd be successful."

This wasn't true for Buffalo, and a year after the team had its best success, having a winning 49–33 record and going to the third round of the play-offs, Donovan announced his departure. He talked about the situation with his normal hesitancy. "I thought something more could have been done in Buffalo than was. I don't want to get into it. But it wasn't a happy situation." Toward the end of the season, as the Buffalo team entered the play-offs, the Knicks announced that Donovan had agreed to join them as general manager, a deal that touches on unethical conduct since circumstantial evidence indicates the agreement between Donovan and New York had been announced before his term at Buffalo ended. He remains touchy on the subject. "I'd like to pass on whether or not New York spoke to me before I quit Buffalo," he said. But he is unequivocal about his reasons for leaving and his judgment about the team's ownership. "I wanted a job; I had to work; and I was interested in working for good people: A team is only as good as its head, and its head is its owner." (The year following his departure, the owner of the Buffalo franchise sold off his major players. Then he sold the scuttled operation to a Kentucky entrepreneur named John Y. Brown. Brown promptly traded the franchise for the Boston Celtics, whose owner moved the entire Buffalo team across the country to San Diego: He wanted a team in his hometown and would have been lynched if he had kidnaped the Celtics. Brown almost was. Several months after he bought the team bumper stickers appeared around the Hub reading, "John WHY?" They became popular items as Brown led the team to a dismal losing record. He quickly surrendered ownership, returning to his native state, where he won the governorship. Meanwhile, it was recently reported that the owner of the San Diego team, having deprived Buffalo of a franchise, is now looking to sell his investment.)

In New York, Donovan encountered a chaotic situation. The team was playing poorly and the ownership was frantic to get a player who would turn the record around. First they signed George McGinnis, a power forward. But the league ruled the deal illegal and the Knicks lost money, good will and draft choices. Then they pursued Wilt Chamberlain, who had recently announced that he wanted to end his retirement. Donovan, Holzman, and Mike Burke, the president of the club, went out to California to speak to Chamberlain, but the center never made the appointment. Donovan claims publicity was the only purpose of the trip anyway. "We went to speak to Wilt. Hey, who wanted to go out and talk to Wilt? We don't want to talk to Wilt. If we've got to talk to Wilt we'll talk in New York. But to talk to Wilt is to sell tickets. And if we don't go to California then the fans will say, What are they doing? Let them do something! Get Wilt! I don't care what it costs! So you go and he doesn't show. That's great: If Wilt had been there we might have worked something out." That season and the next, the team purchased several star players. The expense was enormous and the rewards few, the team managing but one season over .500 and playing poorly in one play-off. Donovan didn't negotiate any of the deals, though he doesn't disassociate himself from them; but he is critical of the team's tactics. "I think we lost sight that there is no shortcut from A to B. In baseball it's different. There are certain players at certain positions and they're not interdependent with one another. You get Nolan Ryan, or a relief pitcher, a left-handed power hitter, or a catcher. But in basketball there are no shortcuts."

The experiment lasted three years until a new owner peremptorily traded all of the team's stars and announced a new era: The team would rebuild itself through the draft, following the path it had taken to its first championship. "I don't know when I thought our plan wasn't working, but I just knew. It wasn't a good situation—not a good one at all. Then you sit down and say, Okay, who's untouchable? Players A, B, C—okay, we'll go with them. Everyone else you can trade. And then you reach a point where nobody's untouchable. We had reached that point." Donovan welcomed the change. "I think every third year or so every coach or general manager involved with a team would just like to whistle, Okay! Everybody out! New group! How the hell are you going to go over the same thing? A new group is more receptive; they think you're smarter; and there's something else: They're worried about their jobs. Every coach has the same feeling. Dick Motta had been with Chicago for a while, then he went to Washington. I asked him how he was doing. He said, I'm having so much fun—this team hasn't heard all the things I say. That's why I think Auerbach did such a terrific job to keep his guys interested for so long—that was more psychology than coaching."

The first season, the new, younger team played wild and exciting games. A fast and frantic squad, not at all like the classic blend of the '69 Knicks, they wanted to win and play the game well, but lacked an intelligent and mature will. They ended the season three games under .500 and out of the playoffs, though many observers saw hopeful signs for the following year, and, indeed, the team began the next fall by winning eleven out of its first fourteen games, the best start the team had made since its last championship year in '72–'73. Donovan deserved a good deal of the credit; directly and indirectly, he had helped make the picks that resulted in the team. But his record for leaving the table without picking up his chips seemed to haunt him: While the team was triumphing, a story in the newspapers announced that the ownership was offering Donovan only a one-year contract and that it was quite likely he would be leaving New York again, a prospect he greeted with his predictable, cheerful fatalism. "It's part of the business to feel insecure in the job," he remarked. "Art Rooney told me the day I came into the business: The day you sign your contract is the day you sign your resignation—all that has to be filled in is the date." Friendly, genial, modest, experienced, he yielded the sum of his professional experience. "Good people," he explained, his eyes squinting, the serious look on his face confirming his words. "You need good people. There are all kinds of different philosophies and you've got to decide what you're going to do and how long you want to take. But what you always need is one good guy, a good person, and then you're set there, that position is taken care of. Then you get two or three more and you're ready: You can go out and compete."

# 5

Cazzie Russell, the sixth man who had dutifully come off the bench to shake up a game with some quick baskets, was the first star to leave the team. Appropriately, his departure was a sacrifice for the good of the squad. The Knicks had been disappointing in the '70–'71 season. The injury that had crippled Reed in the fifth game against the Lakers had healed, but several other ailments bothered him throughout the new term; and the team also lacked the enthusiasm that had inspired them the year before. They finished the season with the second-best record in the league (Jabbar's Bucks did better) but faltered in the play-offs. They beat Atlanta, then again faced their old rivals, the Bullets, losing to them in a tight seven-game series that marked the end of their brief reign as champions. Shortly after, Russell was traded to the Golden State Warriors for Jerry Lucas, a veteran center-forward, who, Holzman hoped, could replace Reed if the captain's injuries prohibited him from playing.

Russell has a different relationship to basketball than either Warren, May, or Bowman. For Warren basketball was an afterthought. His anger at his treatment is justifiable. More famous players than he have complained about the vagaries of Bill Fitch's coaching, and Warren's insistence that he never received a real opportunity to play the game demands attention. The common assumptions that perseverance guarantees success and true talent always emerges are illusions. Every summer, general managers answer letters from aspiring athletes pleading for a tryout; these players pursue their training and careers, but lack the physical skills to make good. And once talent emerges, where does it go? Only an invisible man can play basketball well these days and pass unnoticed because professional scouts reconnoiter neighborhood playgrounds and high-school and college gyms prospecting for good leapers and sharp shooters who might be worth a fortune. But what happens to these players once they are discovered? Their gifts need cultivation—that's one of the prime reasons for coaching—and without the right care their talents are quickly ruined. Warren might well have succeeded at the game in different circumstances: Other players don't take his claims of talent lightly. Still, basketball was never his sole pursuit. Indeed, with the exception of Bradley, only he among the members of the team could clearly see a life outside basketball, a foresight that he later regretted. For May and Bowman, basketball was a path they followed to escape dreary and anonymous futures. Both would have enjoyed stardom but neither seems to believe seriously they deserved it or displayed a passionate attachment to the game, an inescapable need to pursue it.

But for Russell basketball was a devotion. There was nothing theoretical about his relation to the sport. For Warren, Bowman, and May, and the myriad players they typify, basketball was an unfulfilled promise, an unrequited love. For

Russell the game was a body of work, the enjoyment of his youth and his adult profession. He possessed a greater talent for it than most other players, pursued its mastery with an unswerving dedication, and gained his goal. From his college days on, his triumphs and failures were national sports news, his value as a player estimated in the hundreds of thousands of dollars, his style of play—at least his shooting—exemplary, and his presence on court a fan attraction, people paying to see *him* perform. His history in basketball is not measured by "did not plays" and a paucity of minutes, points, and credits, but lines detailing performances in regular-season, play-off, and All-Star games. Other members of the Knicks exerted more influence on the squad than Russell, and he stands lower than Reed, DeBusschere, or Frazier in the game's hierarchy of accomplishment. Still, clearly and decisively, he was a star, someone who possessed the talent, will, and circumstance to achieve what others can only hope for: a life shaped by his success at playing the game.

Ten years after leaving the Knicks, Russell still leads the privileged life of an athletic celebrity, free to pursue his manias. Indeed, when he visited New York for an old-timers' day, during the winter of the team's tenth anniversary, he seemed trapped in a time warp. He arrived at the Garden carrying a bag of gym clothes, shower equipment, sneakers, sweat socks, and his own basketballs. After changing in the Knick locker room, he went one-on-one with the team's present assistant coach, working up a sweat against the younger man as Garden attendants watched admiringly from the stands. Russell showered in the locker room and lazed around the lounge, watching a college game on television. That night, when the announcer introduced him and he walked on court, he received a hero's welcome, even kids too young ever to have seen him perform as a Knick standing and cheering him; resplendently dressed, he waved gallantly and flashed a magnificent smile. He rooted for the team throughout the game and needed no introductions when he went to the locker room after-

ward. "You make me look old," Holzman complained to him.
"You'll be giving me cod-liver oil next," the announcer said,
passing up some vitamin tablets Russell was suggesting he
take. A beautiful woman on his arm, Russell attended a party
in Harry M's upstairs. He planned to leave early the next
morning for Chicago where he would visit his family before
returning to the Coast and his daily workouts, including his
three-times-a-week bouts with leg lifts to strengthen a recalcitrant knee injury that has plagued him for the past several
years. Only one thing that matters in his life is different from
his existence a decade ago. It is an unalterable development
that Russell, with all his worries and planning, never foresaw.
For the past two years, his life as an active professional ballplayer has been over.

Russell speaks obsessively about this change, repeating stories and details with the same avid fascination for getting
things right with which he used to practice jumpers. Talking to
him is like crossing a rocking boat: Having balanced yourself
aright after one wave of details and emotions has swept your
feet out from under you, another sets you rolling. Without in-
terruption he takes his time to get to a point, often betraying
an almost immobilizing insecurity. A disingenuous amazement
informs his sophisticated knowledge of the world and a bedevil-
ing, incomprehensible irony lies at the center of his experience:
He does everything in his power to make things work out right,
and they rarely do, the fundamental pleasure that comes from
being undistracted and reaching your goal always eluding
him. "I like to talk about the issues, the important issues of
basketball," he told me while reviewing (once again) the rivalry between him and Bill Bradley. "I don't like to talk about
the tick-tack garbage that people like to bring up to create
dissension, like were there problems between you and Bradley,
because what that does is blow things out of proportion." Yet
the "tick-tack garbage" does foul the picture, just as dunking
the ball during practice didn't stop the humiliating miss during

the game and all the physical-fitness training didn't preclude career-threatening injuries.

"You know I had experience as a starter and a sixth man with the Knicks," he said, discussing the first four years of his career. "When I first entered the league I thought it would take me time to adjust, but what happened was that I came along when the small forward was blooming, so that helped me, and I played my first three years as a starter. Then Bradley came back from England and I broke my ankle and I missed the rest of that year, my third year, and Bradley played well, and they kept him as a starting forward while I came off the bench, and we won the championship."

His personally most satisfying game was the contest in Cincinnati which the Knicks won in the last several minutes to continue their winning streak. "A lot of people don't realize we were down by nine points and Red put me in at the start of the second quarter and I went something like seven for nine —I think that was the game—and then we went on to win the game heroically, DeBusschere with a great steal, Frazier with a great basket. It was in the old Cincinnati gym." He referred back to the same feats he gloried in ten years ago. "I enjoyed that game," he said about the famous fifth game with the Lakers, "because we were down by twelve or thirteen points and we played with three forwards and I couldn't believe what happened. I even stole the ball if my memory serves me right —I even stole the ball from either Elgin or West. I mean, I was pretty jacked up for that game and we ran the Lakers right out of the gym—we really played well."

His praise of the teamwork is not merely obligatory. The Knicks were always lauded for the fluid nature of their attack in comparison to other teams which rely on only one or two shooters to score; but Russell explained to me the basis for this aspect of their offense. "The best thing about the Knicks was the way we ran our plays and would go to our second and third options. We ran well when the opportunity presented itself—we were very smart, we were a team that capitalized on other teams' weaknesses—but if the other team knew the play we were going to run, we'd go to an option off of it. For example, if the first play was to set a pick to drive off of Willis and if they stopped that play there would be something else happening on the other side of the court. The one thing I remember about the Knicks was the ability to take advantage of all situations. Like if a guy came in and was hot, they'd keep the ball on him."

He is unfailing in his admiration for Holzman. "One thing about Red: I could always talk to Red. That was one great thing I always liked about him. He was an honest guy. I've gone back to New York and we've talked. I think Red is a man who knows basketball—I take my hat off to him. Being young of course I wanted to play, but he was the man responsible for drafting me, so when I look back over it there's no way I can be bitter toward this man. I remember the first big game I ever had in New York. It was against Baltimore. I think I scored thirty-four points, and I ran and passed the ball, and you would have thought that Red had struck it rich—I mean that was his reaction to my playing well."

A good deal of Russell's liking for Holzman comes from the dignified manner in which the coach handled Russell's trade. Russell had suffered a bad injury in early January. Playing against the Bullets, Russell drove to the basket, expecting to meet the Baltimore center, Wes Unseld; instead he met air, and crashed to the floor, breaking his wrist. The injury incapacitated him for the rest of the season and the eventually disappointing play-off games, and toward the end Holzman indicated to him that the team was preparing some sort of deal.

After serious injuries and getting cut from a team, being traded is the trauma every ballplayer fears, and the future exchange troubled Russell. "You don't know how you're going to be received by the other team, and you don't know the town you're going to. Here I am, only twenty-five or twenty-six, and I'm leaving New York for the first time, and I had some very good experiences in New York. I'd met some fine people—I'd even met Howard Cosell—and I had signed my contract and had my picture taken in front of the old Madison Square Garden, and I had played the last game in the old Madison Square Garden, so I was involved with quite a bit of history in New York."

But other considerations sweetened the deal. For one thing, Russell wanted more p.t.; his acceptance of his sixth-man role was a sacrifice he would just as soon have not taken credit for. Also, to gain Russell's approval, Holzman evidently stressed the value Russell commanded on the trading market. "I felt that trading me was almost in line with Willis Reed's knees going bad. They really needed to find another center because they weren't sure what was going to happen. I like to feel that they were trading a quality player. That's what Red was saying: We had to give up a good player to get one."

Shortly after the play-offs, Russell went to a golf tournament in Miami. "I had just made the turn at the ninth hole and there was a message that there was a long-distance call for me at the halfway house. I wasn't playing that well; I had a tough time making any putts and I think I was about two over. The call was from Red. He told me he had traded me for Jerry Lucas. I said, You mean you traded me for Jerry Lucas? I was tickled to death, man. I said, Hey! That's super! I can't believe that! I must not be a bad ballplayer! And we kind of laughed about that. But I was serious because I remembered Jerry Lucas in college in the Big Ten Conference when his team went fourteen and nothing. So I went back to the golf tournament and I shot every par on the back side. Seriously. Have you ever felt the weight of the world taken off your shoulders? Well, that's the way I felt and I finished the tournament with a seventy-four and that was good for me."

Several days later, he returned to New York and immediately visited Holzman to express his thanks to the coach. He related the story in a somber voice that dramatized the occasion. "I had heard that Red Holzman and his wife were in a car accident. I came in and I got some flowers and I went all the way out to Jones Beach I think to see them. And when I walked in and saw Red—well, I can't tell you what he was thinking, I can only tell you his reaction was just shocked, because remember, I had just been traded, and there was some thought that there was ill feeling between Red and I. But he didn't know how much I respected him for taking the time to call me and tell me. I didn't want anybody to know I was out there, I didn't want any publicity. I talked to him for a few minutes and then went to see his wife, who was down the hall. I came in and she cried, and I told her I was so sorry to hear about it, and I wanted her to have these flowers. And ever since then, when I've seen her, I walk up to her and hug or kiss her. I told them I didn't want anybody to know because I didn't want anybody to think I was coming out there to make a big scene; I went out because I didn't know what their conditions were. And she told me, she said, I'm going to keep these flowers, I'm going to put them in my yard or outside, because they were very expensive flowers. It was something I felt very super about because I didn't want them to think I had any ill feelings about a trade. So that mended our relationship and I think my visit to them eventually got into the papers some way, but I didn't want the publicity. I just wanted to tell Red that they were in my prayers and that I was praying to God for a speedy recovery for you and your wife, and that I knew it's a business and that I've enjoyed my years here with the Knicks, and I think—I think—they cried. You see—you look at people like that, and you see them as stern coaches and firm coaches. But then you see them when they have empathy for people and I've always felt that as long as I can have empathy for people then I can feel good."

The Warriors' coach was Al Attles, a short, well-muscled black man known for his throaty, resonant bass voice, longevity as a coach, and fearlessness as a player. Russell had once fooled with Attles about playing for him. "You know I was sitting on the sidelines with a broken wrist and we [the

Knicks] were playing San Francisco, and I said—I was kidding—if you ever need a running forward look me up, and he said, They're never going to let you go." Still, he felt the need to assert his authority and self-respect with his new commander. "Attles called me right after I had spoken to Red at the halfway house. And you know he has that real deep voice, and he says"—Russell's voice dropped several octaves to imitate Attles' famous foghorn and sounded like a fair reproduction of James Earl Jones in *Star Wars* announcing that the force is very strong—"Cazzie, this is Coach Attles. I'm calling you to find out what you think about the trade. At the time, I was kind of cool about it and I said, I think it's great. Then Attles in his deep voice said they would be in touch with me and that they wanted me to come out for the rookie camp. The general manager had heard about me, had heard I could shoot the ball, but he wanted to see for himself, and I thought that was kind of funny, me being a four-year veteran already. I think they were worried that I was going to be a little disappointed, but I took the trade in terms of basketball being a business, and I told them that, and established that with the general manager and Attles."

Russell judges the next three years to be his most productive seasons as a professional player. For once—and, ironically, without his help—his life functioned smoothly. Socially, he enjoyed the veteran members of the team, who palled around more than the Knicks and fitted more comfortably with Russell's own gregarious nature. "We'd go out to eat all the time —Nate Thurmond, Joe Ellis, Jeff Mullins, who was a super, super individual. They taught me to play cards for the plane flights. It was a good family." The playing unit also met his needs. "I had what I considered a very ideal situation because the Warriors were a running team who got the ball upcourt quickly." This style differed from the Knicks, who played a slower, more deliberate game, and Russell pointed out that the freedom given to him helped all parts of his performance. "I remember in one game, I had like fifteen rebounds, and Nate

Thurmond and Clyde Lee [center and forward for the team] said, Listen, don't try to take our job. And it was great. We laughed about it." That first year, he was voted a member of the All-Star team, the only time he received the honor, and for the next three seasons he performed with a statistical excellence, averaging eighty games each season, scoring almost twenty points a game (while hitting 45 percent of his shots) and being credited with almost five rebounds a contest. In the first two years, he helped lead the team in the play-offs, losing his penultimate year to Wilt Chamberlain and the Lakers. Russell enjoyed playing with the team so much that in one season he continued to perform for them even when he was diagnosed as having a broken disc in his back.

Only one trouble spoiled this paradise, a situation that confounded Russell throughout his career. He found himself, after his first year, competing with a white star at the same position. In New York his challenger had been Bill Bradley, continuing the duel the two had started as college stars. In San Francisco his rival was Rick Barry, a former college wonder who had signed with the Warriors upon graduation, then left to play for the ABA, and, in Russell's second year, returned to his first professional home.

Barry differed from Bradley. Barry was a brash superstar, a shooter who demanded the ball when the game was close, a scrapper who argued with referees, players, and fans, never backing off from a challenge, a celebrity who eschewed Bradley's fastidious personal integrity: While Bradley pursued public, civic concerns in private, Barry made public his most intimate personal affairs, including contract and marital disputes.

Still, in relation to Russell, the men were twins. Both Barry and Bradley were forwards renowned for their court sense, students of the game whose combination of instinct and knowledge outsmarted the opposition. Both possessed great reserves of concentration and self-assurance: Barry shot his foul throws underhanded, perfecting the way children naturally toss a basketball, a method shunned by most players but stubbornly insisted on by Barry because, however clunky-looking, the form ensured greater accuracy. Both were prodigal sons returning to their home teams after a sojourn on foreign soil, Bradley in Oxford and Barry in the ABA. Finally, both were white.

Certainly, they affected Russell in the same way: He had to fit his talents into their mold. With Bradley, he was forced to sit on the bench. With Barry, he was called on to sacrifice aspects of his game for his new partner's benefit, taking fewer shots and guarding the opposition's strong forwards, players whose superior strength and height frequently made the ex-Knick's defensive weaknesses more apparent. Although still a starter, Russell was shunted to a decidedly subsidiary position on offense, Barry's enormous talents, and team strategy, calling for the returned hero to be the sole sun around which the team revolved.

Russell didn't seem entirely candid to me about either situation or his reaction to them, expressing any critical thoughts or negative feelings sideways, slipping them between declarations of general good feeling. "I respected Bradley," he said, referring to the junior senator only by either his last or full name. "He was a very sincere individual. We knew he was destined for the Senate because we were always asking, How about me being on the ticket? Can I be this or that? So we had some good experiences. There were things I thought were blown a little out of proportion [by the press] and of course my playing time was cut sometimes. But it's over and done with. I don't want to rock the boat right now or make any enemies or bring up any old material. If someone were to ask me about it I can tell them point blank that there is no confrontation with Bill Bradley. Now, maybe he felt that there was, but if you sat down and talked to him he could not tell you we have any problems." Even a claim that sportswriters fabricated tension between him and Bradley elicited a classic nondenial denial à la All the President's Men. "I don't think I made that statement," he said, referring to a direct quote attributed to him in Phil Berger's book that Bradley made faces when Russell substituted for him during games. "But I won't get off into that. I think there were a couple of times when Bradley came out and he might have been a little disgusted at the way he was playing or that Red took him out too soon. But they [sportswriters] always tried to play things up big. I'm just sorry I wasn't mature enough to handle it at the time. I never said too much about it but if I had to face those guys now I could tell them what I thought."

He was more openly critical of Barry's personality than of Bradley's, but still spoke about Barry with a tantalizing equivocation. "A lot of people think that Rick Barry and I didn't get along. The only problem with Rick is that he is so headstrong, he has such a big ego, that he doesn't really know how much he's appreciated. It was hard to rally around a guy like Rick. But I never had any confrontations with him. We didn't get into any yelling matches or anything. You see a lot of times people try to make up problems, to create dissension. If you went to Rick Barry right now and asked him, Did you have any problems with Cazzie? he'd say no. Like I started calling Rick and I, between the two of us, Salt and Pepper, because we were working together and really trying to play basketball. Disregard the fact that Rick Barry was white. When he played basketball he was a good basketball player. But Rick hurt himself with his attitude and his inability to get along with players."

But it's hard to forget race with Russell. Presently, Russell is remembered as a brilliant but limited performer. This characterization attempts to rewrite history, editorials praising a dead leader whom the papers reviled when alive. Actually, Russell was always conceived by the popular imagination to be what later became the prototypical "black" ballplayer: a physically gifted performer who lacked the mental qualities of will, concentration, and self-restraint that mark distinguished team champions. The constant contrast drawn between him and Bradley served only to sharpen the features of the caricature: Bradley was pictured as the extreme opposite of Russell, a selfless and purposive athlete who compensated for his inferior physical equipment with sterling emotional and intellectual maturity. There's no empirical proof that racial bias informed this comparison. Still, in the years since the two battled each other at Madison Square Garden the specific qualities commonly ascribed to both men have become the general ones white fans mean when they blithely refer to "black ball" and "white ball"—the first undisciplined, selfish, and immature, the second team-oriented, sagacious, and laudatory.

Russell is wary when he talks about race. "I'll tell you about a lot of ballplayers," he said to me. "They have opinions and a lot of them know things, but they won't say anything because they figure it might hurt me, and it might, and they put an apron on it." He isn't totally guilty of this acquiescent silence; instead, he lets his preoccupations intrude, as though uninvited, into his conversation, not taking responsibility for them. "I don't like writers creating all that racial garbage," he said, dismissing the race issue in one breath, only to introduce it again in the next. "Though unfortunately it still exists when you look at how a guy who belongs to the Ku Klux Klan gets so many votes in San Diego. It makes you wonder, and it makes you wonder how the guys playing ball in San Diego must feel. But when you talk about that, they think you're a radical." Similarly, he gave me only a similar peek at the sort of troubled racial relations that must have existed on the Warriors with Barry. "I want to tell you how super the players thought Jeff Mullins was," he said, referring to another white performer for the Warriors. "They had a picture, a team picture, and they cut out every other white guy and left Jeff Mullins in there—that's what they thought of Jeff Mullins, and Nate Thurmond did that."

Russell played in Barry's shadow for two years. Then Russell left the Warriors. Business dictated the move. Russell played out his contract with the team and declared himself a free agent, ready to sign with the highest bidder, eventually becoming the property of the Los Angeles Lakers. Blaming his lawyer, Arthur Morse, the agent Johnny Warren complained about and Donnie May commended, and his own passivity for the move, he spoke about the decision with a fuzzy imprecision. "If I had to do it over again, I would stay my tail in San Francisco. I wouldn't move. I would go against my lawyer's advice. He thought it was in my best interest in terms of financial stability and contract-wise, but I wouldn't move. I really regret that I wasn't more headstrong in saying what it was that I wanted to do. What haunts me more than anything is what prompted me to leave. We got into a contract squabble and yet it wasn't really a squabble. If I had to sit down with the owner and general manager, there's nothing in my mind that would describe exactly why I left or any reason for bitterness. I felt that I wanted some things in my contract and they didn't think I needed them. Really, if I was on trial and had to look for a reason why I left I'd probably be guilty."

The move marked a decisive change in Russell's career. There had always been a comic element in his attempts to shape his destiny. His obsessions with health pills, practice, and performance were like a clown's act: unsuccessful attempts to ward off disasters. Indeed, there was a suggestion of almost self-destructive impulse about him. For all the bottles of papaya juice he carried on the road, Russell was regularly tormented by physical injuries, and at the moment when he could have dunked the ball before a national audience, he fouled up instead and was cast as a buffoon. The move to Los Angeles climaxed this irrevocable tendency toward mishap in Russell. Except, unlike previous times, this mistake wasn't humorous; its timing and consequences proved disastrous for Russell.

The first result of the switch was that he left a championship team. Although the Warriors with Russell had never qualified for the NBA crown, the season after his departure they fought their way to the Western Division championship title and proceeded to beat the Baltimore Bullets in four straight games, capturing the title, a triumph that Russell could not easily have foreseen since the team won only six games over the break-even mark during his last season, and even the following championship year evinced few qualities of a masterful squad. "I left the year before they won the championship. Great timing, wasn't it? My timing has always been super—either I'm early for practice or I stay late after practice. I'm always great on my moves. But it was great for them and I thought they played so well together and then I found there had been some problems between Rick Barry and the rest of the club, but they did play well. I just think Rick—I always told him that the reason he never won the MVP [he did, dominating the series] is that you just can't knock your peers and expect them to vote for you. I wanted to go to him so bad because I thought he played so super, but Rick Barry is not the kind of guy you can go up and talk to, he really isn't, and I felt bad about that because I went out of my way to be friends."

But Russell's future in Los Angeles was more vexing than the lost opportunity of playing with the Warriors. "When I went down to the Lakers, something was nagging at me. It was like something was saying, You're making a big mistake. The money was good—I never boasted about it or put it in the papers because for me just being in the NBA was super. But when I got down to L.A., man, I'll tell you I have never in my life felt so uncomfortable." Almost immediately, his concern manifested itself in the way Russell usually showed inner distress: He got a major injury. "My first year there, I get my knee tore up. We're playing in an exhibition game and here's a guy who runs up and hits me from behind as I'm going to dunk the ball, and I tear up my knee. I had an operation October tenth or eleventh and I didn't get to play in the regular season until February and I thought I made a super comeback. Now, that was a bad injury. It tore up the ligaments on the outside, and on the inside there was a small tear on the meniscus, which is the cartilage, and four years later I had to have surgery on that same knee."

His concern was justified; he couldn't have picked a worse time to join the Lakers. One by one, the members of their impressive trinity had retired and the team was ruined. Russell's first year there, personally noteworthy for him because of his comeback, was a catastrophe for the squad, which won but thirty games. Determined to change the situation, the team's millionaire owner arranged one of the major deals in the history of the game, exchanging four outstanding rookies for Kareem Abdul-Jabbar, the league's premier center who had announced to the press that he no longer wished to play in Milwaukee because he found the city socially, culturally, and spiritually barren. Over the next two years, to complement Jabbar, the Lakers bought, traded, and drafted a wide variety of players, experimenting to find the ones who would mesh with the game's single most powerful player. Russell was subject to this shuffling and performed as best he could. He averaged but eleven points his second year there while the team fell just short of a .500 record; then in his third season, he played impressively, appearing in all the regular season's contests, scoring sixteen points per game, and helping to lead them to the semifinal rounds of the play-offs, where they lost to Portland, which went on to win the title. Russell anticipated he would contribute to the team's progress the next year. Instead he became a casualty of it. The day before the season started, West, Bill Sharman, the general manager of the team, and Chick Hearn, the Lakers' radio announcer, came to him after practice and told him he was cut from the squad.

To be cut from a team is an insult to any professional ballplayer. Simply put, the decision means that eleven other men are better than you, and no excuse offered by any coach or general manager can soothe this hurt: Players may be told that their talents simply don't fit the needs of the team, but they believe, obviously and correctly, that their talents—which include a cooperative sense—are necessary for the team to win.

With his achievements and stature, Russell could scarcely have imagined that such a peremptory and ignominious announcement would end his career, and he expressed his rage by focusing on several aspects of the decision. For one thing, the news was entirely unexpected; the year before, Russell had been a starting forward on the team and its second leading scorer. Second, the timing of the announcement was maliciously thoughtless. From mid-September on, all teams slowly set their rosters, cutting the number of players from the several dozen who appear at the first day of training camp to the final twelve who suit up opening night. These final rosters are delicate mechanisms; few general managers or coaches like to disturb them by introducing a new major talent just as they have finally resolved neatly all their financial and athletic problems. By waiting so long to tell Russell the news, the Los Angeles management effectively denied him a chance of getting a job on another team (even if this was because, as they explained to Russell, they had tried to work out some last-minute trade). Finally, there was the simple matter of the team's rejection. Presumably Russell was sacrificed once again: this time to let younger players get a chance to perform. But his final competition was his old nemesis, a white forward who was a favorite. And now he wasn't beaten by a true star but a journeyman named Don Ford, a mediocre player whom Russell could take absolutely no satisfaction in losing to. In all, the experience left him stripped of his self-esteem, lacking both a job and the means to get another, and he referred back constantly to the rejection in his conversation, analyzing, in his complicated way, the injustice he suffered.

"I'm a starting forward and the team messes around, the team didn't even let me go two weeks ahead of time, they let me sit there and wait until the last minute before they let me go! If they were going to let me go, if they were going to go with youth they could have done me the same way they released another player, letting him go two weeks ahead of time. I'm sure they knew they weren't going to use me—though they still could have used me coming off the bench. But I don't think Chick Hearn particularly liked me, though I don't know why because I never had anything to do with him. Maybe it was because of Don Ford, he liked him so much. If you say it's a racial thing, you know what?—they're going to hit the ceiling. But they let me go the day before the season and it was between Don Ford and I. Now you are going to tell me that I'm going to be your starting forward and I had a good year and you're just going to drop me? If they were a first-class organization they could have come to me and said, We're going to go with youth. But then they turn around and bring in a veteran like Lou Hudson, who is the same age I am. Okay, I know it's a business. But come to me ahead of time, tell me you're letting me go. I played in all eighty-two games the year before; I didn't miss any practices, I worked hard, I played super. Instead they come to me the day before the season and say they're letting me go. They said they were trying to make a deal for me, but you know what?—as a black player they always bring up the contract, saying that you cost so much money nobody wants to take you, though they never say that when they're trying to get you on their ball club. They still had to pay me for one year. That's why I know something was funny: because any time an organization is going to pay you for doing nothing, something is going on."

In contrast to this confusion, he described simply and directly the moment when he was told the news. "They had Bill Sharman, the general manager, and Jerry West—he was the only one to look me in the face—and Chick Hearn. I guess they needed all three to tell me. I couldn't believe what they had said, so I went down to the other end of the gym and shot around. Then I left. I kind of felt that this was it, and I really felt—I wish I could prove this—that they felt, well we let this chump go a day before the season and we'll make it tough for him to get a job. Why they felt that, I don't know, you got me, because I played my ass off for L.A. But that's something I always asked the man upstairs. How you can let people that do wrong and just not be fair continue to exist and to prosper? It's unbelievable. But they're still doing it in some kind of capacity. I look at a situation like that, and you try to do fair and to be fair, but you get the shaft while other people prosper. But maybe it's not for me to say. I definitely can't question the man upstairs. But Sharman and Hearn—there's something strange about them, and I was disappointed in Jerry because he was a player and he knew. I talked to some of the players about it and one of the others even suggested it might have been a racial thing between Don Ford and I, and of course Chick Hearn loving Don Ford ..." He trailed off. "How could I go from a starting forward to being out of the league?"

Adrift, Russell pursued other jobs on his own. "I started calling other teams myself. I called Lenny Wilkens [an ex-player who coaches the SuperSonics] in Seattle, but he never returned my call. I called San Antonio; they never returned the call. Nobody returned the call; nobody was interested." He suspects that the Los Angeles management circulated rumors about him throughout the league. "I really can't say whether they had put out bad information on me or what. If I found that out I could sue for defamation of character; but they could put it out and you wouldn't know where it was coming from." Then he followed his other ambition, broadcasting several games for CBS. "Wanting to be an announcer has always been one of my big aspirations. Walking to school I used to announce baseball games to myself, play by play, like the great announcers, Marv Albert, Harry Carey, and Bob Elston, who used to always say the butcher, the baker, or the candlestick maker, or Marv, who used to say, The Knicks bring the ball upcourt. So I've always had that aspiration. And I could talk to players and when I worked at CBS I could always get into the locker rooms early and talk to the players about what to look for." But playing still lured him and he never committed himself to his work as an announcer. "I should have made a decision, but I just felt that I wanted to play a couple of more years. You know when you do something and you just haven't gotten your fill, and I wanted to play a couple of more years, hopefully on a team where I could be part of a championship and go out in style. But I guess it just wasn't meant to be."

In January, he was hired by the Chicago Bulls. "I had called up one of the partners in Chicago and they were searching for somebody to come off the bench—they needed some help. I didn't understand what had taken them so long." One night they played against Los Angeles and Russell got some revenge. "Los Angeles tried to put out garbage that the reason they had gotten rid of me was that I was a clubhouse lawyer. But I never caused any problems. I think it was that we played the Lakers and I had twenty-eight points. So they had to say something to save face. I think I got nine rebounds that night and six offensive rebounds, and Don Ford was one of their starting forwards." But the satisfaction didn't last. That summer, the Chicago team hired a new general manager; he called Russell and told him not to attend camp because the team had all the forwards they needed. Later the team hired two forwards who lacked Russell's experience. This fact made him again suspect he was the target of a blackball campaign, though general managers swear this isn't so. Instead, as throughout his career, he was expendable: a veteran now lacking that extra bit of talent or fan appeal that would make him an attractive addition to a team, always the sixth man.

Russell again tried to find work. "I talked to some other teams, but I really got no response. I think if I had gone out and looked around, maybe, but after you play for so many years . . . I heard Detroit was looking, he's going to be doing me a favor, you know. But I didn't know what the situation was up there. My agent didn't do anything. They could have sent me to Europe, but they didn't do a thing, and I don't care what they say, they didn't." Finally, he played for the Continental League, the present incarnation of the Eastern

League, where Mike Riordan originally came from. Russell performed for a team in Montana that was owned by his friend, Charlie Pride, the black country and western singer. "I went to Montana in December '78. It was okay. I did it because Charlie Pride was a good friend of mine and I thought I could keep myself in shape and somebody in the NBA might give me a call. I hope I didn't discredit myself by doing it, but I wasn't interested in that. I guess what it boiled down to was that I still had some basketball left in me and I wanted to play."

Several months after he finished with Montana the knee he originally injured with the Lakers required further surgery to remove the cartilage. His recovery has been slow. "I didn't do any running on my leg until January and they operated on it in July. I think age is making everything heal more slowly, because I just turned thirty-six." Even when the muscle returns to its full strength, he will never recapture his former mobility. "You see I'm bowlegged," he explained, "and when you take the cartilage out of a bowlegged guy it's tough because all the weight of his body is on the inside." Now he fills his time with various distractions. "I'm doing a few things with public relations on the quiet side and I play in golf tournaments and I'm thinking of doing some coaching in junior colleges. Right now I'm still feeling myself out and I still work out, lifting leg weights and running two or three miles and occasionally I play some ball."

He tries to put a good face on things. For a black American, he's quite privileged and he laughs that "the bad things work out good for you—you make all the putts on the back side." Still, he regrets the end of his career. "When I look back over my career the one thing I regret is leaving Golden State. And I'll tell you why. I don't think the Warriors would take a ballplayer and just throw him out to pasture when he's thirty-three or -four. I really feel bad about that man, because I really tried to be a good ballplayer and keep myself in good

202 / DREAM TEAM

shape. I didn't smoke or drink, I signed autographs for people, I would always go to practice, I never had any problems—I lived and ate and slept pro basketball, and when it came down to it I got the royal shaft, I really did."

At one point he mentioned the final game in the series against Los Angeles, the last time he would be part of a championship squad. He played little that game and referred to the slight in his offhand fashion, saying it disappointed him. Then, always careful to cover his ground, he gave a few words of explanation. "Let me tell you something. When you feel you're a good player, man, the worst thing that can happen to you, the worst thing that can hurt you is not playing. Now don't get me wrong—I said a good player, someone the general consensus of coaches and players say is good. If he doesn't play that can kill him. It can destroy a guy more than anything in the world—no matter what people say. They can say he's not a nice guy or put out some other garbage. But if he doesn't play that kills him because you've taken from him something he loves and he—he's going to be a tough guy to deal with."

# 6

Bill Bradley, Russell's rival, of course was elected senator from New Jersey in November 1978, around the same time that Russell was preparing to play in Montana. The juxtaposition climaxed the reluctant duel that marked their careers. While Russell chanced returning to professional ball by performing as a famous sideshow attraction in obscure western towns, Bradley embarked on a new career, a focus of national attention and much popular acclaim, the first and thus far only member of the team to gain a success outside basketball that matched the glory and satisfaction he had achieved inside the game.

Bradley has always downplayed the comparison between himself and Russell. In *Life on the Run*, his valuable portrait of life in professional basketball, Bradley notes that he and Russell shared several things in common—"strong mothers," stable families, puritan attitudes toward work, big rookie contracts, and difficult freshman seasons as pros. Still, the differences between them overshadow this list, and contrasts with Russell put Bradley in perspective, a background against which he can be measured. Socially, he is a prince to Russell's pauper. Professionally, his career is faultless, an uninterrupted triumph. Personally, he presents a Roman reserve compared to Russell's rococo indulgence.

Bradley is an extraordinarily hard worker who doesn't take benefits for granted. Politically and socially sophisticated, he is sensitive to the rewards and punishments of privilege. Still, he views his unstoppable progress from academic to athletic to political success as no different from the careers, say, of Johnny Warren or Donnie May: a product of will, gifts, and impartial circumstance.

Yet it's hard to regard Bradley's remarkable string of triumphs without seeing the providential influence of his class position. His professional statistics match Russell's, for instance, almost exactly. He played some five hundred minutes more than Russell during his career, but Russell scored two thousand points more than Bradley. Russell sank a higher percentage of his field goals, Bradley of his free throws. Russell caught approximately seven hundred more rebounds and Bradley distributed an equal number more of assists. The record is a remarkable pairing. Yet no two careers present more different overall outlines: Russell's a zigzag that doubles back on itself, Bradley's a smooth arch of triumph. He didn't merely escape the traps that ensnared Russell (and many other ballplayers); he flew over them. He received early recognition

204 / DREAM TEAM

of his talents and, except for his rookie season, never was faulted for betraying them; he never was traded (or even the object of trade rumors); he won two championships, and performed in play-offs in all but two of his ten years in the league; he ended his career without injury; and he always received the highest payment for his services—Bradley's lawyer, Larry Fleisher, claims that Bradley's first contract with the Knicks was the largest salary an athlete had ever received until then and Fleisher still won't name the sum. And, unlike all but a few other top (also white) athletes, he managed all this without ever receiving any severe public hostility. Russell, for instance, never enjoyed Bradley's vast number of possible career options, his future depending entirely on the money he got for playing. Fans often complained that Russell was paid too much for doing too little. Yet the same fans never squawked about the still greater amounts paid to Bradley even during his last two seasons when, for a variety of reasons, he performed dismally. Bradley wasn't responsible for receiving the benefit of this prejudice; but it did advance his career while hindering others'.

Bradley's and Russell's personal styles also differ profoundly. Contrary to the quip of Bradley's college coach, Butch Van Breda Kolff, Bradley isn't happiest when denying himself pleasure: For one thing, he loves to experience the thrill of winning. (And also junk food; his belly has ballooned without the rigors of training camp and the season.) But there is a hard resistance in him to the profligacy and self-indulgence of Russell. Bradley dresses plainly, husbands his financial resources, disdains the ephemeral accoutrements of popular success. While Russell mixes street and locker-room talk with religious pieties, Bradley narrates events with an almost Hemingwayesque toughness deadened by nondescript phrases borrowed from sociology, psychology, and computer science. Russell is hyper, talkative; his analyses and descriptions of people and events are a journey through a maze of personal associations. Bradley exhibits a painful self-awareness; even about his emotional life he marshals facts as though he were preparing a public speech. Russell's speaking style mirrors his play on court—"I'm always going off on tangents," he says. Bradley is also true to his athletic performances: Entirely un- distracted, he methodically pursues his plan. Russell confuses everything, obsessively trying to squeeze together every detail of argument, fact, and feeling that he observed during an event, haphazardly casting feelings and facts in each other's light. With an obsession of equal force, Bradley strives to sort things out, unnervingly cataloging and categorizing his experi- ence, separating feelings from actions, and both of these from objective circumstance, at times even speaking matter-of- factly about exploring different aspects of his personality as though his nature were a federation of separate states presided over by a government of Reason. He refused, for instance, to conduct the interview for this book down in Washington, in- sisting that the session take place in New Jersey. Eventually this restriction resulted in several postponements and broken appointments. I asked a member of his office staff why the lo- cation mattered so much. The address of the interview was surely a matter of convenience, not principle. Not altogether, replied the staff member, and explained the senator's thinking. When Bradley was in Washington, he was a public servant and spent time with the press only to discuss his senatorial duties— his views on energy, for example. But this interview concerned his career as a basketball player and private person and, conse- quently, had to be conducted in New Jersey, on his own time, as a private citizen. The distinction wasn't a case of Nixonian grandstanding—pulling out the cloth coat for public view while wearing the mink in private; I had to pry it out of Brad- ley's go-between. Still, the logic borders on the sophistical. The most common-sensible attitude to it was given by a secretary in the Knickerbocker office who, when I told her about the incident, threw her hands in the air and exclaimed, "That's Bradley! He is so weird! He is so weird!"

Bradley's passion for order sometimes appears to be nothing

more than a self-serving blurring of reality. He insists, for instance, that his reputation as a basketball player didn't contribute decisively to his election; he speaks and writes eloquently about the factors influencing him to return to basketball when he was at Oxford, but never mentions the lure of the fabulous contract that awaited him as a Knickerbocker. At times even noble efforts border on the manipulative. When Bradley joined the Knicks, a majority of the players were black. That summer he worked as a teacher at the Harlem Street Academy. "He didn't want anybody to know he was doing it," Larry Fleisher, his friend and attorney, told me, "though it came out once or twice later. But Bill really felt that it was something he should do and that it would be a way for him to be better integrated into the flow of what was happening with the guys on the team, understanding them and dealing with them." The method appears rather casual for the concern: an Outward Bound trip to the inner-city ghetto.

The incident reflects the last realm of difference between Bradley and Russell. Russell gives the impression of the world being too much with him when he was a kid; basketball, like religion, provided a sanctuary from the misery that surrounded him, and his devotion to the game provided stability and purpose to his life. But for Bradley, basketball served the opposite function: For him, the game was a bridge from the island of privilege where he had been born and raised to the same real world from which other ballplayers sought relief.

From the first, basketball proved more tenacious than Bradley had anticipated. "When I finished college, I thought I was finished with basketball, and I thought I was going to become a lawyer or go into the State Department," he told me. "I didn't know what I was going to do. I knew I didn't want to play basketball, or I thought I didn't. Then I went to England and spent two years there, and one year I played in Italy and won the European Cup, and then I didn't do anything. And, after about a year without literally touching a ball, I went to the gym and had the experience which I've written about where I realized I really loved the game and decided that if I didn't play professionally I would be denying an aspect of my personality which was perhaps more fundamental than any other, and therefore that I had to play—test yourself against the best, experience it, see who you are and what is important to you, all were a part of that decision. So I decided to play.

"I decided I was only going to play for four years, and insisted on only a four-year contract. The four years were an arbitrary figure. I figured that in four years I'd know how it felt to play against the best, and four years was also a nice-sounding contract term. So I did that, and, toward the end of my fourth year, I started making overtures to maybe go to law school, and when it came right down to it, I had to decide whether I liked doing what I was doing, whether there was value to it. And I really did say at that point, Look, I like what I'm doing, why not continue doing it? There shouldn't be any reason why you can't continue doing it if you use your off-seasons wisely to develop other aspects of your personality and skills. So at that point, I said, Fine, that's what I'm going to do, and that's what I continued to do. As a result, I signed six one-year contracts. And I would say that the period of maximum enjoyment for me in the game was from after the first championship to after '74, those four or five years."

At first, Bradley's main experience of the professional game seems to have been anxiety. The source of his troubles was Red Holzman. By Bradley's account, Holzman bullied him. Bradley responded moodily, not speaking to Holzman, and not even looking at him for a week. Holzman frequently referred to Bradley's Ivy League background, adding that he had gone "only" to the plebeian City College of New York. Bradley reports that Holzman blew up during one play-off, when Bradley requested permission to miss a team flight so that he could take a graduate school examination. "You know, don't you, that your contract gives me complete control over your body for nine months a year," he says Holzman scolded him. "Didn't you know when the play-offs were?" He quotes from a diary he kept at the time: "Recently Red kills much potential joy for me. I don't want to leave New York, but if he trades me what choice do I have? If he wanted to keep me on the bench forever he would. It's always the tyranny of the unspoken. I feel helpless before his power over my life." Originally, Bradley's worries focused on his position on the team. "The first year was a matter of proving yourself, and getting a position, figuring yourself out, realizing you were too slow to be a guard and figuring out where you could fit." His competition with Russell started once he had decided he could best succeed as a small forward. "However much Cazzie and I respected each other," he writes, ". . . every game and every practice became a battle to show Holzman that one of us was better than the other. Our head-to-head competition drained me of much emotional energy, for I was never sure I would win . . . Above all, I could never relax. I felt the tension the moment I stepped onto the court. When Cazzie was on an opposite team in the practice shooting game, we were really shooting against each other. During scrimmages, every rebound and shot was contested fiercely. Each of us looked for any kind of edge, so much so that often we remained shooting after practice until the court closed, both determined not to be the first to leave."

In time, winning the role of starter and getting Holzman's approval became intertwined. Holzman's sarcasm and nastiness toward Bradley were intended to humble the ex-college star. Bradley was one of the league's most highly prized rookies and, at the time, Holzman was only a newly appointed coach with a mediocre history: Making Bradley perform was one test he had to pass to prove his ability. Yet Bradley remained anxious about Holzman's attitude even after he had won the starting position; it wasn't until Russell was traded that Bradley began to relax in Holzman's presence. "Red had picked me," he writes. "The effect was exhilarating." He no longer imagined the coach devising ways to cheat him of playing time, and joshed with Holzman about the references to their respective alma maters. The game appeared to him even more attractive now, and his decision to extend his contract coincided with this newfound enjoyment.

He believes his commitment reflected a new maturity. "The decision to continue playing was an example of growing self-awareness and self-knowledge, of knowing what you want to do because you know what you want and you're not being buffeted and pushed by forces that are really not part of your own internal decision-making process, but are external forces —a sense of what other people thought I should do." But the decision also marked a change in his attitude toward the game. "Probably there was an element of not thinking ball was a worthy profession in the initial decision to play only four years," he said. In time, this critical view softened. "The idea of social utility didn't enter the picture as much after the practical experience of playing as in the abstract, prior to the first experience."

But the game provided more benefits than just pleasure. "I could see that the profession was not just a profession I loved, really did, and didn't just give me a group of friends that I really kind of liked and cared about, but it also gave me the time to grow and it gave me the wherewithal financially to allow that growth to take place at whatever pace I wanted. If I wanted to go around the world, fine, I could do that. I didn't need to depend on the State Department or a company or on somebody else to whom I was obligated. I could go myself and have the primary experience. And I think by the end of the fourth year I saw a real value to the continuation of that process."

For him, there was a distinct division between playing with the team and his life off the court. "To a certain extent when you're the best in the world it helps your self-esteem—to that extent playing with the team was helpful to me off the court. But generally off the court there was another life to lead, other things to do that were unrelated to basketball and the championship. In fact, the first championship, I intentionally left one week after the championship. I flew around the world; I was gone for two and a half months. I had had the experience of winning and I knew what it meant for me, and I also knew that as a result of winning there would be secondary experiences I didn't necessarily want to have—appearances here, this thing, that thing, whatever. And I had gotten what I wanted from the experience and there were things I wanted to do rather than have those secondary experiences: going to Indonesia or Japan or Afghanistan. So I chose to do that and when I got back in August it was all right. We were beginning another season, I was out of shape and had to get into shape the same way—the pain was still there, you still had to go through it, you still had to work, and it was another year."

His extraordinary career provided him with access to diverse groups. "Because of his reputation and the image he projected, Bradley could talk to anybody," Larry Fleisher told me. "He could do things no one else could do. He was accepted at every level you could think of." Bradley himself, however, minimizes the importance of his reputation. "I never really used basketball as a way of meeting people. The only time I ever did that was sometimes when I traveled. I would have a list of fifteen people in, say, Kabul, that I would call up and say, Hello, I'm so-and-so, and I'm here at the recommendation of so-and-so, and I'd like to talk to you for about an hour. Then I'd mention one or two people they'd know and they'd say, Fine, they'd take a chance. They didn't know what basketball was in Kabul. And then it was a matter of how you conducted yourself in the meeting—whether the meeting lasted fifteen minutes or one hour or three. And to the extent that the people I mentioned knew me as a basketball player first that was helpful."

Traveling around the world—"getting primary experiences of various parts of the world"—was only one of his summer courses of study. "Another thing I wanted to do was to spend time with economics, and I had the opportunity, I should say,

I had the *luxury* of doing that on an individual basis, self-study, discussions with people in a semi-tutorial relationship. I wanted to be able to experience various kinds of potential lives after basketball, so I did. One summer I taught school in an urban street academy in Harlem, a social service kind of experience. Another year I was an assistant to the director of the Office of Economic Opportunity in Washington, in a big bureaucracy, to see how that functioned. Another year I spent a large part of the summer with the production of a Broadway play, and for several years—I should say, for two years—during the off-season, I wrote the book. And throughout this time, I spent time involved in various business deals, in various entrepreneurial activities to experience that kind of life, and also, in the years from 1972 on, I was active in politics in New Jersey."

Throughout this period, his role on the Knicks changed, and he began to establish his reputation as a player whose powers of intellect, will, and concentration made him a match for more physically gifted performers. In 1970, he was still something of a curiosity, an edgy, overeducated fellow who had just proved his right to be on the court. In the early '70s, he became an exemplar. He was famous for the deep crouch he took when shooting fouls, one eyebrow slanted upward, the face cocked to the side, a stance that combined the awkwardness of a stork with the mad-eyed stare of a cat about to spring. People spoke of his quick hands—"he was always like this," Eddie Donovan told me, and flicked his hands, imitating Bradley's release of the ball in a high-arching shot—and tireless running. And he became known for his defense. He tugged at other players' jerseys and barged through picks, his arms crossed akimbo, Bradley bellowing such a loud "Ooof!" at the point of contact that you could hear him even sitting halfway between the court and the roof.

At the same time, the team was changing. First Reed was lost. Hobbled by yet another injury, the captain played only eleven games during the '71–'72 season, his spot filled by

Lucas, the prodigious scorer and rebounder who had come to the team in exchange for Cazzie Russell. Then, in November 1971, shortly after the season started, the Knicks traded the other two members of their second team, Dave Stallworth and Mike Riordan, for Earl Monroe, the brilliant offensive guard for the Baltimore Bullets who had so frequently humbled the Knicks during the play-offs.*

---

* Lucas was Reed's antithesis. Lucas had been a nationally known college champion and had a head for business schemes. Bradley reports that when Lucas and his college teammates from Ohio State barnstormed through the state, Lucas demanded 50 percent of all the profits, claiming he was the star attraction the audiences were paying to see. Later, he founded a fast-food chain that eventually went broke, "Jerry Lucas's Beef 'n' Shakes." He was famous for magic tricks and a photographic memory: He could recite the numbers in telephone books, and kept a running account of the wins and losses of the Knick players who played poker during the team's flights. For a while he roomed with Frazier and one story holds that he invented a way for the superstar to improve his vocabulary: He suggested Frazier write five new words a day on the mirror, the only place where the immaculate performer would be sure to see them more than once. When Lucas retired from basketball, he wrote a best-selling book on how to improve memory and founded schools throughout the country that instructed people in exercising their powers of recall. He was considered a handsome man by fans when he played in college, an All-American boy, but as a pro his features assumed a bland, passionless, and almost soporific quality, and although he performed well for the Knicks (and in a difficult position, replacing the team's top member) he was known as a cautious athlete, one who never devoted himself fully to the game or achieved the greatness he promised.

Monroe was scheduled to take Barnett's place in the backcourt and became a starter his second season with the team, when Barnett was demoted to a fourth guard, appearing in but 51 games for a total of 514 minutes, the sort of gradual retirement that Russell was deprived of. Monroe arrived with the same reputation that had haunted the man he was replacing: a one-on-one genius who forced his shots, couldn't pass, and didn't play defense. His offensive strength compensated for these weaknesses, but, seemingly, the Knicks didn't need him to score points because they already had Frazier: Indeed, before the deal for Monroe was made, there had been rumors that Frazier was

These trades altered the team's character. The 1970 team was built around Reed at center. Without him, all the major players on the club had to assume a portion of leadership. (Indeed, the search for a young replica of Reed preoccupied the Knicks for the next several years; the club's consistent lack of success after the 1972–73 season demonstrated how rare a find the center had been and underlined his achievement as a player.) Now no one player was depended on to take the final, game-winning shot, make the big defensive play, grab the key rebound; instead heroes changed nightly. The relationship between the starting and second team also changed. The starters were still the superb general practitioners of the game; but defensive specialists had replaced the powerful offensive unit of Russell, Riordan, and Stallworth. In the '69–'70 championship year the second team had scored an average of 27 points a game, while collecting 9.3 rebounds and making 5.9 assists; in the '72–'73 season, the first during which all the new members of the team played together, the second team scored only 23.7 points a game, but could be relied on to get a little more than 14 rebounds and make almost 7.4 assists a contest.

The new grouping both reflected Bradley's general thinking about basketball and was strongly influenced by his play. A team without peerless superstars that won contests with its intelligence and poise, the squad was known for its defensive

---

going to be traded, and, apparently to demonstrate his value to the team, Frazier went on a tear right after Monroe joined the Knicks, scoring 30 points a game during the next 24 contests and hitting over 50 percent of his shots. Meanwhile, Monroe, like Barnett before him, demonstrated his versatility as a player. He turned out to be a vigilant defender and exemplary team player, using his scoring powers when the team needed a basket, and also creating opportunities for others to shine. In time, he and Frazier became known as—after the chosen vehicles of the two stars—the "Rolls-Royce" backcourt, and for several years were generally considered to be the best all-around tandem of guards in the league.

prowess and combative spirit: After trailing Abdul-Jabbar's Milwaukee Bucks by eighteen points with only six minutes left, the Knicks won the contest by shutting off their opponents, leaving them scoreless until the buzzer sounded. Comfortable in this environment, Bradley, one of the team's three veterans, excelled in his personal performance and reached the high point of his professional career. During the season, he played more minutes, took and made more field goals, was credited with more assists, scored more points, and averaged more points than he had managed before or would ever do again, and, for the first and only time, was elected a member of the All-Star team. Along with Frazier, he dominated the offense of the Knicks; he saw longer periods of playing time than all players other than Frazier, took more shots, made more assists, scored more points, and was also the sole Knick to appear in every regular-season contest.

His storybook season ended in triumph. The Knicks had revived enough in the '71–'72 season to beat the Bullets in the play-offs, four games to two, and went on to defeat the regular-season division-leading Boston Celtics, four games to one, before getting clobbered by the Lakers in the final. In the '72–'73 season, their obstacles to the crown remained the same. They pushed aside the Bullets in five quick games, bullied their way past the Celtics, finally winning a seventh game that Holzman called "the most satisfying victory I've ever been connected with," and finally, faced the Lakers again. All the rituals of combat were enacted. Chamberlain offered his too-gushing compliments to his combatants. "The Knicks," he said, "are probably the most intelligent team that has ever played the game. They have eight or nine men who can do it." Frazier again set himself to best West. And, most important of all, Reed readied himself to perform heroically. His injuries had not healed well during the season and he had played erratically in but sixty-nine games, during which he shared the court with Jerry Lucas. Now, in his last great performance, he employed his art and strength against Chamberlain and led the Knicks to a five-game triumph over the Lakers and their second national championship.

"We were a more mature team," Bradley said, comparing the '72–'73 squad to its predecessor. "We were more in command of our skills." In *Life on the Run* he says that the high of winning the first championship was unequaled. "Well, it was, in my view, certainly the high point of my athletic career —high point in the sense that it was a coming together and an achievement of what I had believed about the game and about my play, and it was a fulfillment of all the work and talk that I had put into the game for as long as I can remember. Winning the championship is the one moment—for however long it lasts, twenty-four hours, forty-eight, maybe a couple of weeks—when you are clearly the best in the world and there is no dispute. That's what I meant by saying it was an unequaled high There was nothing else that could compare to it."

The second lacked this sense of confirmation—a confirmation that climaxed his rookie struggle for respect—and was both less challenging and more pleasurable to Bradley. "The second championship was again a confirmation, but I had been there before—you had been to the mountaintop before—and this was the second time there. In many ways it had a texture that was different and was more pleasant because there wasn't the same kind of anxiety and tension that was involved in the first championship. The year before we had been in the finals but lost, and before that we had lost in the finals of the East, so by '72–'73 I was at a level of professionalism where you tried to get to the championship and you did everything you could to get there and you knew that you wanted to be there, and *that* was the motivation: It wasn't that you wanted to experience what it felt like because you already had—you wanted to re-experience it."

But the victory was a swan song. The following season the team lost three of its most important players and started to decline. Voted MVP for the '72–'73 championship—his presence was decisive, though many believed Frazier deserved the award for his season-long excellence—Reed suffered another injury and sat out most of the year, wondering, along with his fans, whether his knee would require yet another operation. Lucas and DeBusschere announced plans to retire at the end of the season. Lucas played lackadaisically. One of his favorite shots was a push from some distance out, a long shot that was commonly called "the bomb," and that season I recall Marv Albert endlessly repeating a disappointing *haiku* during games:

> *Lucas—*
> *the bomb—*
> *no good.*

His departure from the team occasioned no fanfare, though he had contributed significantly to its success. DeBusschere was another matter. He had accepted an offer to be general manager of the New York Nets, the local ABA competitors of the Knicks, and was honored with nights celebrating him throughout the league and in New York. "De-fense! De-fense! De-fense!" the crowd cried at the Garden as De-Busschere started to speak. Describing the scene in his book, Bradley writes, "My eyes water. Why am I crying? I wonder. It's his night. But it's not, really. It's our night: it's the fans' night. It's all of our nights, under the spoked-wheel roof of Madison Square Garden, an era is ending." Shortly after, the play-offs began. In a seven-game duel, the Knicks beat the Bullets one more time, then were demolished by the Boston Celtics in five barely competitive games. When the season ended, the members of the team split up the bonus they had received for the play-offs and voted Reed but a half share, the niggardly decision suggesting the good feelings on the squad were disappearing with its good record. They lost another quality player to yet another new franchise—the New Orleans Jazz, which later moved to Salt Lake City, where it is called the (oxymoronic) Utah Jazz. Then, during the summer,

Reed's fate was decided: The doctors told him he had to undergo another operation if he wanted to continue playing basketball anymore and he elected instead to retire. The Knicks, as a contending team, were finished.

Bradley writes about this last season of the team's glory in *Life on the Run*. Among basketball literature, the book is unique. Actually written by its author, not an edited version of tape recordings, its subject is neither a championship season nor the life of a superstar. Instead, the book chronicles several weeks of what turned out to be a disappointing season, presenting a frieze of characters and scenes depicting the lives of professional basketball players. "Talk about the same food, the same hotels, the same stewardesses, and how you lose track of the days," Bradley advised Phil Berger when Berger was traveling with the '69 team. Seven years later, Bradley spoke for himself.

The bus enters the Lincoln Tunnel and the lights come through the bus window and strike my black leather bag. The brightness of one light quickly fades as we move through the tunnel. Just as the bag is about to become dark, we pass another light and brightness returns. The variations make the bag look like a neon light blinking outside a cheap hotel.

"Only eighteen more," says DeBusschere.

"Not so soon," I say. "Too early to start counting."

On and off, shining and dull, light and dark; off to another city. Travelers in the dead of night.

He portrays the characters of the team with the same deft touch: Barnett, trying to lose weight by playing (and beating) rookies while his old teammates comment on the roll of fat around his waist; Jackson matching wits in poker with Barnett while talking to Bradley about socialism; Frazier, remote and private; Willis, sleeping all the time, even as the plane lands, his unshakable slumber a testament to his years on the road and his depression at facing the end to his career.

Bradley strives to present himself with a similar honesty. "Fame," he quips testily at one point, ". . . is having strangers constantly test and probe you for the dimensions of your 'real' personality." But he appears determined to exhibit all aspects of his nature as if anxious to prove that though "programmed [by his parents] to become a successful gentleman" he is a diverse and contradictory, fallible and human character. He is prone to melancholy—he writes that there is an "overpowering feeling of loneliness on the road"; *moyen sensual*—he includes a tryst with an anonymous lady in a hotel room; obsessive about details—the locker stalls in the Garden, he informs the readers, are "about three feet wide"; and occasionally prickly—"I am bad copy," he boasts when talking about the press. And he is curiously and happily unequivocal about basketball's value to him. Other stars who have written career autobiographies are always grateful to basketball; but at the same time they indicate a self-destructive quality in their relationship to the game. Bob Cousy, the great Celtic player, relates that after his retirement he would hurt himself while sleepwalking and finally had to be tied to his bed at night. Bill Russell starts his famous autobiography (the first one; not the recent *Second Wind*) with a meditation on death and later states that he endured a spirit-crushing depression during his penultimate years as a player. These demons never seem to have hounded Bradley. Perhaps because he knew that the end of basketball presaged the start of a new career, he is undivided in his satisfaction. The play, the crowds, the life with the team—all fulfill and please him.

Or at least they did when he was taking the notes for the book. By the time the book was published in the winter of '76, he was preparing to leave the team. That season the team won just thirty-eight games and Bradley had his worst year since his freshman debut. He escaped blame for this failure. The columnists said Bradley's poor performance demonstrated what was wrong with the team, rather than contributing to it. The argument had some merit. Fresh to Bradley's ways and less talented than their predecessors, the new members of the team didn't help him realize his ideas—taking the pass, making the cut to the basket, or setting the pick—but waylaid them, frustrating him and making him look bad. Larry Fleisher says the only reason that Bradley didn't complain about the unrewarding situation was that he planned to retire and didn't want to leave on a sour note. "It's a terribly difficult thing for a gifted athlete to play with a bad team," Fleisher told me. "The difference between playing on a losing team or a winning one for a guy who's intelligent is dramatic—it's a different world. Bradley was at the end of his career so he didn't want to look bad personally. But it wasn't pleasant and if he had had four or five more years to play I doubt that he would have stayed in basketball."

But Bradley was also aging. He looked ragged and puffy on the court, an often out-of-breath middle-aged man, and he appeared in only 67 games the whole year, playing just a little more than 1,000 minutes, taking less than 300 shots, averaging just 4.3 points a game. The team didn't qualify for the playoffs and performed its last game in the Garden under nets and trapezes; the circus would fill the arena once the Knicks left. The crowd was spiritless and only a few signs hung from the balconies saluting Bradley. When he entered the game and took a shot, distant voices echoed through the huge, half-filled place, "Dollar Bill!" An audible, regretful sigh accompanied the rebound. Toward the end of the game, the referee presented him with the game ball and Bradley acknowledged the then cheering crowd. The next night, the team played its final game, in Detroit, and he ended his career properly: He had debuted against the Pistons ten years before, hitting his first shot, and 972 games later, he bowed out against them, scoring on his last one.

By then, he had decided to enter politics. He described the choice, like his earlier decision to continue playing ball, as a result of "broadening self-awareness, self-knowledge. I decided politics was the most fulfilling thing, the thing that engaged me on more levels. I really found that in the latter two years of my career I spent time on the road differently from before. I used to spend time on the road experiencing the town, learning how to deal with people and circumstances, and kind of saying, Isn't humanity incredibly various and interesting, and taking furious notes, and so on. But now I found myself on the telephone talking to politicians back in New Jersey, or I found myself talking about various campaigns in the cities where I was, and my interest was growing in that area of public service. At the same time, I found myself reading less novels and spending more time reading reports on energy or welfare reform—not that I didn't read them before or that I never read novels afterward, but there was a shift. At the same time, the experience with the team was deteriorating somewhat because the commonly accepted bonds of caring and team effort were lessening. There were a lot of changes in personnel and I clearly saw what had to happen if we were going to make that team into a team. I would have to go through the same kind of process of relating to individuals that I did in '68, and that was almost eight years earlier, and it might take three years—by that time, I would be thirty-five. So all you could do was say, Look, I don't think we should do this play that way and if someone did do it that way they did it. So all that made my experience of professional life less enjoyable, and, at the same time, the other was becoming more enjoyable."

The following spring he entered the senatorial primary in New Jersey. He ran as a liberal Democrat whose political consciousness was shaped by the major events of the past decade and a half. "My politician benchmarks begin, I suppose, with the civil rights movement in the early '60s, when I was in college. They were of course upgraded by Jack Kennedy's assassination. That was followed by a summer internship in Washington in 1964, the summer of the Gulf of Tonkin resolution, and being present in the chamber when the 1964 Civil Rights Act was passed and leaving the Senate that day realizing that something of monumental importance had been achieved and that things can actually happen in that body that can change the course of events in our country and the lives of its people. And then, after that, it was probably Robert Kennedy's assassination and Martin Luther King's, and the war, and the belief that if the best don't go into politics then policy will reflect that and that politics required the best of people and they must give it. So a political interest and direction was framed in part by 1970, and then it took a new direction once you began thinking about problems, particularly energy, after the embargo of '73–'74, when it became clear that we are incredibly vulnerable to an oil supply cutoff and what do we have to do? And from that the whole direction to solar energy, the need to shift, the need for conservation, the need for reasonable environmental standards, the need to think through how our system works and how our interdependence with the rest of the world forces us to do certain things and allows us to do others."

He met instant success in both the primary and regular election. In the primary his opponent was a McGovern man who couldn't match Bradley's financial wealth or celebrity; his Republican competitor was a conservative, campaigning in support of the Kemp-Roth proposal for a 30 percent tax cut. An experienced political journalist who followed both campaigns said neither dramatized many issues, including Kemp-Roth, which few voters believed in. In his view, the campaign was planned and orderly—when some aides decided Bradley needed to liven up his basic speech they canvassed the reporters for good jokes—and predictable in outcome. Bradley was a superstar in the state, a legend not only from his Knick days but also as a Princeton man, and the voters idolized him; running against him, the journalist told me, was like trying to cut down Goliath.

Bradley doesn't like to think he has unduly benefited from his celebrity status. At first, he denied his basketball career significantly influenced his electoral success. "I don't think I was elected as a basketball player. People listened to me, and maybe more people listened to me, because I was a basketball player. But if I was saying things on inflation, energy, defense, environment that they thought were bad, they weren't going to agree and they wouldn't vote for me. So it's true that being a basketball player put three hundred people in a hall instead of fifty, and gave me a bigger opportunity, and I could either fall flat on my face or convince them. But I don't agree with the argument that I was elected because I was a basketball player. It was helpful. It gave me an initial advantage in name recognition."

Then he claimed that his past had helped people to decide in his favor, but only for admirably rational reasons. "They had a series of associations formed over a ten-year period while watching me in a very intimate way on television screens under all kinds of pressures and all kinds of circumstances, and they had formulated a conclusion about what kind of person I was by the way I conducted myself—not just the way I shot a jump shot from the top of the key. And so to that extent having played and having been subjected to that kind of scrutiny for ten years was helpful." When I asked him whether he would claim the same justification for an actor—was he an East Coast Ronald Reagan?—he continued the argument. "No. The difference between an actor and a basketball player is that an actor is acting. A basketball player is confronting real-life situations under enormous pressure where he's on the line and either he delivers or he doesn't deliver and he must react to that and you don't just make a performance. I mean, if there's anything about it, it's that there's a clear-cut resolution, either you win or you lose, either your man has scored or he hasn't scored—that is a real difference."

The argument finesses the facts of Bradley's record. He has picked the times and issues about which to speak out. His concern that people would overestimate his views because of his athletic prowess and glamorous appeal didn't stop him from touring and speaking for the Fellowship of Christian Athletes

—a kind of proselytizing, however benign. But he was much more cautious about expressing publicly his opposition to the Vietnam war and his concern over racial conflicts in the '60s. "At the time, I was twenty-five, something like that, and I expressed my opinion, but I wanted to express it in a way that would not be blown out of proportion by the people. I expressed it in ways that I felt were consistent with the way that I wanted to express it. So you make your statement and it's a statement you make. Just like during the championship. Everyone said then, after you win you'll do X, Y, and Z. No, you do what you feel you must when you win the championship and you're not going to do what other people say you must. When you are outraged with a circumstance in the world you do what you feel you must do, not what other people say you must do." But on examination this individualism amounted to precious little practical activity: a march against the war during the October Moratorium in Cincinnati, the incident DeBusschere mentions in his book, and then vagueness. "I participated frequently in discussions with friends and continued work in the race area—that was the summer I was in Washington at OEO—and also, the summer before that, I was working in the school in Harlem, and I think you find ways to express your own outrage and your own feelings that are consistent with your personality."

In the Senate, Bradley established himself as a respected, responsible politician. A rookie, he kept a low profile, deliberately trying to avoid press stories focusing on a basketball star's first year in Congress. When his colleague Harrison Williams was caught in the Abscam scandal, Bradley sidestepped any public mention of the issue. (Though unless Williams is found innocent, he will be ruined as a politician, leaving Bradley as *de facto* head of the New Jersey party.) He remained neutral during the Kennedy-Carter primary struggle, although both men had campaigned for him during his election. He became expert in the field of energy and while he kept away from the potentially disastrous issue of gambling in New Jersey, he worked hard on another local matter of national importance, the dumping of toxic chemicals, receiving credit for helping get passed a bill to create a national fund to pay for property damages incurred by these poisons. He impressed one senatorial aide I spoke to with his preparedness during committees; he asked good, common-sense, practical questions and also sophisticated ones and had the "ability to ask follow-up questions." The aide, who worked for Democratic Senator Gary Hart, recalled that Bradley had proposed the "concept of an energy doctor." Experts working for utility companies would advise homeowners, especially poor ones, on conserving heat, the utilities being compensated for any lost revenues by tax credits applied to new facilities. "The Senate embraced the concept," the aide told me, adding that "it was impressive for a freshman senator to come up with a new and innovative approach on a major subject area." In his view Bradley is an important member of a new group of younger politicians who, though the aide described them as eclectic and non-ideological, seem generally marked by liberal attitudes in domestic policy and hawkish ones in foreign affairs, in short, the new version of essentially John Kennedy Democrats. Shortly before fighting for the bill about toxic chemicals, Bradley wrote an article for the *New York Times* suggesting America intervene militarily in Afghanistan. The ADA gives Bradley a 68 percent rating for his performance in the 1979 Congress, thirteenth highest on their list, and after the Republican sweep in the Reagan election, his importance in national Democratic politics seems to be assured. In short, his political career has repeated his progress in basketball: a quiet start, then gaining more prominence after a veteran is knocked off, a rise into good repute for his thoroughness, a sure knowledge of several things, little risk-taking, and what seems to be a certain graduation into being a key member of the eventually winning team. It had been suggested, when he was only a Princeton undergraduate, that he would be President before reaching fifty; now, thirty-eight, he seems ready to start proving the prophecy true. "I don't know if he'll stay in politics," Fleisher told me. "I'm not certain I could see Bradley being a senator for twenty-four years. And what would be another aspect of politics? If he's not President what else would he be?"

Bradley's election ended his interest in the game. He sees only a few of the Knicks. "Earl [Monroe] and Willis and DeBusschere were very helpful in my campaign. They made appearances, they contributed money, they came to rallies. There was one rally in Newark with Mondale which Monroe came to. We had the governor, Senator Williams, myself, a congressman, and the Vice President, and Monroe got the biggest applause. So that helps keep things in perspective. I see Jackson [Phil] because we kind of kept up. He came down to the Senate when we were debating the windfall profit on the floor. I was going to give a speech on energy security, but then things happened and I didn't. So I keep up with them as much as I do with anybody under my present circumstances. But I haven't seen Lucas or Cazzie or Clyde or Stallworth."

He doesn't follow the game at all. "I haven't seen the game; I don't watch it; I have no interest in it. Since I've retired—which is two seasons, this is the beginning of the third—I've seen two games in person. After the campaign was over, I went to Philadelphia to see a game with Fitz Dixon [the owner of the Philadelphia 76ers] because he was a contributor, and I wanted to see San Antonio play the 76ers. And I went to the last play-off game between San Antonio and the Bullets in Washington. But those were the only two games I've seen. I think I haven't watched it, not because the game has changed, but simply because basketball is an experience I've lived through and concluded. In a way, the book was a means of saying good-bye. I had come to terms with the whole experience. It was put down; it was recorded; and now it was time to move on. I think it might be different if there were more players I knew still playing or if there was an unusual team. The Portland team in '77 [NBA champions led by

Bill Walton] captured my imagination. They were doing things right and were fun to watch because they executed such complex group interactions well, and that's what is fascinating to me. And I'll watch the final game. I remember the night after my primary, June 7. It was the final game of Seattle-Washington [the '78 contenders for the crown] and I went out to dinner with my wife, my campaign manager, and the guy who did my media. We had a big steak dinner—steak and lobsters, a celebration—and came back to the house to watch the game and almost all of us fell asleep. Partly because we were fatigued, but partly because it wasn't that interesting. But I will always watch the final game because of the personality interaction which I find the most interesting thing and which I think I have insight into and which I can read into just seeing it on TV. But I'm not a fan. I don't care who the leading scorer is. I'm not interested. I'm interested in those people who perform under pressure at a time when if you win you make it and if you lose you're on the side. Has the game changed? I don't know. I'd be repeating a lot of things I hear other people say."

Yet nothing has influenced him as decisively as the game. Basketball opened the world to him. Because of the sport he left the provincial, hermetic surroundings of his youth and came to New York; as a player he first earned the respect and friendship of men from backgrounds different from his, for the first time not being met with immediate reverence; he practiced his first lessons in politics representing the players during the long battle over the merger, lobbying against the proposed plan and testifying before Congress; and, most important of all, it was because of basketball that he came to share the lives of working and poor people, and especially black people. "Nothing," he writes in *Life on the Run*, "... had prepared me for the impact my [black] teammates have made on me." He goes on. "I have changed in some ways because of my black friends. It is hard to say exactly how but after witnessing their joys, fears, perceptions, and spontaneous reactions for seven years I am different. I regard authority a little more skeptically than I once did. I am more interested in experiencing life than in analyzing it. What happens to me today and tomorrow is more important now than it used to be when I worried about the next decade. And I feel less guilty about the black man's experience in America, realizing that though some of my friends have come from a poorer background, it did not lack in the richness of family love and joy." Similarly, his friendship with DeBusschere opened to him a new world of loyalties, attitudes, and experiences among white working-class people. Bradley often appears to romanticize both. The fact that blacks raise loving families testifies to their moral and emotional strength and not the social conditions that surround them; there is something in Bradley's comment of the social voyeur, the young man who taught in the street academy to learn how to talk to his teammates, practicing a sort of emotional and social slumming. But Bradley's pleasure and fascination with those who haven't shared his privileges are genuine, undiluted.

"The people," he answered immediately when I asked what had most attracted him to political service. "Coming into contact with people who had problems, who wanted to talk to somebody, who don't have anybody to talk to, who could be helped by imaginative government action. It was the people. I mean, I liked the public policy, I liked trying to draw up the perfect residential energy efficiency plan, which is what I'm doing—okay, I liked that. But I also liked the late-night phone calls, the fakes, the dead-end streets, the performance aspects, all of those things I've just enumerated being different things, not all one thing. So I liked all that. And I liked trying to communicate because in many ways a politician is a communicator and communicates in a lot of different ways."

Indeed, it is his relationship to "the people" that inspires his political work. During our talk, I mentioned my impression from his book that he had a strong emotional and moral commitment to blacks. The last scene describes his visit with Willis Reed and Phil Jackson to a Sioux Indian reservation in South Dakota. "... cars lie abandoned and rusting in the fields," he notes in a powerful image, "as if the Indians drove them to death taking out their fury on the white men's machines." The three players run a clinic for the Sioux children and the book ends with Willis Reed offering an enraptured audience his view of life. There isn't much these days that hasn't been done, Willis tells them, but one of you has a chance for a real first: to be the first Indian to play in the NBA.

My comment pleased Bradley. "I'm glad you got that," he said. "A lot of people read the book and not all of them see that. There is a part of me, I think, that believes that if I had never played basketball I never would have been a politician." Never a politician, or merely a different sort of one? "Maybe never," he answered after a pause, "because the decision was based upon what you enjoyed and what you liked. One of the things I think I talked about in my book is that you learn there is an awful lot to learn from different kinds of people, and you come to appreciate and love all of those aspects of personality and of different kinds of people. That's true of blacks, whites, Indians, whomever, and it's not just racial, it's true of class and ethnic origins. You know, a lot of times I go through events as a U.S. senator in New Jersey that are not dissimilar from events that I went through as a basketball player on the road, where you find yourself in situations, whether it be a—I don't want to name one because it would be exclusive of others—but where you say, I've been here before, I've been here with DeBusschere on the road in Detroit, or I've been here with Willis. Take a bar in Detroit in a working-class neighborhood that DeBusschere's family ran, and compare it to bars in Elizabeth, New Jersey, that you go into to campaign and where you want to communicate with the people in it. The situations aren't unfamiliar. And I've spent ten years doing it, I've spent ten years loving these people. And that's why the campaign aspect, going out to meet the people, for me, is a rejuvenation. A lot of politicians when they go out to meet people—well, this is what you've got to do to get elected. With me, there's a real enjoyment of people in these places, and I think in part that enjoyment comes from my experience in sports."

# 7

Holzman supervised the changes in the team. After Donovan left, Holzman added the duties of general manager to his coaching responsibilities, negotiating the trades that kept the team a contender while continuing to lead his daily life by the squad's schedule of practice, game, travel. At the end of the '76–'77 season, after the team had finished under .500 for three consecutive years, he was retired and named a consultant, a meaningless, but salaried, front-office title. He still attended games regularly, but sat with the crowd, behind the bench, graciously accepting the compliments of well-wishing contemporaries and giving his autograph to kids. Then, after little more than a year of this exile, the management sacked the team's new coach, and needed someone who could take command quickly and expertly. Holzman had first assumed leadership of the Knicks under similar circumstances a decade earlier; now he got the nod again. Originally merely a stopgap appointee, he had become as associated with the team and its glory as its superstars: DeBusschere, Frazier, Reed.

Holzman is an old-time, professional basketball coach. However proud of his accomplishments, he conducts himself with extreme public diffidence. He dresses in conservative Ivy League clothes, never criticizes his players or management in the press, and doesn't talk about his personal problems. He offers no panaceas or new strategies to the game, claiming that nothing needs to be invented in basketball, execution is all, and insists that coaches are only as good as their players and not the other way around. Loyal to his team, he has never joined in the musical chairs that usually ends each season, the coaches circling the teams before dashing to each other's previous positions. He loses without complaints—unless he lodges them against his own performance—and wins without crowing. And he does win. Among all NBA coaches, he trails only— have you guessed by now?—Red Auerbach in total number of career victories.

Like his partner Donovan, Holzman is essentially a simple man. But he doesn't share Donovan's piety. He is a representative New Yorker. His journey from a Lower East Side childhood through City College to Long Island, his home for the last twenty-five years, summarizes the progress of a generation of Jewish Americans, and he has an edge of sophistication and irony unknown to his colleague. "He's a gentle type of guy," he said to me in his gravelly tenor about Walt Frazier, one of his favorite players. "But he can be vain about his body and himself. That's why he works so hard to keep it looking like it does. To do that to your body, I think you need a certain amount of vanity. Anybody that goes out and kills himself dieting and running—you've got to have some vanity to do that." His explanation for maintaining a personal distance between himself and his players demonstrated a similar probity. "I really didn't have any relationships with any of the '69 players," he told me. "For one thing there was a big difference in our ages. But, generally, I never socialize with players. Besides the age thing, I just don't think it's good. I respect their right to not want to be around me. When you coach, no matter what you see a guy do, if they're winning it's going to be cute, and if you're losing it's going to be terrible. You see a guy combing his hair and he's using a brush instead of a comb. If you're winning, you'll say, Let me see you use that brush! And if you're losing, you'll say, What the hell are you doing with that brush? That type of thing. And in this business you're together so much that if you get some time alone it's good. That's not to say that you don't occasionally go to a guy and say, Hey, you're doing all right! Or to some other guy, Hey! You're not doing it! And there are always players you like more as people. But you still have to treat all players basically the same. I may have liked one player more than another, but I can't show that because you want to be fair. I think that's one thing players appreciate more than anything —fairness. If there's anything they appreciate it's that." When I finished our talk and thanked him, he demurred, commenting, with typical modesty, that he didn't know whether his comments were helpful. At least I believed them, I joked. Well, that's what makes your job so tough, he answered, squinting at me while he leaned forward in his chair, his lit cigar cupped in his hand: You've got to know what to believe. Often the oldest man on court during games, he never appears ill at ease among the young black and white athletes he instructs during time-outs; instead, at these moments, his slight but surprisingly authoritative presence presents the pleasing anomaly of a street-smart sixty-year-old who knows the nuances of the playground game and dresses with impeccable taste.

Holzman's importance to the championship team has been debated. During the team's heyday, opinion split into two camps. The first was manned by the daily sportswriters. They drank and joshed with Holzman and lionized him. Because they were his peers, perhaps they imagined that his success reflected some glory back on to them: They were fans, after all, and self-aggrandizement is a fundamental part of rooting for a team. Ambiguously called "the pack," they presented Holzman in their stories as a cagey, wily fellow, in the jargon of the sitcom story editor of the movie *Network*, a crusty but benign coach who could figure out how to win any game. Their opponents were free-lancers. They were wary of Holzman. He disappointed them. Pressing him with questions, they received seemingly disingenuous answers. Through them players voiced their complaints: Holzman enjoyed power, didn't coach offense, played favorites, acted officiously. The criticism upset Holzman, who believes that team relationships should be kept private. In 1975, Phil Jackson wrote an autobiography that criticized members of the team. "We [Holzman and Jackson] got into a situation over my book that was difficult," Jackson told me. "He thought that what I had in my book was bad for the team and I had to agree with him—if I was the coach I'd hate to see a ballplayer put out a book like that too. He said, What you wrote should line garbage cans. That's where that kind of stuff belongs. It's not good for the team. I said, You may be right. I didn't argue with him."

In time, a balance was struck between these two views. Some players, front-office people, and writers remain cool to Holzman; Donnie May, who has some reason for bitterness, twitted him for vanity, claiming that Holzman always wanted to be a movie star. But people generally agree he is a superior coach. Bradley's judgment in *Life on the Run* is representative. He calls Holzman a "genius" in handling players, praises his delicate but straightforward relations with black players, his clever dealings with the press, and his insistence on coaching defense, concluding—and Bradley clashed with Holzman —that Holzman's role "in the development of unselfish team play was crucial."

Still, even this appraisal is incomplete. Of all the members of the team or men who worked with it, Holzman had the most experience in professional basketball: When Eddie Donovan debuted as a professional coach, in 1961, Holzman had already been a player, coach, and scout in the NBA for the past twelve years. He was a realist about the game and business. His past and attitude might have been romanticized by the press, but there was nothing precious in his relationship to the team. Each member of the Knicks brought some trait to the team—Frazier's frisky genius, DeBusschere's doggedness,

Bradley's intelligence, Reed's strength and will. But as a collective unit they were marked by their professional coolness, their ability to get the job done—the way, as Eddie Donovan said, "they didn't jerk you around—they just beat you nice and easy with basketball"—and also the pleasing modesty they displayed about their accomplishment. They exhibited a tough, economical, and measured intelligence, and only Holzman could claim this prime collective trait as his distinctive, individual personality.

I spoke to Holzman one day while he was at work, during the first week of the 1979 Knick training camp. He was just starting to form the team. Twenty young men were playing in the gym; five of them had contracts with the team, and of these only three had assured salaries and jobs for the season. The rest competed for probably only one open slot; their success or failure would be the resolution to years of childhood and adolescent work and hope. Dressed casually for the practice in shorts, a long T-shirt, crepe-soled shoes, and with a whistle dangling around his neck, Holzman stood on the sidelines opposite the players' bench. He commented only rarely as the players scrimmaged: "Slow it up, bring it back out—bring it out, damnit!" Other than these commands, he said nothing to the players and ended the practice telling them when the bus from the motel where the athletes were staying would leave for the next practice: Punctuality matters to Holzman and throughout the practice he kept nervously checking his pocket watch. Some reporters following them, the players trudged off the floor to the showers: Except when their team is winning, practices always exhaust and defeat players. Some hopeful rookies tried for extra credit and stayed on court, waiting to be the last to leave just as Bradley and Russell had done years before. One shot fouls; another fell purposefully to the floor and started performing energetic push-ups. A third commented scornfully to me: "Coach don't care about push-ups, man. It's wind that he looks for. I never lean over to catch my breath because then he knows you're not in shape. I just lean up against a wall. I think I've got a good shot at making the team." Holzman ignored all this; in the middle of the court, he and Donovan conferred, trading notes on the practice and arriving at the decisions that would shape the team.

Later, freshly showered and sportily dressed in designer jeans, moccasins, and a tattersall shirt, Holzman conducted interviews with reporters at the motel that served as team headquarters during camp. The room was furnished in inhospitable nondescript. Holzman sat at a table piled with several stacks of the team's 1979 *Rookie Guide* and adorned with a basket of fruit. Courtesy of the management, the fruit was covered with green Saran Wrap, its lifeless arrangement managing the impossible and making the natural items seem plastic replicas. Quarters like these are home to Holzman for two thirds of the year and he was welcoming and casual, immediately offering us all fruit while unwrapping a plastic-tipped cigar and turning on the air conditioner (a fetish, evidently; Frankie Blauschild, the team's press secretary, and an old buddy of Holzman's, told me that when he chauffeurs the coach he cools the car several minutes before Holzman arrives). Peering at the physical specifications listed for the individual players in the *Guide*, Holzman answered the questions of two reporters from some local New Jersey papers, his truncated snatches of observation indicating the probable futures of the players—he's a big guy, he likes to mix it up underneath, he didn't show us much that was new, he seemed slow. Never refusing to comment on a player, he also never dismissed any.

His gaze constantly returned to the rookie guide. After games in the Garden, Holzman meets the press in a cubicle next to the players' locker room. There he sits behind a small, plain wooden desk, stat sheet in one hand, cigar in the other. While he patiently answers each reporter (often repeating himself) he studies the sheet, his attention focused on the statistics that profile the performance of the players and team. He performs the inspection using the same concentrated diligence that an athlete employs when practicing a motion to perfect a shot; like players, he believes a material reason always accounts for a victory or defeat. Now he looked up, a detective having found the tell-tale clue that would crack the case. "No centers," he muttered about the present batch of rookies, "that's the trouble we got here."

Two veteran reporters, a generation apart, entered. Holzman greeted them warmly; during the season, they are his buddies on the road trips and at the Garden. "Hey Red," the younger one joked to Holzman about his older peer, "he's got your year's roster set already." The older man took umbrage. "Come on, Red, you know these guys can't make it." But Holzman wouldn't be persuaded. "Well that's the way you see it. I can't see things that way. I've got to give each one of them an even shot and judge what they can do." The older man sighed at this piety and his young partner argued with him: "Come on, you know they cut guys with guaranteed contracts." He mentioned the name of a once-prominent player released by the team even though still on contract. The proof disgruntled the older man even more. "All right," he surrendered and referred to one of the promising rookies on the team. "Speak to me about Demic." Holzman laughed. "You're not even asking questions anymore?" The younger one broke in: "You want a tip on the tenth race?" The older reporter was insistent. "I know you too well to ask questions. How's Demic? Tell me about Demic." The younger man interrupted again. "The real question is what are you going to do for leadership on this team?" Holzman puffed on his cigar, intrigued by the difficulty. He suggested one young player for the position, but the younger reporter argued with him—the player was a kid who played the radio in the locker room all the time. Holzman listened to this without judgment. "You don't know," he finally suggested. "He may change. He's gone through a shaky last couple of years." The kibbitzing of the reporters was work to him. Of the trio, he was the only one to view the coming season with enthusiasm and curiosity.

The reporters left and we began to talk. In the sports world, Holzman is known as a difficult interview. He will spend time with reporters, but his rules of professional conduct limit his comments and he doesn't speculate about players or games: For him reasons in basketball are clear-cut and final. Besides these inhibitions, he only wants to discuss basketball and ignores attempts to make him talk about anything else. Phil Berger recounted his troubles with Holzman in 1969. "My sense of Holzman was that he wasn't extremely interested or concerned with the world outside. There was a period when he soured toward me. I think he thought I was digging too much. I remember I was in the locker room and something was going on and I went to take notes in the hallway because I didn't want to make the players self-conscious and he made fun of me: Oh, there you are with your notebook, that sort of thing. Then I had an airplane interview with him which was a total washout. I remember asking very simple biographical questions and he wouldn't answer anything. He told me he was in the Navy. I asked what ship. He said, What do you need to know that for? Then I asked about college. Who was the coach? What did you study? That sort of thing. He didn't want to reveal anything about himself, but he was also suspicious of me. What do you need to know that crap for? I remember him saying that in his grating voice— What do you need to know that crap for? What does that matter? I could see he had no perception of what a guy like me should be doing. I was perplexed and finally I thought, This man doesn't like me."

Time, winning, and custom must have either changed this temper or Berger misread it. During interviews, Holzman will challenge you to discover his secrets, his frequently short responses seeming only to suggest what he thinks. Sometimes he seems to skirt the truth, his self-effacement often smacking of false modesty. Generally, however, his manner belies his convictions. He really doesn't think his personal life affects his behavior on court—an unexpressed criticism of managers and coaches, à la Billy Martin, who use their personality to promote themselves into celebrity—and responds simply and directly to the complexities of his office.

I was impressed by this the first time I met him. During Holzman's last year as coach, the Knicks bought Bob McAdoo and Tom McMillen, two players from Buffalo, whose talents, it was hoped, would make the team respectable. The team held a press conference to introduce the players to the local press. The conference was a silly affair: The news ended once the players said hello. Manfully trying to earn their salaries, the reporters asked absurd questions. The trade resulted in a new multimillion-dollar contract for McAdoo, yet one writer, pressed to find some angle for his story, asked the player if his transfer to New York had soured him on basketball. McAdoo is a tall, sleepy-looking fellow who passes through all public functions wearing a mask of indifference. Still, the reporter's question shook even him. "No," he replied, looking incredulously at his interrogator, "why should it?"

Holzman was a lame duck at the time; he hadn't announced his retirement, but a story with the imprimatur of the team's corporate owners had appeared in the *Times* claiming that management wanted to hire a new coach. Still, he performed his duty graciously, sitting on a couch in the press lounge talking to reporters. What he was doing when he heard the news? "I was just leaving the office and in a restaurant about to eat with my wife," he answered good-humoredly. And she told you? "No, I got a telephone call." Then: "You want to know what I was eating? Scungilli. A cold scungilli salad. You know what that is? Conch. The inside of a conch. They take the meat out"—he pretended to cut and scoop the muscle from the shell with his hand—"and you can have it hot or they cut it up, mix in the garlic, onions, parsley, and it's wonderful. I still smell of garlic." The arrival of the two new players had forced another Knick off the roster. How had the expendable squad member taken the news? "I told him myself. I called him up this morning. I think we have the responsibility to do it, but I hate it. Especially this time because I used to fool around with the kid a lot and he was a good kid. I think he'll be picked up by some other team. He didn't like hearing it. People ask how did he take it? How the hell do they expect a guy to take it?" Did he expect a sudden progress in the team? "We'll start these guys playing and see where we go. What are we now? Twenty-four games into the season? A third of the way done?" Had he anticipated the team to play better? "I don't know. We had a shithouse of injuries and that may be some of it. It's hard to know how these things affect guys. And all the talk about the trade [for McAdoo] might have had some effect—at least on a subconscious level. You can't tell. Like that thing that was printed about me in the papers. You can't worry about it. You just got to keep going and not let it worry you."

He offered the same undeviating simplicity in his hotel room three years later. "The big thing about coaching," he explained, "is figuring out how much time a guy gets." Holzman had made himself comfortable now; he sat in his own room, his stockinged feet propped on the bed, smoking a cigar whose tip he neatly brushed against the edge of the ashtray, trimming the ash. "Of course during a game you've got to adjust. A guy gets injured, another fouls a lot. But all you really want to do is establish a regular order of playing time and duties. When things are going well and you have people doing the things you like to have them doing, and the right people are thinking properly, the guys know when they're going in and coming out and what plays they're going to be playing. I don't coach these guys any different than I did the guys in '69. The difference is that the guys in '69 would make the plays regularly, every night. But with a bad team or not such good players" —he never treats talent lightly, a residual respect perhaps from his own playing days—"the pattern breaks down. And then you've got the clock. It's always going. I mean, we always tell the guys to shoot, shoot. Because you'll always be better off taking the shot. Who knows? Maybe you'll get

lucky and make it. So the play doesn't work and the guy's
under pressure and the clock's going and the whole thing falls
apart. But with the '69 team, Reed knew he'd get forty minutes, and Frazier a little more, and then I'd bring in Riordan
or Stallworth. See? A regular pattern developed."

He unstintingly commended the players for this mastery.
"You know what's a great feeling when you're coaching?" he
asked rhetorically while remembering DeBusschere's first days
on the team. "You get some guy who's been around a few
years, maybe not a big star. But when he comes, you tell him,
Look, we're going to try this, and bang! right away he's doing
it, or even before you say it, he's saying, Should we do this?
or, Are we going to try this now? Like that, you know? And
the guy just makes you confident, gives you the confidence.
See, really, when these guys came, like DeBusschere, well, we
all knew he was a hell of a great ballplayer, but we didn't
know he was as good as he was in those other departments—
we just never thought he could do all these things as well as he
could." He refused to take credit even for Frazier, although he
is generally held accountable for Frazier's development as a
player. "When Frazier started, I guess I was sort of a teacher
to him," he said. "But after a while he just came along so fast
that he was ahead of me. He was such a smart basketball
player! He always knew everything that was going on. He
had no trouble picking anything up."

The intelligence and expertness of the players made the
team the easiest, and also the best, he had ever coached. "They
played the game the right way," he said, repeating an old
maxim of the basketball world. He squinted and leaned forward, the gesture toward intimacy he takes when he wishes to
impress a truth on his audience. Holzman's noticeable calm-
ness on court is not coolness toward the game. Indeed, at least
in interviews, the game remains the only subject that will ex-
cite him, and the classic judgments about the championship
team still seemed fresh to him. "What was good about them
was that they won with all the old-fashioned virtues—unsel-

fish, good team basketball. They helped each other, they had
the smarts, they did all the sacrificing things, which was good
for them because some of them were older and couldn't be
running around all the time, so our style of play made them
shine—but still, they achieved it that way. They weren't that
flashy. Some individuals were—Barnett, Frazier—but we
really worked just on getting the thing done. We had no guys
who were in the top ten players. We had great players, but
the balance was there. Maybe you score tonight, and we work
toward my end of the game the next night because that's what
the other team lets us do. We didn't force it to you because
you were our top scorer; we worked it to you if things were
going to you or to me or to the next guy." The team's final
triumph simply confirmed the excellence they had practiced
throughout the whole season. "Toward the end of the year I
worried. They lost four straight and I worried that I had let
them get too loose. But, really, our winning didn't surprise
me. You see what a team can do during a year and that's all
there is—you try to achieve it, to achieve it, to achieve it, and
we did."

Besides personal satisfaction, the championship rewarded
Holzman with long-term financial security. From his first
days in pro ball, Holzman has viewed professionalism as a simple equation: You get well paid to perform your best. "When
I started playing professional ball I was one of the good players in the National League. I was a good defensive player, and
a good team offensive player—things like that, just fundamental team things. I wasn't a flashy player or a superstar and I
never thought I would be: I always just wanted to be appreciated and get more money. If I was appreciated and got more
money for doing what I was good at then that was fine—that
was good." He has the same attitude toward his record as
coach. "Winning the championship didn't have any great effect
on my private life, it just made everything great—everything wonderful, better," he said as though this were a self-ev-
ident truth. "I earned more money—that was important. My

contracts were better—that was good. As a young man, I never expected to be as comfortably off as I am today. Never. I never looked to make a lot of money. I was always looking for security, I lived from each week to week. I was always one of those guys who if someone comes over and says, I'll give you ten thousand for life, you grab it, you don't look for any reason not to. I was always one of those guys. And when I was secure it was nice—it was very nice."

Afterward, the only change in his life was that he didn't keep winning. In Holzman's first six years as coach, the Knicks won 347 games, lost 189; in the next three seasons, they failed to reach the .500 mark. "The big change in my basketball life is that we haven't had every year as good as we would have liked—that's been the change. For a couple of years things were going very nicely for the team. But for the last few years, it hasn't been going that great—so in that way there's been a real change." Curiously, during this final period, when he could be fairly blamed for the team's poor showing, Holzman was hailed as a genius, his standing rising as his team's sank lower. These applauses were like cheering a fireman who extinguishes a conflagration he has started. The general manager of the team, Holzman had picked the players who performed so disappointingly.

Holzman dismisses the extravagant praise he received. "It's bullshit that I'm a genius," he told me. "What kind of genius? I don't even try to appear like a genius. I try to appear humble." But he defends his record as a general manager. He claimed the trades for Lucas and Monroe had helped to result in the '72–'73 championship—a point well taken—and wouldn't criticize the players on the losing teams. "He had a flashy reputation," he said about Frazier, the veteran on the team who carried its offense and was frequently faulted for shooting too much and slowing the team down during its losing seasons, "but I think he was a solid ballplayer. It was what he did off the court that gave him that reputation—the clothes, fur coats, and things. There were two ways to feel about his play later on. You could feel disappointed sometimes. But then you had to realize he was not in the precision type of thing with guys he had been used to playing with, and that made it difficult. He sort of got into more of a one-on-one type of thing because the plays broke down: The guys he was playing with just couldn't execute them right all the time. It really wasn't his fault to a degree because he wasn't the leader type." Another player he remains loyal to is John Gianelli, the thin, tall player from the University of the Pacific who took Reed's place at center and met the ire of the fans. "In my book, John is a good player," he told me. "I like him. He can always play for me. The first day John came in we had a workout and he blocked every shot, he did everything. Boy, were we excited! We thought, This guy is the next Bill Russell! He just got too much heat here. It affected his game. He has his deficiencies, but overall he's a player, on certain teams he could even be a starter. But not everybody's going to be a starter and you know, really, that's overdone. The starting team is really not as important as the finishing team. But they always say, Are you a starter?"

The acquisition of McAdoo was intended to reverse the team's decline, and the Knicks won the first games he played with them by exhilaratingly promising wide margins. It seemed Holzman might end his career on a winning note. Then the team began to lose. Before, their defeats had been lamentable but understandable: They were simply overmatched too much of the time. Now the losses were unpleasant and hard to watch because the Knicks enjoyed so much talent. The collection of players simply didn't jell and they stumbled to defeats in a frustrating, maddening way, blowing large leads in the final quarter, missing the foul shots that would ice the game. Stalling on offense, fumbling on defense, the team played itself out of a winning record and the new coach was announced.

Shortly after, Holzman appeared in what would be then his last game at the Garden. He and Bradley had joined the team in the same year and were also leaving together. From the balcony hung one sign:

HundREDS of wins!
Thousands of points!
Thanks a million!

Still, no ceremony marked his departure. By the fourth quarter the Knicks were losing again and he had stopped coaching. With several minutes left, he took some gum out of his mouth, stuck it under a chair, and motioned for Bradley to leave the game, giving the crowd a chance to show their appreciation. After the refs presented Bradley with the ball, they handed one to Holzman. "This had better be the last one to give out," joked the ref, "because I don't have any more." Holzman joked back, "If you give me another T [technical foul] I'll throw this at you." The press secretary for the team, who sits next to Holzman during games, joined the repartee: "I get the next one." Minutes later, the Knicks lost and Holzman walked off the court, ready to hold his usual question-and-answer period.

During those last months of his career, I wondered about Holzman as I watched him coach games. For the undemonstrative Holzman games are largely forty-eight minutes of adjusting his posture. The game begins and he sits upright, one hand folded over the other, a skeptical uncle. As the action progresses, he leans forward, his arms resting on his knees, his chin resting on his palm. Then, excited, he squats before the chair, yelling out much the same instructions shouted down by the coaches in the balconies: "Hold for one! Get up on him! Press!" When he calls a time-out he immediately rises from his seat, standing as the players take theirs, a gentleman waiting for the lady to sit before he begins his pitch. He kneels and speaks earnestly as the players look alternately interested or with a glazed exhaustion or boredom. As he sends them back onto the court, he presses his lips together and checks the clock overhead, pondering possibilities with an aggrieved,

worried expression, and before the ball is put into play, begins
to shout his ancient instructions to his performers—urging, directing, and correcting them. The entire performance is predictable and, as I observed him go through it during these final
contests, I tried to imagine his inner life. I wondered whether
he was anguished or relieved to give up the game, imagined his
anger at Frazier, his protégé after all, who had performed so
poorly over the last season, pictured his frustration at the
players for not understanding and being able to execute his
commands. In short, I imagined him engaged in a rich inner
monologue.

But actually, the season didn't trouble him at all. He measured his failure the same way as his triumph: in largely financial terms. "My last year with the team wasn't difficult for me
because my situation was fairly well set. I had another year to
go in my contract and I wasn't planning on coaching beyond
that anyway. And I was set up because I had a five-year contract as a consultant. So it wasn't like the ownership was coming over to me and firing me and I had to worry about where
my next job was. It wasn't that situation. I was content. I was
professional enough that when the thing started that I wasn't
coming back, I tried to do as much as I could do then, work as
hard as I could under those conditions and go on from there
—in other words, I didn't just stop."

After the team's last game in Detroit, he thought that his
life as a professional coach was over. "I wasn't anxious to
coach again. I honestly never thought I would. I thought that
this was all I was going to do as a coach. It comes to a point
where all of us have to stop doing what we're doing—maybe
not in your profession—but athletes and coaches don't go on
forever. So I was realistic, you know." He faced the first free
stretch of time in his past thirty-five years. "I adjusted very
well to the year off because, thank God, I had a salary. So I
didn't have to worry. Things change and your money isn't
worth as much as it once was but I didn't have the economic

problem. I had a job, so to speak, because I was on payroll. I enjoyed the year. I took up tennis—filled some of my time that way. I spent more time with my wife and family. I was able to come and watch the games, completely relax at them, eat dinner before them, which I never used to, drink before them, which I never did, watch them in a completely relaxed manner, get away from storing things to a degree—you always do that somewhat—and watched the games as a fan, and I enjoyed that life. It was nice. I thought I was at the point where I could do it and I enjoyed doing it."

Early in the next season, however, the new coach was fired after fighting with the management. The management called upon Holzman again—a temporary position, it seemed, just as his first had been. Holzman never equivocated about accepting it. "I came back because I feel this way: The people I've been working for asked me to do it. Now, they didn't hurt me by asking me to come back—they took good care of me, so I'm doing it." He won his first bunch of games and was again hailed as a genius, the old chief and his magic. But the team was intractably ornery, a group of players who didn't complement one another, a flighty, offensive unit that never won more than a few consecutive games. The stars were traded, the team accumulating three first-round draft choices for the next season, and Holzman entered the training camp where I spoke to him as the head of a largely unknown squad. "What I'd like to do," he told me, "is build something so that whoever comes in after me can have a starting lineup and not have to begin all over. If it comes quicker or we get better quicker that's good. If we are suddenly a winning team that's great. But I'm not just coming here and killing time. I want to build a winning team; if I succeed it will be wonderful."

He got his wish. The Knicks opened their home season to an only half-filled arena. Reporters expected little of them, and questioned the wisdom of Holzman and Donovan in selecting what turned out to be an all-black team. Holzman dismissed this talk. "I don't feel any questions about race at all. Once we start working, I don't know who's who. I know only the guys who are playing, who can contribute. Or at least I like to think I can tell who's helping and who's not. I don't know what a guy's color is—that doesn't concern me. You hear there's trouble because of the number of blacks, but I don't think that makes any difference if the team plays the right kind of ball and wins. I think the only time you start hearing things like that is when the team doesn't win."

He proceeded to do his job. The Knicks performed eagerly and well, taking their opening game into overtime and eventually winning it, presaging their performance for the year. A collection of talented, willful young performers, the team was often both inspired and out of control. But, though they lacked the experience and poise needed to win close games, they fought hard on court, making Holzman's comeback a success and promising more the following season. At the start of the '80–'81 year, Holzman was voted Coach of the Decade by the Professional Basketball Writers' Association of America, and his team, unexpectedly, won twelve of its first fourteen games, demonstrating a degree of certainty, determination, and craft they had not done before. With another year to go on his contract as coach, Holzman was postponing the final decision.

"I don't need adventure," he told me that day in his motel room before those flush times. "I'm satisfied easily. My wife and I live in the same house for the last twenty-five years. We could afford a better one but we're comfortable there. What do I do different now than I did before? Maybe eat out more." Then why even contemplate continuing to coach with its round of flights, dreary motels, depressed reporters, unhappy players? "I get excited by it," he confessed. "Yeah. As you approach it you get kind of ready to be excited. I'm not going to get as excited as a guy doing it all for the first time. Still it's new. It's exciting what you may see or find. The guys we really knew were good or we thought were going to be good—that's not so much. But, you know, some of these guys really come in and show they should play. Sometimes all of a sudden there's a guy there who can do this or do that. He makes what you want to do work or picks up something quickly. My God! It's marvelous!"

# 8

DeBusschere left the team before its bad times began, retiring at the close of the '73–'74 season. He finished his career in style. The statistical profile of most basketball players describes an alpine landscape, sheer peaks and valleys marking the triumphs and reversals of their careers. DeBusschere's overall performance shows a high, even plateau of consistent achievement: Year after year he averaged approximately 35 minutes, 11 rebounds, and 16 points per game. He matched this level during his last season and even demonstrated his characteristic doggedness: Suffering from a severe muscle pull, he led the team during the play-offs against Washington and Boston. His last game was a one-sided loss to the Celtics that secured the Eastern Division championship for Boston. In the final minutes the camera showed DeBusschere on the bench, one hand holding his side, his face squinched in pain, annoyance, and frustration as he checked the clock. To the end, he unflinchingly presented himself as a steadfast, determined competitor who suffered no nonsense: the working-class hero of the team.

He left for the business world. He was named general manager of the New York Nets, the local ABA franchise, the new league's champion that starred Julius Erving and a fine supporting cast.

At the time, basketball's domestic drama of the misalliance between the NBA and the ABA was reaching a climax. The NBA was set to destroy the younger league; the ABA—its owners certain a marriage would vastly increase the value of their teams—was intent on joining the older one. Both parties acted with a provincial greed and desperation. Afraid that public competition between the players would destroy the myth that the NBA owned all the best basketball talent, representatives of the NBA refused to let ABA players join with their NBA colleagues in a charity game. Meanwhile, two ABA teams, having sworn fealty to their partners in the struggle for the NBA's hand, unilaterally applied for membership in the older league, effectively saying they'd deny their whole family for just a nod from the groom.

As a general manager, DeBusschere had only a peripheral involvement in these proceedings. Then, after a year running the team, he was named commissioner of the ABA and became a central character in the drama. Eventually, he oversaw a marriage between the two parties. For a dowry of twenty-four million dollars and a solemn vow not to share in any television revenues for several years, four ABA teams were permitted to join the league. The agreement matched greed with stupidity: The expansion of the league thinned talent dangerously and only one of the four ownerships that originally acquiesced to the deal has managed to profit from it. Out of work, DeBusschere got a job with a television company called Trans World; among other things, it produced neologic athletic events, "trash sports," competitions designed solely for video audiences that pitted entertainment celebrities (including some athletes) in bizarre events. Finally, he started his own firm, Total Video, a production company that both packages and produces television and feature films and specials.

His progress is both predictable and surprising. Players often retire into business. After the Second World War, industrial companies often fielded teams; intelligent and aggressive players on them would graduate from representing Phillips 66 on the court to representing its products in board meetings. Other players were helped by local businessmen, an "old boy" network that secures sinecures for retired heroes: Walt Bellamy is the present doorkeeper of the Georgia Senate. In the last decade, the expansion of the game and its increasing dependence on television have integrated the sport into the world of corporate entertainment. The lines that previously separated businesses are blurred. Actors become athletes competing in television contests, while athletes become entertainers. Businessmen, such as George Steinbrenner, become sportsmen, while sportsmen, such as Ted Turner, become businessmen profiting from their multiple investments in teams. Increasingly the ethos of the entertainment industry rules sports: the action of deals, the love of gossip, and, above all, the magic of money, athletes such as David Thompson or Reggie Jackson commanding public attention not just because of their physical gifts but also because they are paid astonishingly vast salaries.

DeBusschere was particularly suited to succeed in the business world. "Dave may have been more exposed to the business world than any other athlete in America," Larry Fleisher, his friend and lawyer, told me. "Coming from Detroit and because of certain friendships, he knew most of the major corporate executives in the automobile industry and dealt with them on a personal and social basis and the same with union leaders." When his retirement approached, he followed the path of many predecessors—it simply led to a different executive suite.

Still, his conversion does contain an element uncommon to these transformations. DeBusschere, after all, was the quintessential jock of the Knicks. He excelled in the game and the life of the professional athlete. "Dave was an athlete for a very long time," Fleisher said, "and a bachelor for a long time, and therefore a real athlete." (Donnie May: "DeBusschere was a bar man; he was never one for the ladies—not like Barnett or Frazier.") He lived in the midst of an admiring public, responsible only for his duties on court, a single-minded individual famous for downing six-packs of beer after particularly strenuous games. On the team, Barnett was covetous, Frazier flashy, Bradley moody, Reed overwhelming. DeBusschere was determined, steady, unfailing, undistracted, unselfish, the disciplined, spartan ideal which high school coaches urge their charges to emulate. Precedent suggested that his behavior on the court preceded a cautious and passive existence as a businessman, a life in which he was essentially taken care of. Instead, he has acted aggressively and with a winningly adventuresome, even quixotic, spirit. Following in his family's footsteps, he has opened a bar—not the working-class local pub of Bill Bradley's romantic recollections, but a swank East Side joint patronized by athletic and entertainment celebrities. He publishes *Ring* magazine, the indestructible journal of boxing. And a television film he helped develop was an attack on scandal-mongering newspapers, a thinly veiled allusion to the *New York Post*'s exploitation of the Son of Sam murders. For a jock, he is an engagingly sophisticated, informed, and uninhibited entrepreneur.

At the same time, he has not lost his most impressive quality as a player: He is without artifice. Physically, he is a large and powerful six feet six of arms, shoulders—a wall of flesh and bone—and legs: DeBusschere could have been created to let boys know what western sheriffs should have looked like. His hair is a natural, soft white and his eyes a bright hazel. His feelings find immediate expression on his face. On our second interview, I encountered him unexpectedly in the lobby of his office building. We had spoken on the phone several times, but hadn't seen one another for a while, and DeBusschere didn't recognize me right away when I walked up to him. He squinted and lowered his head, thinking. (DeBusschere squints often and hard when he's thinking, his eyes turning into concentrated slits; he squints with more energy than most people exercise.) Do I know this guy? his face said. What's his name? Maybe I don't know him and he's just a fan. His confusion and possible annoyance were almost painfully palpable. I introduced myself again and he instantly eased up. Pleasure, distaste, puzzlement register with the same immediacy—you never wonder about his mood.

His social manner is equally frank. We held our two interviews at the office of Total Video, a suite of rooms in a midtown Madison Avenue building. Both times, there was no delay in setting up an appointment or waiting for DeBusschere to finish an important phone call, the two devils that, with the monosyllabic answer, are calculated to drive a journalist mad. On my first visit the office was in unsightly disarray. The company had just taken residence and a Hogarthian disorder ruled: The secretary sat on a large cardboard carton. DeBusschere's private quarters weren't much more regal. He sat behind a desk on a high-back chair that fell over every time he leaned back. The walls were blank; unopened boxes and stuffed cartons filled the floor along with a stereo set, phones, and file cabinets. The chair he carried in for me was another monstrously tall and dangerous swivel model: For most of the interview I perched on the edge of the seat, my feet clamped to the floor, afraid the slightest movement would cause instant collapse. DeBusschere apologized for all this without embarrassment or arrogance and for about an hour and a half we had a casual and unrestrained discussion. When we left, the company's new stationery had just arrived, lackluster blue paper on which the name was printed in a bold, sans-serif type, creating a squat and ugly, bulldoggish design. DeBusschere inspected a piece. "I like it," he told the secretary. She immediately rejoined that she didn't; the paper should have been brown. DeBusschere frowned and reconsidered. "No," he finally concluded, putting the paper down. "I like it."

Order reigned by my next visit, the office now a handsome suite, DeBusschere's walls decorated by photos of him and Bradley, and an intriguing, framed blueprint that seemed the design of an old ship and, on inspection, turned out to be the plans for renewing Yankee Stadium. Still, the pleasant informality of my first visit prevailed. DeBusschere introduced me to all his colleagues, including his secretary. When we spoke he kicked his shoes off, putting his stockinged feet on the desk, relaxing. When I asked to use his phone, he obligingly dialed the number I wanted. Later he apologetically asked his secretary if she could go by the bank for him after her lunch; he planned to leave with his family the next day for a month's vacation in the Michigan woods and needed to pick up a certified check. "How come you don't invite me out to lunch?" he kidded his banker while telling him on the phone that his secretary would be coming by. "I must not give you enough money to play with."

We spoke for another hour and a half, DeBusschere conversing in the frank fashion he had shown on our first meeting. DeBusschere's talk lacks color and quirkiness. He doesn't exaggerate his ideas or emotions and seems to be a stranger to ambivalence: "I don't sit under a tree and figure out how I feel about something," he told me; he simply feels it. Yet he is never dull. He speaks with a pleasing and undemonstrative conviction; he attacks subjects directly and pursues them until they yield their point. Earnest, intelligent, and genial, he is a particularly indivisible character, a trait that he shares with Reed and Frazier: These men have followed the paths of their natures without deviation or hesitation. DeBusschere's tale is the simplest of the three and I have reconstructed what he told me.

"I always wanted to do things well and that included basketball. If you were going to rebound, rebound as best you can; if you were going to make a jump shot, make it the best. I would watch professional games on television. I would look at different things if they were good—if a guy had a good jump shot, what made it so good? Bailey Howell was one player who would get free of his man to take his short jumper. He had lots of tricks to do that and I studied him—the way he would run his defensive player into another player and free himself, and that also taught me how to free other players. So I watched things like that and learned.

"I played both professional baseball and basketball and after college the big thing was deciding which I would do. I was a member of the White Sox and pitched for them. I was in Triple-A, which is as high as you can get in the minors, and sometimes I joined the majors. I won fifteen or sixteen games a year, as good as you can do in the minors, so I didn't worry about making it as a pitcher. Sometimes I still wonder how effective I could have been if I had chosen baseball instead of basketball.

"But after four years I decided for basketball. A couple of things made up my mind. First, I had to make a decision. Growing up, I had played every seasonal sport and this was the same; but now I had to choose, because I was a professional, and playing both was a way of continuing my life as an amateur athlete. Another thing was that I was the player-coach in basketball and I could see the game was going to afford me more opportunities and responsibilities than baseball. And there was something I didn't like about baseball: waiting for the three or four days for your next pitching start. I mean, what do you do in those couple of days? Pitch batting practice for ten minutes? Run around in the outfield? Sit around in the dugout playing word games? It gets to you. I couldn't stand the inactivity. Maybe I would have felt differently if I had played another position, but I never tried to do that. I just wanted to play—that's what I was there for, because I loved to play, and basketball afforded me that all the time.

"Also, by then, I guess I knew the professional game. There's a big difference between college and professional ball. College is an emotional game—you have terrific ups and downs: That's what makes college ball so special, at least to me. That's why I don't like teams that play slow-down ball— Princeton, Army, remember them? You were lucky if you scored fifty points a game. I think that's the wrong way to play—it's boring. But professional basketball is a percentage game. You learn over time not to take the left-handed hook shot from twenty feet. You learn always to make the plays that have the best chance of succeeding. So it takes someone four or five years to know the professional game, and I thought by the time I was ready to make my decision that I did know it—what to do and what not to do, the players, the arenas, and so I decided for basketball.

"My trade to New York happened under funny circumstances. At the time, I had been replaced as coach of the team and once again was playing with guys whom I had coached, a situation that might have made some people uncomfortable—maybe, maybe not. Regardless, the trade was good for me in terms of extending my career, and I was far too young to coach anyway. I thought a trade was coming—it wasn't something I didn't think would happen—and I was very concerned where they would send me. I didn't want to go to an expansion team. I wanted to end up with a contender or a team with that potential, and you felt that about New York—you felt that they were really close, all the players in the league did. They had a lot of talent; they just didn't have the perfect mix that comes together in a championship team.

"We finished my first season with the team terribly strong. Even our defeat to Boston in the '69 regional finals didn't really affect us. They just overran us and we were extremely tired. And we had already gone far by beating Baltimore, who had had a great year that season. In any event, it didn't change my expectations of the coming season. I had definite expectations of winning: We were going to spend an entire training camp together, getting to know each other, plus we had Stallworth back, and each year Bradley and Russell were getting better and better and Reed was going to have a full year at center and Frazier at guard. So I really felt good about the season; I felt we would be right there.

"We started the winning streak and it snowballed—you felt you couldn't lose. It was inspiring to play that season. I looked forward to every game—I didn't care if they were four in a

DREAM TEAM / 255

row or anything. We were playing well and clicking like a unit and I enjoyed the whole game—it was actually fun. We would frustrate our opponents; we worked so well, we would frustrate our opponents terribly. Everybody had a role and everybody accepted it—we were a team, and that feeling heightened throughout the season.

"We became the darlings of New York. That kind of adulation was new for me. I had received some in Detroit, but in New York there was a feverish adulation of the team. You were a celebrity because you were a Knick. Even the guys who didn't play that much were looked on in awe. You had a sense that the whole status of basketball was changing. An entourage of media surrounded the club and there was an unbelievably enormous interest from major magazines, television, documentaries, all focused on the Knicks. We were under a microscope. I remember when the Jets and the Mets won, but with the Knicks there were fewer guys and we were more visible. With basketball players, there's a feeling that you can reach out and touch them. The audience participates a lot within the game. There's a tremendous give-and-take between the fan and the player. During games, there was a tremendous electricity in the Garden. You went to a game there and you got goosebumps—I did as a player. The first half of the game no one sat down—people standing all the time, just cheering. It was an emotional outlet. There was a tremendous love affair between the fans and the players, and I suppose the fans really helped us—an inspiration that really carried us on. And all this feeling got into the press coverage. It was terribly flattering and obviously I enjoyed the attention—even if sometimes it could be something of a nuisance.

"The feeling that we were a team heightened most at the finals because they set Chamberlain, Baylor, and West—best center, best forward, best guard—against a team of just guys. We weren't supposed to have a chance. So I think our victory represented a very unique thing in sports. The fifth game, of course, was the critical one. We all felt that we could survive for a short period of time without Reed but not for any serious numbers of games. He was the bedrock of the team, the center. He had to be. You have to have a big man. He doesn't have to be Chamberlain and he doesn't have to be Russell, but he has to be the guy who can get the ball up the floor, set picks, passes, and scores. Without Willis, we could improvise here or there, do things to complicate and make things difficult for the other team—I played center for a while, then played over there, and they didn't come out of their pattern and so we were able to take advantage of them—but you knew that eventually they would catch on and if Willis had been hurt in the second, rather than the fifth game, I wouldn't have liked our chances.

"For me, that win was the most memorable and exciting one of my career, the high point of my athletic life. Yet, from a professional standpoint, the '72–'73 win was a little more gratifying. We went through all kinds of hell that year. Earl [Monroe] was injured, Willis was injured, we didn't have a terribly great season, we were a battered club. But we were a very professional club and though we were given no chance by the so-called experts we felt, all of us, that we would win the championship. We felt—all right, the season is eighty-two games long. But in a short series, though we didn't have the big horses, we have the know-how. We knew how to disrupt teams and really pull off anything. And though it's impossible to sustain that intensity without the big guys in a whole season, we could do that in a short series. And that's what we did. So from a professional standpoint, it was the most gratifying win, it really was. It was the culmination of a lot of good ballplayers who had confidence in themselves, in knowing that they knew what to do and how to do it, a really interesting team.

"The next year I retired. I first got the offer from the Nets in the summer of '73—after the championship—and I told the Knicks about it then, so actually I gave them more notice than most people get. But my decision to retire was also influenced by Willis's injury. That season my knees were giving me trouble and I pulled a stomach muscle. Every night I'd feel the pain in my knees. Jesus Christ! I had been injured before, but they had been little things, nothing that would limit my performance or make me afraid I'd be crippled. But now I was afraid because my knees were really bothering me and seeing what Willis was going through, watching him go through his torture, magnified the fear. He always had weak legs—you look at his powerful body and it's supported by very thin legs —and I'd see him dragging his leg down the floor and think, How is this man doing it? It's not just the physical pain that you go through, but the worry of never being able to run again and intense mental pain and anxiety, with six doctors around you poking this and shooting that and taking X rays. And I would look at him and think, Hey, there's no reason why this can't happen to me. There's no reason why it should. But only a fool can think that you can play and play and come out unscathed: Sooner or later your body must give way and there's a time and place when one must walk away. So I felt it was in my best interest to go for the long haul and see what life would hold for me and leave the game at that point. So when the Nets made their offer it was attractive— moving to a young team with a young league where I could learn a lot. There was some anger from the management about my leaving. They didn't want me to play more; they just didn't want me to join another league and another team in the same city. But what could I do? They didn't make me a counter-offer. I don't know if they had made another offer whether I would have taken it, but the chance never happened. All they kept talking about was my playing more—and I didn't want to. Finally, I said, You guys don't understand, I don't want more money for playing, I don't want to play, but they never caught on.

"My first season with the Nets was a sort of Cinderella year for the team, because the team won the championship right away. I didn't have much to do with the team. It was a good team—Doc [Julius Erving] and Billy Paultz, Larry Kenon, John Williamson, and Brian Taylor. People ask me how they would have done against the Knicks and you can't be sure, but they would have given us a fight. In any event, I didn't have a whole lot to do. People think that general managers sit around all day dreaming up great deals, but most of the time you're dealing with arena management: ticket sales, concessions, ushers, parking lots. That's what I learned about, and it was interesting. I hadn't known anything about it before.

"About three months before the season ended, the owners asked me to become commissioner of the ABA. At first I wasn't interested. I thought I wasn't qualified for the job. I didn't know what the responsibilities and functions of the job were. Then I was made an assistant trustee and started going to the meetings, and I saw what the job entailed. Finally I agreed to do it. Partly I agreed because of my unhappiness with the Nets; for whatever reasons—I don't care to elaborate on them—my job with them hadn't worked out as I had imagined it would. Probably it was more difficult to work under someone than I had thought. Every job, after all, has some illusions.

"In becoming commissioner, I thought, in some kind of boastful way, to help the league. I thought I could help make a contribution to basketball. There were two possibilities—making the merger or stabilizing the ABA itself. My initial aim was to stabilize the ABA. We didn't have any television markets—there just wasn't time on TV for two leagues—but I kept saying, Look, if the league becomes strong there will be time, we'll have a Super Bowl, you don't know what other channels will open up, and with cable there'll be lots more time on the air. I just wanted to make the league strong, and I still think that there were markets and players to allow that many teams and still provide good sport—I don't know whether there were enough good coaches to coach them, but that's another story.

"But the owners ran scared. I kept telling them that if we

worked at it we could get a situation where it wouldn't cost us a cent to join the NBA. But they pursued their own goals and when it became inevitable that a merger or amalgamation would take place and when the judge presiding over the suit ordered that talks about a merger be begun, I followed that path. But as soon as the owners smelled that they could join the NBA, they just acted like dogs in heat, and soon enough the deal had been made. Afterward, I was wrapping up the odds and ends of the league—there were too many lawsuits to end it all at once—and I kind of felt sorry for the sport: even if the merger had been in its best interest. All of the inter-workings of both leagues and even the Players' Associations of both leagues were distasteful to me—everyone was so self-interested. I just didn't understand why they couldn't have arrived at some form of mutual coexistence—it didn't make sense to me; and to see all these self-interested parties pulling in all different directions—it was shocking. What is the mentality that leads to that kind of behavior? There were a lot of times when people really shocked me by what they were doing—I couldn't even begin to tell you some of those things.

"After that two-year crash course as commissioner I didn't pursue basketball. I didn't give it up, but I didn't pursue it. I had a bitter taste of the inner workings of the league and it had nothing to do with the game I played—and I was in a state of, I really don't know what the hell makes sense right now.

"Now I don't go to games frequently. I watch some at home. I have mixed emotions about them. I think there's no question that in 1970 there was a higher quality of play and I guess there are a lot of reasons for that. There was a higher level of intensity then—more rivalries were created and we were able to sustain these rivalries, build up things, and create a lot of drama. You had match-ups versus team philosophy, slow down versus fast breaks, all these things, and you don't have them now. There are too many teams to have it. Who are we playing tonight? We're playing San Antonio? Oh yeah

—who plays for them? Who you playing tomorrow night? We're going to Kansas City. Oh yeah—who plays for them? Who you playing then? San Francisco. Oh yeah—who plays for them? It's too much with twenty-two teams. And the game has changed a lot too. Teams run more now than they did when I was playing—I don't know if they run more with control but they do run. Plus you don't have the same degree of professional ability in the players because of expansion—both physically and mentally. There are glaring examples of guys who are so important to the franchise that people are forced to put up with their antics, even when they are detrimental to the team. Years ago, you wouldn't have stood for it. You just would have said, Time-out, get your head together, we're playing basketball. Now everyone is a franchise maker and babied. You know years ago there were very few franchise makers; except for guys like Wilt [Chamberlain] or Oscar [Robertson] very few came along. Now people talk like everyone can turn things around—and every kid who comes out of the draft is a franchise.

"I don't watch the Knicks with any particular sympathy. Now I don't have any close personal attachments to the team —other than Pearl [Monroe] of course, and the general fact that I think it's important for the league that the Knicks do well. There's not that much attachment to Red. We're not close, though we're also not far apart. But we don't have terribly much in common because he's older and has different interests than I do. And anyway I was never terribly close to any of the players to begin with.

"But I have a lot of good memories of the team. Bowman and Russell used to make me laugh. You know Russell was always so concerned with looking good. He was a nut about his body. I thought he should open a Nautilus Shop when he retired. Sell the equipment, run the gym. He'd be all set up. He could work out there and show off the machines to everybody. It would be perfect for him. Cazzie is a very smart guy, a very very smart guy; he just has these obsessions. Bowman would always call him dumb and he'd call Bowman dumb. Cazzie would come in and say, I'm dating the daughter of a very well-regarded preacher. Oh, Bowman would say, was that the bitch you were body-slamming last night? She was moaning like she needed religion, Russ. And Russell would say, What? Shut up! and turn away. I used to cry with laughter. I can imagine Bowman selling something—I'd never buy it, but I'd love to hear his pitch. Barnett was also funny, but in a different way. Bradley and I have talked about it. I've told people stories about Barnett that I thought were hysterically funny but they don't get them. It must have been his delivery. He had these eyes that slanted down and then they'd pop open as if he had been asleep. He would say things that were very apt and funny and quite deep really. And he knew the game—he could analyze things and know what to do. I always thought he could be a good coach. Frazier was a very intelligent guy—very smart and extremely honest.

"I'm still friendly with Riordan, Monroe, Jackson. I'm friendliest with Bradley. We have common interests. We speak once or twice a week, open-ended telephone calls. I think he's crazy to be a politician—anybody is. But I think lots of things are crazy. I think it's crazy to be a writer, but what do I know about writing? People say there is the attraction of power, but real power is always wealth. And to always have to watch over your shoulder and think about owing this one or that one! Bradley's different than that. He really didn't pay his dues as a politician; he made it easy. He suddenly became a person of real importance without having to step up the ladder and because of that he doesn't owe anybody. Bradley wants to stay in politics, and his position is pretty ideal because the two places you can get to in politics and stay for a long time are either the Senate or the Supreme Court and I don't think he has the legal background to do the Court. I don't think he wants to be President, but who knows? He believes he can help, he believes he can do things that will help people. We talk about everything, just exploring things. Like

262 / Dream Team

tax cuts, not Kemp-Roth, but what would be the implications, say, of establishing an across-the-board fifteen percent income tax? I just pick fifteen—it could be twelve or ten. Originally the progressive income tax was supposed to be progressive—but now the idea that the rich will pay more has become a justification for them to spend all their time figuring out ways for them to pay less. I think people would be amazed at the number of millionaires in this country who pay no taxes. So I say fifteen percent and no dodges—what would that do? You make a million dollars, you pay one hundred and fifty thousand, you make ten thousand, you pay fifteen hundred. What are the implications of that for wealthy people and corporations, etc?

"After leaving the ABA, I didn't have any problem financially and wasn't in a bind to get a job right away. I wanted to get a job that would prepare me for another facet of the business world. So I took a job with Purolator as a consultant for three months while figuring out what I wanted to do. Then I went to Trans World for two years. It got me into a new field and at the same time I was still attached to sports. I think originally I was brought on because of my connections in sports, but after a while I learned the trade. I didn't know anything about points and ratings and selling time, but I learned—it took about three months. We did Wimbledon and the U.S. Open and 'contrived sports events'—what you call trash sports.

"Now I'm here. We started to concentrate on video but we don't like to cut off our options. We put together the package of the U.S. Olympics team against the NBA and we do other things—we have a feature movie in development right now. Sometimes we sell the air time, calling up people and getting them to buy, and sometimes we act as producers or packagers. We all work together, each of us getting our own ideas and then working them out. I like the work. It's a people business. One thing about basketball is that you're sequestered with a group of guys the whole year and you don't have an opportunity to develop relationships with people outside the basket-ball world. But in the business world, you meet different people who do different things. Right now I'm working on a special with Marcel Marceau. I'm going to sell it to a cable network. He has an international audience—he just came back from a trip to Japan where he sold out forty-one nights in a row, and its like that for him everywhere—yet he's never been on television. He's in his early fifties and has a great body—just like an athlete. Really, he's amazing."

# 9

Walt Frazier stayed with the team until 1977. Then, just before the season started, he was traded to the Cleveland Cavaliers, the same team which Johnny Warren, the twelfth man on the bench, had gone to seven years before. The only player who had lasted through the team's cycle of triumph and decline, Frazier had become the symbol of the Knicks. He matched his flawless, graceful performances with a tantalizing lifestyle. The Beau Brummel of the team, he wore fur coats over extravagantly designed fashions, and dated beautiful women, driving them to clubs and bars in a burgundy-colored Rolls-Royce. Far from his 1970 New Yorker hotel room where his gorgeous apparel hung from a clothing rack, he rented an East Side penthouse, sleeping in a magnificent round bed under a curved sign that spelled his now-famous nickname: Clyde. His manner was imitated for its cool, his unyielding self-possession being translated by the public into a *macho* self-assurance and arrogance. Masterful, magisterial, he became the dream of fans, a living magical mirror who transformed viewers into a perfection they would never know in life. In the '74–'75 season, both Willis and DeBusschere gone, he inherited the team. He was named captain, inheriting Willis's mantle, and played brilliantly in the All-Star game, winning MVP honors. But these were individual triumphs. The team was performing ineptly, losing games regularly, and ending the season in the Houston debacle. Frazier suffered the fate of celebrity. The object of the adulation of the fans when the team was winning, he became the target of their resentment when it lost. He promised to adjust his game to meet the new demands of the team, but injuries hindered his progress and the impossible was suggested by columnists and fans sooner than one had imagined: The team would be better off without him. The following season didn't stop the slide, and the trade to Cleveland was arranged. There he followed a fate not very different from Warren's. Frazier's debut was a triumph. Early in the season, the Cavaliers played the Knicks at the Garden, and Frazier dominated the game. First he was introduced to the sellout crowd, who gave him a standing ovation that delayed the contest; then, when the game ran into overtime, he won it with clutch baskets. But injuries and bad relations with his coach hounded him. He took time recovering from his injuries, and his critics became testier: They said he let his opponents make too many shots, took too many himself, lacked courage, lacked desire. On October 21, 1979, a decade after the season in which he had claimed glory, he was waived by the Cavaliers and returned to New York. A final tumultuous and triumphant tribute at the Garden awaited him along with a profitable future in business, but he had finished his playing career. His accomplishments as a player had been prodigal. He had been a member of the All-Rookie team, four times selected to the All-NBA squad, and appeared seven times in the annual All-Star games, once winning MVP. In the statistical archives of the club, he was peerless, holding eight out of a possible eleven records: the most games, minutes, field goals, assists, free throws, attempts from both the field and the foul line, and the most points. Now he added one more: He was the last of the championship players to leave the court.

As a fan, I followed Frazier closely. He was a hero to me, the expression of the intelligence and beauty I saw in the game, the standard by which I measured excellence. Even today the few guards who display Frazier's physical form and overall excellence claim my allegiance powerfully. Indeed, they even make me a traitor. This past winter I watched the San Antonio Spurs take on the Knicks. My team had gone into their usual January hibernation—the month saw them play poorly even in 1970—but this night they had a chance to win, and were playing hard when a bearded, muscular guard named James Silas took over for the Texans with an all-around clutch performance that included fifteen for fifteen from the free-throw line. His display so reminded me of vintage Frazier that I watched the last two minutes of the game rooting him on to win even though a victory for my home team might have brightened what promised to be a gloomy month.

In 1976, I met and observed Frazier close-up and off the court, one of my first thrills as a journalist. I anticipated a commanding, regal man. Physically, he didn't disappoint me. Frazier's looks and physical presence dominate his surroundings. He stands taller and broader than on the court, and he has a spectacular feature you never notice on television: broad and heavy-lidded eyes, the pronounced, commanding, sensual eyes you see on Babylonian sculptures, unblinking brown pools.

But his behavior was utterly unassuming. He had been laid up the previous season with a back injury and appeared eager for the season to start, practicing with almost puppyish enthusiasm. After a scrimmage, the squad broke up to shoot fouls. Frazier had been missing free throws in exhibition games and now the ball again spun in and out of the basket. He cursed himself and concentrated on the task until he made several consecutively. Then, feeling good, he went to midcourt and loosened up some more, bending over from the waist and touching his hands to the floor as he skipped across the court from side to side, a veteran eager for action even when rookies were wandering exhaustedly to the locker room. His voice impressed me most of all, an inordinately calm, unhurried tenor flavored with a mild southern accent that lent him a boyish air, alternately either happy, watchful, or self-assured.

The same emotions colored his behavior during games. Early that season, I was sitting courtside when Frazier obstructed the view of a referee as a ball went out of bounds. The referee called in favor of the Knicks. Taking the ball, his back to the refs, Frazier winked broadly at the press table, knowing we had witnessed his sleight-of-hand and proud to have pulled it off. Some eighty games and many disappointments later, I sat near him at the team's last outing at the Garden, the final game, as it turned out, in which he, Bradley, and Holzman would be Knicks. During half time a drunken young man stumbled in front of him on the bench. "Clyde, Clyde," the fellow implored, "put it there." He stuck out his hand while tilting from side to side, an aggressive, angry, and threatening drunk. But Frazier followed his orders, offering his hand while keeping a watchful and suspicious eye on the man. Later, toward the end of the game, Holzman benched him as the team collapsed before their opponents. Frazier talked with Earl Monroe. A group sitting behind Frazier cursed and abused him. "I hope you're having a good time making a million while your team loses!" one called, finally catching his attention. Frazier stared at them without blinking and continued his chat with Monroe as the game—and, unbeknownst to him, his career as a Knick—wound down.

The next time I saw him was for the first interview for this book. We met in his office. Although Frazier's off-the-court fun made people frequently imagine him a thoughtless person, he actually organized his career quite thoroughly. After the championship, he asked a lawyer named Irwin Weiner to represent him in his contract negotiations; rewarding Weiner for an excellent job, Frazier gave him money to set up a business. Now Weiner heads Walt Frazier Enterprises, an agency representing many top athletes, including Julius Erving. Frazier works here, recruiting college performers, his office a side room facing a narrow street. We met only days after he had been waived from the Cavaliers; the office was unnaturally blank and bare. "I'm a rookie again," Frazier joked about the dreary-looking suite, "I have to earn my stripes." We began the interview and he gave maddeningly mono-syllabic replies; then, as inexplicably as he entered his deep freeze, he came out of it, answering even intimate questions with a relaxed flood of words. We spoke for several hours, touching on the different sites of his life, New York, Cleve-land, and St. Croix, where he spends most of his time at pre-sent. Frazier said he enjoyed the talk and we chatted for the last hour. Frazier explained that he believed in "color ther-apy," the science of determining how people feel by what col-ors they wear. He said he had a small sailboat in St. Croix and frequently went down the beach meeting women. I confessed my fear of boats: I am a powerful swimmer, but am seized by a momentary panic when first over my head. He sympathized with my anxiety. He had recently seen *Jaws* and the picture had chilled him. "On earth, I fear nothing," he told me, "but in the water *Jaws* still freaks me out." He related a recent nightmarish incident: Out beyond the island reef, his boat had capsized, and he and his young woman companion had thrashed about trying to right the vessel and get on board while he fought off fantasies about killer sharks.

Our next time together was some seven months later. Now his office was decorated with a variety of plaques and a mys-terious number of dead plants surrounding his desk: Frazier can't always manage to do what he thinks he should, and I guess the pots filled with two dying cane plants, four dying spider plants, and three seared and unrecognizable stalks were a testament to a misguided notion that some greenery should enliven his otherwise dingy room. (The worst was a perfect little bonsai that sat on his desk. I exclaimed over its brown needles; bonsai are rare and costly. "I know," Frazier explained. "But it's so hard to take care of.") We repeated the routine of our first talk, his curious, cautious, robot-like answers, preceding a sudden ease. But just as he was relaxing, he left to visit Weiner, who was meeting with representatives of natural-cookie manufacturers who wanted to name their brand after Clyde. "Taste it," Frazier offered, returning to his office after a forty-minute delay. Annoyed at the length of his absence, I told him the cookie tasted too sweet—too much molasses, I judged. He considered the opinion and agreed, but thought they were making others that weren't so sugary. I forgot my annoyance. We spoke about his work and aspects of his past career. "I'm older," he told me. "I meet attractive girls now and they say, I used to follow you when I was ten." By the end, I had learned a good deal about him, certainly more than I had ever imagined I might when I first watched him perform on television. There was nothing he didn't answer and I censored myself only a little: Two of Frazier's sisters died reportedly of drug overdoses and I didn't mention the tragedies. I had spent more time with him and watching him than I had with most of the other Knicks and, actually, found his conversation, though charming and pleasant, neither the most compelling nor provocative. Yet the man continued to fascinate me and even after my exposure to his more mundane features, he holds my imagination: It is his presence on the court that I still feel is most inimitable and which consequently I still most miss as a fan.

This fascination with him is common. He has aroused the imagination of more fans than any other Knick—indeed, than any other basketball player with the exception of the magisterially mysterious Abdul-Jabbar. Invariably, Frazier is the player whom fans most want to talk about and they want to know the answer about him, the detail that explains what makes him tick. "Reporters call me all the time about him,"

Ira Berkow, the co-author of one of Frazier's semi-autobiographical books told me. "You wouldn't believe the things they ask. Does Clyde throw games? Is Clyde homosexual? Is Clyde sleeping with models? Does he take drugs? They suspect him of everything." Nate Bowman, who roomed with Frazier, repeated the same theme. "Frazier is a very nice guy who's misunderstood. People always assume he's a certain way—they assume he's this, assume he's that, assume everything. Nobody knows where he's coming from—just him."

Irwin Weiner offered a more comprehensive view of the same phenomena. "He's basically a very shy person. People don't pick up on his shyness. They read all the things in the paper about him but when they meet him they find someone much different from what they read, and I always get a chuckle out of that. He's a very honest person—in his behavior. He does a lot for people that he doesn't get credit for. When his grandmothers were alive he used to support them. His sisters, his brothers, he used to support them all. But he would never talk about it. He thinks that's his private business. I remember one game against the Bullets and he came in and scored six or ten points and everybody blasted the hell out of him. And his grandmother had just died—she had raised him—and he had just come back from Atlanta, and he really shouldn't have come back but he did because he felt he had to because of the play-offs. Yet the press knocked the hell out of him and then a week later, they said, Gee, we found out his grandmother died. So he's a very private person and I think inside he's very sensitive. Outside he might be cool Clyde but inside I think he has a lot of things going on. The fact that he was such a private person helped him become an object of fantasy for many people. People were used to guys being on the street saying this or that and here was a guy who moved around quietly. You felt his presence but he didn't have much to say. Everybody wanted to know what Frazier thought, but no one really did. His talent, the times, and the way people related to him, the mystique about him—which he didn't put on; it came to him naturally—and all this with the way he played, the way he looked, the way he walked, the way he conducted himself, created a mystique: You never heard him rant, but he would be there and so people became fascinated."

But for all the confusion and suspicion about him, Frazier's most characteristic visible feature appears to be his inwardly most compelling one: He needs to control himself and his environment. There is nothing threatening or dominating in his manner—he makes no attempt to master others—but over himself and his passage through the world he exerts an absolute reign. "He was the oldest of nine children and he was responsible for them," Ira Berkow told me. "He changed diapers and cooked and cleaned for them. He was the man of the household. He used to sell peanuts or something at the Atlanta Braves games, and his mother told me that even when he was a little boy he used to take care of his own clothes. He would iron them and set them out all folded the night before school so that everything would be nice and neat in the morning. She says he always took care of himself." The deliberate quality in his manner (that appears haughtiness) stems from a simple desire to order himself and his surroundings; being caught off-guard spooks him and he has the will and imagination to force circumstances to his wishes often enough. This marked him as a player—what are those marvelous fourth quarters about except controlling a game?—and as a private person. He wants to defy circumstance not with luck or mere persistence, but by doing right, and channels all the energy that others expend on anger into this insistence on performing correctly.

For this reserve, he received the unrestrained adulation of the fans. Frazier's career has its disappointments and his final moments as a player were unquestionably sad. Still, careers aren't fairy tales following ideal standards of circumstance and character, however much we Americans are inclined to see them this way. Realistically, Frazier's career ranks as a supremely satisfying one. He enjoyed a marvelous talent that was recognized and nurtured, gained wealth and social importance, and never suffered a serious injury. Finally, he got a sort of affection special among all the Knicks. Bill Bradley calls the applause of the crowd "love vibes," and for Frazier those love vibes were without reservation. They didn't just celebrate him as a contributor to a winning team, excellent player, or admirable person, but also as an incarnation of a basic, flawless beauty of person and spirit that we all imagine we possess. In this sense, nothing was extenuated in his career as a player. For him, as for no other Knick, the prize held out to everyone in our society was won: He was a star.

As a child, he wasn't particularly ambitious. "My goals as a kid were to be a pro athlete in any sport," he told me, "that's all. I prayed to God every night that I could become a pro athlete. When the Knicks drafted me it was a dream come true. I didn't think it would ever happen. I remember once a guy at my school got drafted eighth by Detroit—that gave me hope. Then coming out, being drafted number one, it was a total shock. Then to end up here, in New York!"

In his book, he writes that his selection by the Knicks was an unpleasant surprise; the team was already stocked with good guards and he wasn't sure he would make the squad, thinking they might trade him. This was a misreading of the situation, but his feeling of being slighted helped him to perform better, he thinks, because he believes he always does best when people expect the least of him. "Like coming to the Knicks," he writes in his book, "it was always Bradley getting the notices, Bradley who was going to save the Knicks. Bill was going to do this, Bill was going to do that. I was never mentioned, but I knew what I could do if I had the chance. I probably tried harder than if Bradley had never been there." The resentment—not toward Bradley but toward the team's management—still lasts. "They all waited on Bradley," he told me when I asked about his first arrival in New York. "I didn't feel wanted. Willis Reed picked me up at the airport and said he was surprised I signed because there was so much competition in the backcourt. And that didn't help me much with my confidence."

He was lonely and unsure. In an exhibition game, he missed three consecutive foul shots, and, trying to compensate for his mistake, rushed for the rebound and sprained his ankle. For the next month and a half, he sat through games, watching the team lose and observing Bradley's debut in each new city. His enthusiasm also hurt him socially. "I'm a loner," he explained to me, "because people who would be nice would also be plotting against me. It used to hurt me when people I'd like would betray me. It creates a lot of bullshit—and I hate bullshit and static. That's why I never got into the team camaraderie. When I first came to the Knicks, guys would be friendly, but they wouldn't trust one another to spend time with their girlfriends. I decided, these guys are phoney, don't get into it."

His spotty play and loneliness caused him to be depressed, a constant theme in Frazier's career, enervating lows marking his progress as distinctly as exhilarating highs. His first depression was during his sophomore year. His teammates ostracized him on the court, refusing to give him the ball, the coach benched him, and he was dogged by the blues. ". . . I wasn't happy," he writes in his book. ". . . I couldn't make contact. I stopped going to classes. I just didn't show. I'd sleep late and mess around playing pool or watching TV. My roommate had a set and I'd stay up late watching The Late, Late, Late Show. I knew I was letting a lot of people down, most of all myself, but that didn't stop me." His confidence was shaken again when he first joined the Knicks. "There were times at camp," he writes, "I was depressed because I didn't think I was playing up to my ability—I knew I wasn't. I was nervous, too. I knew I could be playing better, but somehow I couldn't shake loose. I was handling the fast break all right, but I wasn't shooting at all, so naturally I wasn't scoring. And if I did get a setup I couldn't make an accurate shot." Even after his injury healed and he started playing regularly with the team, his depression remained. From the bench, he watched the team lose regularly, his confidence ebbing steadily away. "It's very easy to lose your confidence when you aren't playing," he writes. "You start to downgrade yourself and it's difficult to stay mentally ready. For a while ... I never wanted to play. I would sit on the bench and think, 'I hope he doesn't call on me. I don't want to go in.' "

Holzman saved him. In the middle of Frazier's rookie season, Holzman was appointed interim coach. Shortly after, he challenged Frazier and began to restore the player's self-confidence. "Red was important in my development because he wanted defense," Frazier told me. "That got me playing time because I was a good defensive player—at that time, I wasn't known as an offensive player at all. Red called me over once and he told me he knew I could play better than I was because he had scouted me in college and I wasn't doing shit now, so he knew I could play better. I was nervous. But the fact that he had confidence in me gave me confidence and it stirred up my pride. I wanted to show him how well I could play and I knew better than he did that I wasn't playing to the best of my ability. Up to then I was just depressed. But after he spoke to me, it shocked me, like an awakening, and I tried harder and it worked." He finished the year averaging 9 points. He still was a sub, but he enjoyed coming in for Komives. "I liked Komives starting," he said, "because I was tense when I started." When Komives left with Bellamy for Detroit, Frazier moved easily into the starting spot, doubling his minutes, points, assists, and significantly improving every other aspect of his game. "I developed as a player once Komives was traded because I got more time," he told me. "And after that I got better each year. My main thing was being in shape. I knew that out of that my shot would come and the rest of my game would be there." His casual public relationship with Holzman blossomed, and also his pleasant, eager-to-please public personality. "I used to lock the locker room up," he told me. "There was always one more writer wanting a quote."

Winning the championship climaxed this first act in his professional career. He anticipated the triumph in a way. "I never worried about being on a championship team," he said. "Maybe because I was always on them. So when we won on the Knicks that was what I was used to. If we didn't win, I didn't know about losing. I had only played on one losing team. So I never had a championship jones. Winning wasn't an obsession with me like it was with, say, Dave Bing or Jerry West because they had never won. Even before we won I never said, Hey, I'm here to win a championship. I was just glad to be a pro player." Still, he feels that the management and the press overlooked his personal contribution to the team's victory and resents them for the slight. "I was always responsible for the team," he told me, a natural enough feeling for an oldest child who used to iron his own shirts. "Even when the veterans were there—Willis and Bradley and De-Busschere—the responsibility for running the team was always on my shoulders. I was the quarterback." He feels this particularly about the seventh game, rightly arguing that Willis's appearance, rather than Frazier's spectacular performance, is remembered about the contest. "The last game of the first championship I played great. It was probably the greatest game of my career and it was a game that mattered—not just any game, but the last and decisive game of the championship. But the next day I don't read about that in the paper, but about Willis Reed because he sank two baskets. I had no recognition. I could walk down the street and everybody wouldn't know me. That next day when Willis got all the press I was hurt. They always jerked me around. When I didn't get the MVP that year they told me it was because they judged by the season; and when I didn't get it in 1973 they said it was because they judged by the series. Finally, one year I played great. I was having lines all the time. And one day I picked up the paper and it said, Walt Frazier—Superstar, and that made me feel good. But I had had to play a lot of super games before they finally recognized me."

By then he had become Clyde. The transformation started the championship year when his fashionable clothes provided nice copy for the sportswriters. "I was always like Clyde, but the press didn't pick it up until I became a good player. I always liked to dress and I always liked to go out and have a good time—though not in college: In college I was quiet and wasn't like that and, plus, I had no money so I couldn't dress. But in New York, it all happened at the same time with the movie *Bonnie and Clyde* coming out, and I bought this big hat and it started from there. I think Danny Whelan gave me the name and then the players picked up on it—you know, the way I used to dress, the night life, the party, the clothes." Frazier didn't buy the clothes for publicity; as with so many instances of his famous traits, his consumer sprees were motivated by personal, psychological reasons. "I started buying clothes because I was depressed because I wasn't playing well. That's how I pacified myself. Every day I went shopping. I bought a new suit, a new shirt, and that got me happy. And every time I went on the road I bought something: It was my way of getting over my frustration."

The clothes were accompanied by other attractive qualities. "I became a celebrity because of my lifestyle. Cars, clothes, women. Even on the floor—my behind-the-back passes, my steals, my cool, how I never got excited no matter what was going on. So guys liked that. And I was doing something all guys wished they could do. Like if I walked into a bar, it was thought I could have any chick there. Most guys think that. And when I come in they disappear because they think: Hey, he's going to get any girl he wants here. And the girls are saying the same thing: He can get anyone here. So that's where the fantasy starts. I had mink coats—lots of guys wish they had that. I epitomized what New York is all about. Plus we were winning. And I would stay out late at night and still play up to my standards and people would think: How can he do all this and still be scoring, forty-five minutes a game? It intrigued them."

But Clyde was not just a happy invention of the press and public imagination, an urban sports hero for the '70s. He was a creation, the product of Frazier's natural talents, the demands of the marketplace, and Irwin Weiner's natural salesmanship. Frazier's person was a business, a profitable enterprise that kept growing, value creating value. First he was worth money because he helped win games. Then his value doubled, audiences paying to see him play whether or not his team won. Finally, his influence extended off the court altogether. Producers began to solicit his endorsement for non-basketball products, believing that consumers would select one item over another because it was associated with Frazier. Presumably he embodied certain qualities (or was considered a good judge of excellence) and people purchased things given his stamp of approval to gain those attributes for themselves.

Weiner was the alchemist who performed this transformation. He and Frazier met shortly before the championship year. "Irwin was my friend first," he said. "He was always giving me advice. He used to book guys at shopping malls and different appearances. I did a few and liked the way he had things organized. I told him a few deals I was in and some details about my contract and he thought I should be getting more. But that was normal. Everybody you talked to always thought you should be getting more, every guy you met would say, Oh, I can do better. So one day eventually it dawned on me that maybe I could get more and I said, Let him try it. And he did do better."

Weiner's account differs from this only in tone, not fact. At the time he met Frazier he ran a local Long Island newspaper, the last of several botched enterprises pursued by the energetic entrepreneur. (Once Weiner manufactured dresses. Stuck with an unpopular design, he sold a few to a department store and sent some models to buy them up; the department store quadrupled its original request.) His association with Frazier rescued him from a world of unpaid bills and small-time scrambling, and he speaks about his benefactor with gratitude and respect. "We met and he never talked much the first six months," he told me. "We'd go somewhere and say good night and that'd be it. He had a representative then, Norman Blass. I was representing athletes then, but just in endorsements, not contracts. Frazier used to come and tell me different things: What do you think of this? What about that? I told him I thought he could get more and told him to get himself an attorney. He said I have one. I said, Get another one. He said, No, I have the confidence in you, I'd like you to try it." He negotiated the contract—"I think I got him three times more than he was offered"—and several weeks later Frazier started him in business, giving him a reported forty thousand dollars to clear his debts and another fifty to ensure his future credit. "When he did my first contract, I gave him more than I would normally give an agent," Frazier explained. "I was thankful to him and I liked him as a person and wanted to help him out." Weiner matches this humility. "Frazier made me," he said. "He gave me a lot of money out of his pocket when I was flat down on my ass in '69–'70 and he stood by my side and paid me well and he really did a lot for me."

The partnership was magical. Both led the other to success. With Frazier's money, Weiner opened an office on Park Avenue. "It wasn't a plan of mine to start this company. That was in his mind, not mine," Frazier said. "You see, that's the problem. When you're playing you never see anything beyond that—you get so involved in playing and having a good time and being young that you don't think of the business aspect of your life." The firm was a quick success. Negotiating summoned Weiner's competitive zeal—"When I negotiate a contract, it's a contest for me," he said—and he displayed a natural talent at getting excellent deals for his clients after Frazier. "I know the dollar mark," he told me. "At knowing the value of a player, I really think I'm the best in the business. I really think I care. When I negotiate a contract, I make myself the athlete. I go in and bargain for myself. But I didn't know I had the knowledge and natural talent to negotiate a contract until I did Frazier's—knowing the people, knowing the player, knowing the market, knowing where the player is going and how important he is to the team."

Through Weiner, Frazier became a superstar, a person whose name or presence endows things with value: from the arena where he plays to the pants he wears. People in basketball frequently say that Weiner molded Clyde, the name by which this transformed version of Frazier came to public prominence. But Weiner rejected this accusation. "Nobody can turn somebody else into a superstar," he told me. "The player and the representative—I hate the word agent; I represent the player, not just negotiate a contract and take my four percent and kiss them good-bye—must complement each other. I think that Frazier had to have talent. The same for McGinnis, Erving. These are talents. If you get on with them and move with them you can really merchandise and market them. Frazier has certain qualities about him and an agent can't give them to a person. He attracted a gate. There are some great athletes who can't do that—Bobby Dandridge is a talent and he can't pull at the gate. Monroe pulls, Frazier pulled—they're just athletes who have that off-the-court charisma. He was different. The clothes, his talent, the way he moves like a ballerina on court, the appeal he had for women, his legs—they all loved his legs, they all talked about his legs —he had his own natural charisma."

Still, Weiner was the rocket that sent the superstar into orbit, who (to use his word) "merchandised" him. He talked about the process referring to Greg Kelser, a new player who Weiner hopes will repeat Frazier's success. "Take Greg —now coming out. Now he can be merchandised because I think he's going to be a superstar. He's a good-looking fellow, he has great discipline, he's very smart, and he dresses well, and I just think that as he catches on he's someone that a manufacturer will absolutely want as an endorsee. But this doesn't happen overnight. You get the normal sneaker deals and the basketball manufacturers and so on, but in getting merchandise you've got to give things time to grow. They want you when the product is hot and if you're black you've got to be a crossover. You see Frazier and Julius are crossovers: They're accepted by the black and white audiences. So your crossover gives you a bigger market—that's very important, your crossover, because then you've got a national market."

In this universe of created stars powers are exerted by ineffable and immaterial substances. I asked Weiner how much the Frazier company was worth. "The company is worth Irwin Weiner," he answered, "that's what it's worth." But what are its assets? I insisted. "What assets? Its only asset is the person who does the work. It's a service business. It's a one-man business. It's worth what I say it is. It's me. Who knows its value? Pick a number from one to ten—that's its value." The powers of transformation even affect Weiner, his stars pulling him into orbit with them. "Now the most amazing thing is that people tell me, You know, you're half a celebrity, Irwin. You go out into the street, people want your autograph. It's crazy. Why would you want an agent's autograph? If they came to me and said, I want Walt Frazier—that I understand. But I've been on planes or other places for the company and people come up and say they want your autograph and you know it's nice for your ego, but it makes me wonder. These people don't see my talent. But they see an athlete's. You can appreciate something you see. But they only know about me through the media. I haven't figured it out. I was on a plane. A guy comes by and says, Are you Irwin Weiner? I say, Yeah. He says, I didn't want to wake you up but can I have your autograph? It makes you feel good. But I don't walk over to a representative in the movie business and ask them for their autograph. But I'd ask a star. It's funny. I go to a restaurant and I hear, There's Irwin Weiner. I chuckle to myself about it because they say it but won't approach you —it's amazing. It gives you a buzz, but you wonder who's doing the buzzing."

For Frazier, the distinction between private and public personality became almost palpable. He became two people, Walt Frazier and Clyde. For him the difference between the two was primarily psychological, not economic. Referring casually to himself as either Walt Frazier or Clyde, he divides up his attitudes and behavior between the two. "Clyde was my night-life self," he told me with an unnerving off-handedness. "An arrogant guy who played on the ego trip of the crowd. Walt was my basic self—down-to-earth, quiet, and shy, the way I started out." The characterization of the two reminded me of another duality in Frazier's earlier life: the contrast between his hard-working, staid grandfather and his loose-living father. "I'm sure that's not it," Frazier replied when I mentioned the similarity. "I never considered it that way." Earlier, startled by the Jekyll-and-Hyde-like description of his character, I asked what brought Clyde out. He joked that he didn't know—sometimes, he thought Blue Nun brought Clyde out—but added that one thing about Clyde disturbed him: Clyde would appear under the influence of other people. Still, he never disowns Clyde. "I'm not critical of Clyde," he explained later on. "I just view it as a third person. Clyde, yeah, I say, that's the Clyde, Clyde will do that, as though Clyde's someone else. But it's still me. I'm not critical, but I'm normally not like that. Sometimes the situations make Clyde come out—you know, like when I'm out at discos or parties, I like to be loose and just have fun. Whereas basically, I'm not like that—I'm more withdrawn."

Clyde's triumphant days were the early '70s, when Frazier was the team's most consistent dominant force, leading them, along with Bradley and DeBusschere, to the '73 championship. Frazier hadn't set himself the goal of another championship. "After the first championship, I never said, Now we've got to win two or three. If it happened, it happened. I just set personal goals: making the All-Star team or twenty points a game, five or six rebounds, the same with assists and steals, and being a good all-around player in the team concept." Unlike the others, he barely recalls the '73 triumph. "That team—we'd just knew we'd win. I can't remember the second championship well at all. I guess that's the price of winning too much."

A season later, the team's decline started. Frazier began his fall from grace with the fans, the image of Clyde now suggesting boredom rather than studied mastery, and the star's conspicuous signs of success a heedless egotism. But in most important ways Frazier was blameless for the team's poor showing. With the depature of Reed, Lucas, and De-Busschere, Frazier remained the natural leader of the team: Bradley could never dominate games by his own play and Monroe was still acclimating himself to the team. Frazier simply took on a responsibility he couldn't meet. "After '74 I had to do more—scoring, more work on D," he told me, repeating Bradley's complaint about his last years on the team. "It's more frustrating playing with less talented guys at times. When the game's on the line, I had to coach and try to score and rebound, whereas with the guys we had before I didn't have to do that."

The change in the team and fans surprised him; with a naïve assurance he had imagined that he and the team would always succeed. "I always thought we would win and get the players to be competitive. When we got new players, at first I thought they would make us competitive and were the right picks, but once they got to the team I didn't." He felt beleaguered. He was criticized for not demonstrating leadership as a captain. "I'm not a rah-rah person," he explained to me, answering the charge. "But if you see me play, I'm rah-rah. But in the warm-up, I'm not, Let's go! Let's go! I do it on the floor. I lead by example, because if you're a basketball captain what do you do? You go out before the game to speak to the referees and if you're losing you call team meetings: What's that?"

He also suffered his first major injury, an incident which again made him resent the management of the team. "I can't remember exactly when I was injured, but before I was traded, I had a bad back—the first injury that put me out for a long period. I was surprised because I had never had any major injuries and this was very serious because I had trouble putting on my pants and my legs were numb. But the thing was that no one would believe me. I would go to the team and tell them and they'd look at me like, All right, all right, yeah, okay. So I had to check myself into the hospital. I told them I wanted to go into traction, and Donovan, Holzman, the whole brass went, Oh yeah, okay. So I told them I wanted to check into a hospital and I did for a week and it helped my back but not to the point where I could play. The front office kept giving me a sense that they didn't believe me—when I told Danny or Red they didn't act concerned." Reed also criticized the management's attitude toward one of his injuries, but Frazier said the situation of the two players wasn't similar. "They *were* concerned with Willis' knee: They sent him to a thousand different doctors. But they didn't send me to a back specialist in California or anything like that."

The injury exacerbated his already bad relations with the press and his teammates. Almost from the start of the '76 season, the press, which molds fans attitudes, had begun to suggest that Frazier was hindering the development of the team. Frazier thinks animosity inspired the criticism. "The press picked on me," he told me. "Some of it was probably jealousy. They didn't like my lifestyle. It couldn't have been from never talking to them. I always talked to them, win or lose. So it couldn't have been from a professional standpoint. It had to be from something deeper than that."

The new Knicks also betrayed him. "When I had my injury the players started talking against me. You know, it was

—well, the team is five and one without Frazier, or Beard [Butch Beard, the guard who substituted for Frazier and the present assistant coach of the team] is doing things that Frazier could never do, and just a whole lot of crap going on, and I wasn't out there. Guys were telling the press: We're a better team without Clyde, we're doing this without Clyde. You know I can take criticism from the fans. But coming from the players it's harder because this is like a family, whatever you say to them should never get out. So it's like your family speaking out against you when players speak out against you. It hurts."

The following season began more auspiciously. Rehabilitated from his injuries, Frazier played with enthusiasm. One pleasure I got from watching Frazier was that he communicated a primary, sensual enjoyment in playing the game. He loved the feel of winning—the ball leaving his hand for the final bucket, the extra second he lay on the floor after the man guarding him had made a frantic foul. He relished those moments and I enjoyed his gratification. This delight had disappeared the previous year as the team lost, replaced with a dogged indifference, the opposite side of his boyish enthusiasm, the game causing him pain and disappointment. Now his old charm reappeared. The Knicks had drafted a meaty, determined player named Lonnie Shelton, who quickly demonstrated his speed, strength, and agility at forward. The team won its first three games, almost holding their opponents to under 100 points, a token from the past, and on their first road trip—the test of excellence for any club—played respectably, a considerable improvement over the previous season. Sounding a note from the past, one columnist cleverly called the Frazier-Shelton combination the Lonnie and Clyde show. Then, in December, with the team skirting the .500 edge, they acquired McAdoo. Now they appeared to have a powerful combination in the front court, finally replacing Reed and DeBusschere (albeit with different sorts of talent), and they won their first several games, clobbering one team by some thirty-odd points. "The pack is back," Frazier told the press. But the promise disappeared within a month, and Frazier was again blamed for the defeats. Toward the end, his continued presence on the squad became an exercise in humiliation. He stopped talking to the press, resigned as team captain, and, finally, was benched as the team blew its chance to make the play-offs.

Frazier believes this downfall was partly inevitable. "I think people get what they deserve," he told me, and continued to say that he had been proud and arrogant when he was a success. "Some guys they cushion," he said, referring to management, the press, and all shadowy others who control the careers of players. "But they move the cushion. Some guys they bring down soft, and some they bring down hard—they move the cushion. I don't know why, but yes I do—it's because if you're really successful you create enemies who plot your downfall." He has less animus, but feels more disappointment, toward Holzman, whom he believes changed the nature of the team, creating a unit in which Frazier could not use his talents well. "The guys were selfish. It changed when all the old guys left. The new ones were scorers. They weren't team players and the team lost the team concept. I thought at first that we could make it a team, but then Red changed the team, all of a sudden he changed the whole concept he had before. He wanted us to run and get the ball downcourt. It was entirely geared to McAdoo, instead of just coming down and moving the ball and whoever gets the ball gets the shot. He just started giving those guys more shots and taking other guys out of the offense, especially going to McAdoo a lot, and the guards just became guys to run plays." In the end, the game robbed him of any pleasure. "The experience of playing on the team wasn't fun anymore." Then Holzman was replaced by the new coach. Right before the next season, Frazier was traded, exchanged with Cleveland for a player named Jim Cleamons, a publicly modest fellow with a taut, long, thin, alert face who played a steady, undramatic game and

who countered, in his appearance and performance, all the pa-
nache, beauty, and daring that Frazier had brought to the
Garden.

The press had predicted Frazier's departure from the team
for some time; still, he was surprised by the move. "When I
was traded, I was disappointed. I hadn't thought I was going
anywhere. I knew there had been trade rumors, but then it
had been silent for a time and so I was surprised. Besides, the
team had had a good pre-season and I had had a good pre-season. I was looking forward to playing. So it was disappointing.
It changed my whole life after ten years. It was disappointing." He found out about the trade from Weiner. "I can remember it like yesterday. I had been shopping and I pulled
into my building and saw Irwin. I said, Why is he here? He
had a very bewildered look on his face. He said, You've been
traded. I said, Damn!" For several days, it seemed that Frazier
might retire. Then he announced he would go to Cleveland.
"After I got over the hurt of being traded, I analyzed everything and on paper it seemed that Cleveland was the ideal
team for me." Fitch was a disciplined, intelligent coach who
believed in a strong defense and patterned offense, the sort of
ensemble play that Holzman had inspired in the championship
team and that the recent Knick squads, to Frazier's unhappiness, had abandoned, and the team had been playing quite
well, a contender for the Eastern Division championship
which, with Frazier, it seemed they now had a good chance of
winning.

New York fans got their first look at Frazier as a Cavalier in
the fourth game of the season. Frazier was uncertain about
what sort of welcome he could receive. "I was apprehensive. I
didn't know what to expect. I knew I'd get some applause—
how much I didn't know." The Garden was sold out, and
when Frazier's name was announced by the public-address
man, the crowd stood to honor him, cheering and applauding.
On the Knick bench, Ray Williams, the rookie who was Frazier's heir apparent, joined in the ovation, looking at Frazier

with awe and joy: Maybe this homage would belong to him one day? Frazier, standing by his new team's bench, lowered his head, thanking the crowd. But the cheering didn't stop, the noise subsiding for a moment, then starting anew, a rumble from above that gathered force, tumbling down through the crowd. With each new wave of hurrahs, Frazier lifted his head higher, until he claimed the moment totally, raising his hands to the crowd, his face as radiant and thankful with pleasure as a child's. Frazier then played with his astonishing brilliance of old, two hours later, in overtime, winning the contest with a jump shot and raising his hands again, this time forming two fists of triumph. "It was a great night," he told me, remembering the occasion. "It was like a Hollywood script—like everybody thinks the way I should have gone out. You know, it was a super game. It went into overtime. We won. The fans were happy. Everybody went away happy. Except the Knicks." He laughed mildly at this. "But that was just ego on their part. Because, you see, they thought, Hey, this guy can't do it anymore and then I came in and played a game like that, looking like the old Clyde. And they were really hurt because I had put on an exhibition like that. Whereas they would have liked me to play poorly and then would have looked justified to the fans, you see? But for me that night was enough—for my ego."

It had to suffice; the game marked the end of his glory. In Cleveland he suffered. A foot injury plagued him. After playing 51 games and averaging 16 points, he sat out the rest of his first season; the following year, he played 12 games, averaging 10.8 points before his injury benched him.

Then Fitch, the coach, claimed that Frazier was dogging it, exaggerating his complaint, really too old to play. Frazier implied he was being scapegoated for the team's disappointing performances. Their sense of mutual betrayal became public, each trading charges against the other in the papers, and finally Frazier stopped speaking to Fitch entirely. Frazier had already stopped attending games. His life was the gray depression he had suffered earlier in his career. His daily schedule was crushingly dull. After breakfast, he drove around shopping, went to malls, returned to his house, did sit-ups and push-ups, then ate dinner and watched television. He looked forward to Mondays because he could set the dial to Monday Night Football and concentrate on the game for three hours; other days he had to look in the papers to find out what he would watch. He didn't go on the road with the team, and he drove to the Coliseum on game nights only when he wanted to see other teams play. He was living with a woman whom he liked a lot but didn't love. But she was important: If he hadn't been with someone, he told me, he would have died of isolation.

The summer following his second season with the team, he worked hard to get into shape. His contract ended with the '79–'80 season and he had already decided he would then retire. "Rather than like saying, Hey, I'm caught off-guard because I didn't expect something," he told me, "I was expecting my career to be over because I knew when my contract was up that that would be it. So I got my life in order. I put my priorities first, cut down on expenses, and started saving my money and getting into things I wanted to do. I was very enthusiastic about the year. I was looking forward to having a good year." But when the preseason began it seemed clear that Frazier's career would end sooner than he had imagined. The Cavaliers had changed coaches and the new one wanted a quick team and felt Frazier dragged on the squad's speed. On October 22, the Cavaliers announced they were waiving him: Frazier was available to any team interested. There was some speculation that a play-off team might pick him up, but, for all his passivity, Frazier remains a strong personality on the court and teams didn't want to change their rosters. He returned to New York.

As with his trade, Frazier had not anticipated being waived. He hadn't been reading the papers—"they started me to hate people and I don't want to hate anybody"—and he didn't suspect his career was over until the coach told him. "I thought they'd just keep me," he said, "that I'd be there for the whole year. It was obvious that I wasn't going to play that much. But I did think I'd be there." Still, when I spoke to him several days after the news, he seemed to insist to himself that he not take the development too hard. I suggested the main result of being waived was missing the emotional satisfaction of enjoying a final year in the league. He agreed. "But then, when I look at that," he added, "that's all ego too because I don't really believe in the principle of most people that you've got to go out in glory. I don't feel that has anything to do with my life right now. I'm happy. I'm happy because I played twelve years. I'm happy because I'm leaving the game the same person I was when I started. I'm not injured, and I'm still a very down-to-earth person, I don't have any hang-ups. I have everything, I have a clear conscience, and I enjoyed it, and I have no regrets. Of course I would have liked to have gone out better, playing or whatever—but to me once you're dead, what's the difference how you die?" I asked him whether or not he missed the nights that different teams would have organized to honor him. He laughed. "I had my nights. They can't give me a night that I haven't already had there, man. See, all that to me is ego."

Later he even claimed that the whole Cleveland episode had been beneficial. "The two best things that ever happened to me were coming to New York and leaving it," he said in a neat turn of phrase. "I think the trade was the final development into making me a man. When I was traded, it was more than a cultural shock. It was sort of a put-down. I had to regroup mentally. I did a lot of reading, a lot of soul-searching. I decided that all this was something that was meant to be: It was part of my destiny." In his curious scheme of personality, he was now more Walt Frazier than Clyde—60 percent Walt Frazier, the "quiet, shy person," who after years of "being a receiver now wanted to give back to people what they gave to me."

In December, the Knicks organized a night to honor him, and a sellout crowd cheered as representatives from the city and the team gave him plaques commemorating his performances, signed by his old teammates, several of whom looked on. One was a citation from the Police Athletic League showing a picture out of a Boys' Town past with a white cop and white girl and boy, a surrealist vision for New York in 1980. Another was a scroll presenting a resolution from the New York City Council commending Frazier and including in its whereases his "ability to penetrate, pass to his blind side, steal the ball, start fast breaks, rebound, and score." The last was a silver serving plate signed by his teammates including Nate Bowman, who added parentheses enclosing the word "great" under his name, and Danny Whelan, the trainer, whose melismatic signature covered almost a quarter of the platter. Frazier thanked them all, received another magnificent ovation, and disappeared from the court.

He began working in his office. He still didn't mind his manner of leaving the game. "It didn't bother me that I was waived—that has nothing to do with your life afterward. You know, like I hear guys say, This guy's a loser because he went out this way—that has nothing to do with it. I know guys who went out winners and they're losers, because they haven't adjusted, so I wasn't concerned about that." Still he was depressed. "I was uncomfortable in the office. It was new for me. I felt strange. Right after I was waived, I felt fine because I was so glad to leave Cleveland. But it was too soon to determine what my real reaction would be. Once I was here, I was depressed: when I started reading the paper about the games, the guys playing. Basketball was something I had done for twelve years, not counting grade school, high school, or college, and even though I had planned to retire anyway that year, it was an adjustment for me. That had been my whole life—basketball."

Now, he didn't surrender to the depression. "I tried to get busy here, compensate for feeling bad, learn the business, get

out, and meet people." His job is to help recruit college athletes to sign with the firm. When Frazier was in school only
the top professional athletes had agents; the commercial value
of athletes has increased so much since then that agents want
to claim them as their property even before they enter the
market. "There's a lot more pressure now on players than
when I was in college—back then no one tried to sign me as
an agent. Agents weren't that prevalent. Now everyone's an
agent. It's almost like deciding on a college—the agents are
after you all the time. Everyone is an agent because all you
need to get is one top player and you'll make a lot of money."

Frazier holds out the unspoken promise of repeating his
own success for the young athletes and obtains a certain cachet
from his celebrity status, but still must pursue them as all the
other agents do and hasn't scored any particular triumphs. "I
contact the players to convince them my company is the best
one for them," he explained to me, enjoying the topic. "I give
them a couple of reasons as to why they should join. First of
all, I've been there, I've been a player, I know what they
should expect from their own careers, and I can guide them in
saving their money. The company itself, even without me, is
good. It's a complete package company: We do endorsements,
commercials, financial advice, taxes, etc. They buy a house, a
car—anything they do with money we can advise them. I call
the guys. I know the top ones who are coming out. Everybody
does. So you've got to get to them, that's the problem. Last
year, I worked out of this office and we didn't sign anyone. I
was learning the ropes. Now I know that to sign these guys
you've got to be in the field. I'm like a social worker: I've got
to go out and meet them, beat the bushes, so to speak. I tour
the colleges and go to certain games, but once I visit a guy I
just keep in contact by phone. Personal contact is important
because I want to know what a guy is like. Even if he has talent, the guy may not be what we want: level-headed, conservative in their spending, dedicated to the game and their
family, that type of stuff, just good people in their hearts first.

I find that most of the guys we represent are like that. I take them out to dinner, meet them in their room, whatever, see if they're interested. A lot of players say, Hey, I don't want to talk until after the season. So then I go to their mother, father, cousin, coach—you've *got* to go through someone else because you can't wait until the end of the season because someone's going to get to them before it's over. The kids are impressed to meet with me. When I call and say it's Walt Frazier they all listen. But that doesn't mean I can sign them. Sometimes they're already committed. We flew in forty guys to see the company and everything last year, but we got nothing because they were already committed."

He is pleased with his company. "I decided it was a blessing I have this company because if I didn't have this, I would be bored like other ex-players who have nothing to do, nothing to call their own. I'm my own boss, keep my own hours, have my own company. In a way that's a high. Like you say, Hey, I don't want to go to work today, and you don't. So it's a real blessing. Best move I made." But his former success as a player gives him a cooler view toward it than a businessman would have. "See, my thing now isn't money. I know if this [the company] doesn't work, I still have enough to be comfortable. So there's no pressure on me here as there is in a game where you rise up to meet the situation. Like last year we signed only three players. Maybe this year we'll sign only five. But there's no pressure to sign five. If we don't, we don't. We're still balancing the books by doing other things. My personal goal is to have this company be the top agency in its field. But it's not a necessity. If I don't do it, I won't see it as a great loss. See, most people when they have money seek power. I don't. I have money, I'm happy, which is the main thing, and I have a job, which is what I do."

Without the game, and since his trade to Cleveland, his life has changed. "I've cut down my personal life. I might go out Wednesdays and Fridays. And if I do go out, I've got to rest a night. I can't do one after the other. When I played with the

292 / DREAM TEAM

Knicks I was a night person. I wouldn't leave the house until
eleven, then practice, go home, lay up, then the game, and my
night would start. Now I'm a day person. It developed in
Cleveland. It was too cold to go out and there was no action,
so I just stayed in. I go to a play and at twelve I'm ready for
sleep. I feel better when I go to sleep early, get up, run, rather
than staying out all night. I just like that lifestyle. I'm happier."

He is pleased by the public recognition he still receives. "If
you were with me when I walk down the street in New York
you'd think I was still playing, and I think that's great because
I gave the Knicks my best years and I think it's wonderful
that people still remember me. Now I haven't played in New
York for three years or so and the adulation is still there.
I didn't expect that. I didn't know what to expect because I
know once you leave you're most often forgotten. So when
I came back—myself, I figured, Hey, I'm no longer a player so
no one will recognize me. So when they do it catches me off
guard a lot." He is often also noticed on his frequent travels
for the company. "I don't ride first class because I don't drink
and I don't eat the food"—Frazier likes health foods—"so
why spend the money? Just for the ego trip? No. So I ride in
coach. People come up to me, especially New Yorkers because New Yorkers are everywhere. Last week I was in Detroit and people ran up to me. They asked me for autographs.
I'll tell you a funny story. I was in Vegas and a guy comes up
and asks if I'm Walt Frazier. I said, Yeah. He said, Wait a
minute and I'll be right back. So another guy comes up and
says, Are you Walt Frazier? I say, Yeah, and he says, Damnit!
I just lost a hundred dollars!

"The thing I miss most about the team is the camaraderie
with the players. Bullshit in the locker room, just fooling
around. My social life isn't as much fun now because this is a
business. You don't hear the 'motherfuckers' coming out of
here like you do in the locker room, where every other word
is a curse. And the experiences the other guys are going

through—it's hilarious, man. You know, after the games, the funny things that happen. Like a guy like Barnett who played so long is always funny—I miss that. Or Red or Danny—they're always keeping something up, there's never a dull moment. I liked traveling with those guys because of that. I liked talking to Danny with his stories. Red, Barnett, Lucas, when he was there, with his card tricks and all. Bradley having holes in his socks. Have you seen him recently? He's got the chin, everything, he's gained like a hundred pounds. I saw pictures of him and I couldn't believe it. He loves ice cream and the junk food—he loves dessert. Mike Riordan never sitting down to eat a meal, always standing to read a paper. All these things were really funny. Plus we were winning so that made it all great. And the practices were light because Red never overdid it. He had everything under control. Once we started to lose, he would make it harder; once we were winning, it was easy. And then too you have no problems because your life is mapped out. Like I used to say, All you have to do is show up. You just ride and play and everything's mapped out for six or seven months."

Since being waived, he hasn't played basketball at all. "Not even shooting around by myself in a gym. No shooting around, no fantasies of ever coming back. I just accepted it."

Not playing has deprived him of a satisfaction he found only in the game. Frazier dismissed the idea that he could save himself for the crucial moments in games. "I wasn't that great," he told me. "People used to say that I could reserve myself for clutch situations, but I didn't have that control." Indeed, his excellence came from pure excitement. "I just got turned on during the fourth quarters. I think that's why I never excelled in Cleveland—because there were never that many games that had pressure situations." This excitement gave him a pleasure that has proved irreplaceable and inimitable. "I miss the excitement of the game, the last five minutes. That's the only time my palms get wet and I really get into it—when the pressure is on. I was always a good clutch player. When I was in grade school, high school, and college, I was always the leader of the team and when it was a pressure situation the coaches would always say, Frazier, take the ball, Frazier. In college, I was a guard, but during the game I would never bring the ball up-court; but at the end, the coach would tell me to handle it. That made me feel good inside, to meet a challenge and do it, or even if I didn't do it, to know that I gave my best, that I didn't choke. So I was used to handling the pressure and I liked it because it was the time of my greatest concentration: My head was clear and I concentrated totally on what I was doing. I had moments like that before but never so intense and I loved them. There's nothing I've found to take the place of that."

# 10

And Willis? The big man, the center, the captain—what happened to him? He became coach, of course, the man picked to replace Holzman and restore the team's glory. His return was Napoleonic: heralded, brief, disastrous. Given command in spring '77, he drafted the players he wanted, won his Garden debut, and directed the team to a respectable 43–39 record. Then his defeats began. Performing poorly in the play-off tournament, the team closed the season with a series of embarrassingly one-sided losses that disappointed even the faintest hopes of the fans. His attraction as a celebrity already worn thin, he was picked on by the press. The management didn't defend him. He squabbled with the team's owner, saying the Knicks needed a center to win, a call for reinforcements that sounded like an excuse for the team's poor showing. Fourteen games into the new season he challenged the management again, now demanding they deny any rumors he might be fired. This time he was promptly fired, Holzman being summoned to replace him. Within less than two years he had gone from hero to disgraced loser. His triumphant return had resulted in the only failure he had ever experienced with the team.

Reed's story follows the standard plot for classic heroes. Like a mythic character, he arrived without fanfare to the team—the city he would eventually rule. He met a challenge —first beating Barnes and taking the center position, then fighting Bellamy for it. Receiving early acclaim as Rookie of the Year, Willis fulfilled his promise when he finally was granted his rightful spot as captain, and under his rule, the team thrived. But then a mysterious plague struck it—his numerous injuries. He resisted the plague for a while and even managed to reclaim some past glory, the second championship, but finally was forced to surrender to his disability and left in some confusion and disgrace. When he returned to re-establish his rule, his powers were fading and his character betrayed him. He was outcast. Other similarities can be pointed out—Reed's strength and will represent the superhuman qualities with which mythic kings were endowed. But the point doesn't need to be stretched. Reed is a genuine American folk hero—not a modern man, driven by inconsistencies and equivocations, but a classic figure of ineluctable qualities and single pursuits.

In basketball, Reed occupies a special niche. He is the big man. The phrase is a special endearment of the game: Hey! It's the big guy! It refers both to a player's size, his responsibilities, and the scope of his accomplishments, or, at least, what other players imagine will be his accomplishments. The big man is the leader and is expected to stop the other team from scoring, hit clutch baskets, and set the tone for the team: partygoer, family man, or religious devout. He is imagined to be both invulnerable and indefatigable, and at the same time must always prove his worth. He fails relative to his prom-

296 / DREAM TEAM

ise and no one attracts more bitter resentment than the big man who doesn't measure up to his promised greatness. In a game dominated by height, he is the quintessential figure, and Reed is the quintessential big man. What he lacks in height—he stands a slight, by the standards of his peers, six feet ten—he compensates for in width and might: His torso is so thickly muscled that his powerful arms and legs seem delicate in comparison. This size and his reputation as a scrapper make him a physically intimidating person. When Reed was hired as Knick coach, writers implied he would discipline recalcitrant players better than Holzman because the athletes would be afraid to contradict him. The idea seemed ridiculous to me: Adults, the players weren't small themselves. After meeting Reed, I changed my mind. He's no bully, but his natural, physical force is a constant presence, and my unconscious tendency in his presence was not to provoke him.

He is also a commanding person emotionally. Part of his appeal is a simple, old-fashioned manliness. "There are three things I like to do," he told me. "I like to hunt and fish, and I love basketball and I love chasing girls." During our first meeting, we were standing in the elevator of his apartment building when a woman walking a small poodle on a long leash joined us. The dog sniffed Reed's foot—his shoe was longer than the animal—and immediately set to barking vociferously at the giant towering above him. Reed asked the owner if the dog was male. When she answered yes, he admonished the pooch: "Don't be afraid of me. Men aren't supposed to be afraid of each other." This was silly and there is an almost clownishly simple aspect about Reed's devotions, except that—at least in the presence of another man who was no relation to him—he applies his principles so democratically that you end up feeling an unusual freedom with him. In his presence, you feel no constraint about acting properly or thinking correct ideas; there is no worry about what is right. He presents himself with a remarkable ease, free of all self-consciousness. He yawns and mumbles when he speaks about his injuries, and livens up when he recounts past triumphs, smacking his thigh and talking animatedly, re-creating the past. He suggests a kind of Whitmanesque decency—*Not 'til the sun excludes you, do I exclude you*—but without Whitman's preciousness or morbidity. It is as though Reed is so large that he needn't bother protecting himself against the faults and anxieties most people worry about, especially failure, which he seems to face fearlessly, accepting it as neither shameful nor disastrous, but as a necessary part of people's social careers. His physical size is an emblem of his emotional being: Without bombast, he defies pettiness.

Partly this openness is a public display, Willis acting the role life has assigned to him. Larry Fleisher, Reed's agent and friend, told me that, as Willis prepared to end his career, he really didn't pursue jobs outside of basketball. Fleisher believes that Reed's reluctance stemmed from the unusual respect he enjoyed receiving from fans. "There have been very few athletes in the history of the world who have been as idolized as Willis Reed was in New York. He was in a different category than DeBusschere or Bradley. Willis was just loved. He would walk down the street and people would run out of the doorways to say hello to him. People respected DeBusschere and Bradley for the kind of person they were, but the only time I've ever seen anything close to the kind of feeling Willis got in New York was when I went to a convention in Las Vegas with Havlicek [the Boston player] a month after he retired. It was awe-inspiring to see the people running over to shake his hand and thank him for the years of enjoyment he gave them —he reflected all the things they wanted their kids to be. Willis had that kind of respect in New York and I think it was hard for him to step away from that."

He still can't. His life remains shaped by the game. Since the Knicks fired him, he has pursued other coaching positions. He continues to show up periodically at Knick games. This past winter, he worked for his friend, Lou Carnesecca, the coach of St. John's, instructing the big men on the subtleties of front-court play. He discusses basketball and his experience with the Knicks in almost endless detail. The game even determines his domestic life. Divorced from his wife of nine years and the mother of his two children in 1969, he still lives alone, a condition partly desired because it leaves him free to lead the single life demanded by the game. Over his bedroom door— you get a glimpse of a vast bed opposite a wall of home-entertainment equipment—hangs a sign announcing "The Captain's Quarters." In the living room, a bear's head and a deer's stare from one wall; a breakfront filled with plaques and trophies commemorates his basketball career; a replica of Rodin's "The Kiss" decorates one coffee table. Reed moved here when he got the job with the Knicks, and the location suggests the dramatic crisis he confronts in his life. Situated on the upper floor of a high-rise, East Side midtown apartment building, it is an island of exile: When you look out the large living-room windows you see a fantastic cityscape of lights and traffic that lead straight across town to the forbidden kingdom of Madison Square Garden.

Still, Willis and his predicament isn't simply another story of a ballplayer unprepared for middle-aged spread and bad knees: Cazzie Russell's saga is the epic poem of those unhappy tales. Being fired from the Knicks certainly hurt Reed's ego. "Here's a man who has enormous pride," Fleisher said to me, "who always wants to succeed in anything he does and he thinks—because of what the world feels—that he's a failure: He got fired and he's a failure. So he would like to show that it [his dismissal] was a mistake."

But for Reed basketball is more than a profession at which he has been successful. The game is an art. He loves the craft and discipline of his labor, not just the adulation of the crowd or the sudden moment of inspiration, but the slow struggle by which mastery emerges. "I played against players with more skills," he told me, "but they didn't have my powers of concentration and analysis. Everyone rates me as a great player, but I am a product of work." Later, discussing his early years in the game, he said, "The only thing I had when I started was a decent shooting touch and my height. Everything else I developed. And because of my family background I always gave one hundred percent. It might be only equal to ninety or eighty percent of yours, but it's everything I have to give. So that helped me, and I went out and learned the game."

At times, this insistence on practice and devotion seems a kind of athletic Reaganism: the self-satisfaction of a financially and socially secure man who attributes the failings of others to faults of character, not circumstance. But again, for Reed, the satisfaction of work is in the striving, not merely the reward, the effort—always, to his mind, a collective one in basketball—and working out of detail, never the prize. His predicament has a dignity denied to other players because of all his colleagues only he, when talking about basketball, articulates a vision of life. The game is not simply a means of survival, understanding, or gratification to him, but the practice by which he realizes his imagination in the world, and he speaks about his performances in these terms. "Life changes," he said to me while talking about the uncertainty of his future when he was a player. "That's the excitement life gives you. That's the excitement of getting up one day and reading in the paper that the Knicks have won the world championship or that people nowadays speak of me as a great basketball player. But when you start out, nobody knows the limits of your abilities and your accomplishment. You're only limited by your own imagination and the amount you're willing to pay for it. And for me there were no limits because I always felt that no matter how well I play tonight I can play a better ball game tomorrow. You asked me who was hard to play against? Hell, they were all hard. You think if they weren't named Russell or Chamberlain that I laid back or said I could go out and stand around? No. I had given a commitment that I was going to give one hundred percent of myself every night no matter who I played against, no matter how much we got beat by or by how much we won. That was my job. And I worked long enough from the time I was a kid not to need anybody standing over me when I do a job. My job to me was always very important. I took pride in it. Sportswriters used to ask me what I wanted people to say when I retired. I said, That I gave one hundred percent. Because that's all you can be sure of because no one knows their ability until it's all over."

Later, we were speaking about the effects of winning the championship. Reed mentioned that he had been challenged more rigorously by his opponents and played harder game by game the year after winning the title. "When you went into an arena and they said, the World Champion New York Knickerbockers, hell, every guy on the other side said, Hell, if we win tonight we'll make our week, our month, our season. And they'd get hepped up to beat us." Hadn't teams felt that way the year before, when the Knicks were so lauded by the press? "Yes, it was somewhat true," he answered, "but let me put it this way: Until you win it, you haven't won it. Like people would always say Frazier was a great player. They'd rate him with Jerry West and Oscar Robertson. I'd say, I can't. Once he plays ten years then I can rate him with those guys. But I mean he might go out and have two great seasons and maybe no more. Hell, now, I rate him as the third best guard I ever saw, but that's at the end of his career."

The end of Willis's career started at the peak of his athletic triumph, during the championship year. He was injured then for the first time in his pro career, the start of many disabilities that eventually forced him off the court. Occasionally stretching out on his couch, leaning back and rubbing his hands over his face as though he were a sleepy child, a depressed and uncharacteristically fatigued manner for him, he told me the tale of these difficulties in an almost singsong, by-rote fashion.

The first injury was to his knee and prepared the way for the famous fall in the fifth game of the championship. "I had injured my left knee in November 1969," he said, starting the recital of dates and incidents that are his by now well-memorized litany of defeat. "It bothered and bothered me and eventually I had to have some shots of cortisone in it. And in the fifth game of the play-offs there was some discussion about whether I should have a shot, and I really wanted one; and I favored it as I pushed off, going for a drive to the hoop against Wilt, and pulled some muscles in my hip.

"Going back that fall, I didn't have much problem with that, but in November 1970, it started bothering me again. So the doctor said you can't do any damage playing on it and so I did. We got into the first round of the play-offs and we beat them, and in the last game I hurt my shoulder. Then we struggled through a series with the Bullets, who eventually beat us in the seventh game on a last shot. My knee, the left one, was still bothering me so we decided to have an operation and did rehabilitation. I came back, but it was still bothering me a little, and I guess around November I couldn't play anymore. So I went to Oklahoma City to see a specialist and he told me not to play again and put the knee in a cast for six weeks and then start rehabilitating it again. And that year the team played without me and went all the way to the play-offs but lost to the Lakers."

At first his progress was discouraging. "I struggled along through it, playing some good, then playing bad." He felt abandoned and isolated. "My own determination got me back to play. If I had been a very weak person, I don't think I would ever have made it back. If you read all the print and had to go through all the pain—a lot of people wouldn't have been able to handle it. And the press doesn't make it easier. They don't know; they write ignorant stuff." But he had successfully worked himself back into shape by the play-offs and led the team in their victory over the Lakers, a surprising and personally rewarding triumph. "You remember the first girl you fell in love with? The first championship was like that. Everybody in New York was all hepped up about it and you knew it was going to happen. In '69 we lost [to Boston] because Frazier got hurt, and we lost by just a few, and that night in the locker room DeBusschere said, Hell, next year's ours, and I felt that way and everybody felt that way. We started off good in camp and everybody played well and it was a glamor year: Everything fell into place and everybody came together with the right frame of mind. But the '73 championship was more gratifying because I had been through some hard times and coming back to play was good. We won in '72–'73 because I was healthy. We took the same identical team and we played the same team that we had lost to a year before and there was only one player different: me. They voted me most valuable player. As far as I was concerned, I think Frazier deserved it. They said I had a better series, but I thought that he had played so well before that he was the one who had got us to the final series. I think he was upset—his agent was—but for me winning most valuable player wasn't important because basketball is a team sport. But to come back to play was a great thing, a personal triumph."

At the time, he imagined his career would last three more years. The year before, while still recovering from his injury, he had negotiated a new contract with the team. "I hoped to play to the end of my contract. It would have given twelve years altogether in pro ball, which was enough. Larry [Fleisher, his lawyer] said to me, Well, we'll tack on another year. I said, Larry, don't tack no more on. He said, What? I said, Don't tack anymore on. If I can live up to these four more years that's all I want. I don't need any more ball—not to play. I don't want to play unless I can contribute and I don't think after another four years I'll be mentally and emotionally able to contribute."

But his comeback ended abruptly. "The next season we went out to the West Coast—I guess it was November again— and I was running down the floor and I hear something snap in this leg, my right knee. Up until then, I had never had any problem with it. So I ran up and down the floor two more times and called a time-out and told Red there was something wrong in my knee. That night, the team went on to Portland, and I came back to New York. The doctor looked at it and he thought it was a sprain and didn't think there was too much wrong with it. So I took some therapy and went back and played a few games and it got to the point where it was beyond playing on it. I returned to the doctor and I took tests and it came out negative and they couldn't determine what it was. So I went to Oklahoma City and the specialist there said he thought I had a torn cartilage. I had an operation on it and I started the rehabilitation process, figuring we would make the play-offs, and I did a lot of work hoping to come back to play. But really I was very ineffective and after we got beat by Boston I took off for the summer. Finally I went back to Oklahoma City. The specialist looked at the knee. I told him I had some pain in it during the play-offs. He said he thought I was going to have it operated on. So I said, Well, I don't know about that, and finally I decided I didn't want to have the surgery."

The decision ended his career. Essentially, he made it alone, defying everyone's advice, even Fleisher arguing against it. "I told Larry I wasn't having the operation and he got upset about it. He said, No no, don't say that. I said, This is my life and my career and I don't want my career to end this way but I want to be able to walk the rest of my life." He believed he had sacrificed himself physically for the team. "I had too many shots for my lifetime. I used to sprain my ankle all the time and the doctor would give me an injection and I hated them. He used to laugh. That was great! He's sticking the needle in me and he's laughing! Sometimes I thought about sticking the needle in him!" Now he simply no longer wanted to submit himself to the pain and anxiety of an uncertain rehabilitation: The failures of his body had exhausted him. "I said to everybody, I'm not opposed to having surgery, but is anybody going to guarantee me that if I have surgery it's going to be all right? The knee was already to some degree arthritic and I wanted someone to give me some guarantee and when nobody did I said, Well, I'm not going to mess around with it. I didn't want to go through what I had with the other knee. I played on my knee all that time and went through that and I said, Well, if the doctors aren't willing to make a commitment, there's no sense of me going out and endangering myself. I did it the first time, and I was lucky and came back and played, but this was a different kind of problem."

The peremptory end of his career frustrated him. "I knew basketball was going to end someday. I knew I'd have to live and do something else, and I prepared for that by not spending all my money. That's always the most important thing. In fact, I'm living now better than I lived then because then you never knew when the water would be shut off. But I was disappointed that I had to quit. You see, players get older and the question is whether they can contribute to a team as they age. And that's what I wanted to do. You always have the dream that out there right now there's some kid practicing and getting ready and that one day he's going to come and take your job, and when it's all over you'll just clean out your locker and enjoy it. But I didn't walk out the way I wanted to. I had a very successful career, but it did leave me with permanent damage."

He returned to Louisiana and his other love, hunting. Reed frequently compares hunting to basketball. For him, both activities are studies in chance versus skill, disciplines of pursuit. (Though he is no sentimentalist. He doesn't only hunt, but also kills. Similarly, the trophies from those presumably unimportant victories fill an eye-catching wall in his apartment.) Still, the hunt didn't replace basketball. "I had thought of doing a lot of things when I quit. Originally, I had been in several businesses, and I went down to Louisiana and I did some of them. But after a while when I was away from pro basketball I really started to miss it. Which I hadn't expected. I hadn't thought I would want to be involved with management, though I was always interested in coaching because I was the captain and I did other things because Red didn't have any assistants and so I had to listen to everybody's problems and I had been a captain a long time. But I started missing the game. I never missed playing because I'm satisfied I did as good a job playing as I could and I always knew sooner or later I wouldn't play anymore. So I wasn't disappointed about that. But I still enjoyed working with the guys, teaching them how to do certain things with the ball."

Within the first year of his retirement, Reed spoke to the Knicks about a job coaching. Holzman still had a season outstanding on his contract and the management suggested Reed work as his old coach's assistant. "Eddie" [Donovan] was instrumental in getting me to coach. There was talk about me being an assistant. But I felt I had been an assistant already when I played for Red. I had watched him coach and ninety percent of everything we ran on offense didn't come from Holzman anyway. We came into the time-outs and said, Hey, I got a play for me, or I got a play for you, and Red would say, I don't give a damn what you guys want to run, just run it. The only thing he did was the defense—we played defense the way he wanted."

Insistent on working alone, Reed negotiated with another team. "I started talking to people in Buffalo for a job and we came a long way. I went up to see the owner in the middle of a snowstorm—you know, when there were mounds and mounds of snow up there and everybody was digging out? And then I went to see the man again and we talked coaching philosophy and then we got to the point where we talked money and it was pretty much set that I would go there." But the Knickerbockers fought to keep their symbol. "Then the Knicks said that Red was going to retire. So I talked with Mr. Cohen and Mr. Burke [then the owner of Madison Square Garden, and the president of the club] and I said, Well, if I'm going to be coach, I don't want to be coach in June, I want to be hired and go to work now because there's a lot of work to be done—scouting teams, scouting talent, and preparing for the draft. So I got hired on and got a chance to look the league over."

The new job ordered Reed's life. As a player, he had lived

by a strict schedule, his natural appetite for pleasure curbed by his conscientious attitude toward the game. "I always put business before pleasure. If I had a game the next night, I'd meet a girl, have some drinks, fool around. But the day of the game, no. I'd try not to do anything that would get me nervous—any bullshit on the outside. We'd shoot around, then I'd hang around the house, do errands, take out the laundry, and cook my own meal, lay down, and try to get my head ready to play. My priorities were very set. Temptation? If you can let yourself be tempted to do something that would be detrimental to you and the team, then you're not the right player for the team on a certain level. You'll never get to be what you could be if those temptations get in your way."

As a coach, he resumed this discipline. "When I played basketball, people would say, You're great. I'd say, I don't know. Greatness is a word I'm awed by because what's great this minute, month, or year won't be the next. You have a great game this night and you win. But that doesn't give you any privilege when you play tonight's game. You've got to always prove it. I feel that the main thing about being in basketball was that I knew I had a lot to learn and I spent a lot of time working. When I was coaching we had a scouting service and they'd tell us, This guy's great and this guy's good. But I'd say, I want to see this guy, and I want to see how good he is. There were days when I came back from Chattanooga, Tennessee, from seeing a game at four in the morning and go to a practice at the Garden at ten."

His insistence on picking his players stemmed from his natual pride and his experience in the game. "You see, some coaches think that their strategy is more important than the players. Obviously both are important, but the greatest play in the world is no good unless you have someone to execute it, and you've got to get the players disciplined enough to do it. The bottom line is always the players." He told me a funny story about Julius Erving to illustrate the point. "You know Lou Carnesecca [the coach of St. John's] and I are good friends, and when Julius Erving was coming out of high school in Roosevelt, Long Island, Louie called me up and said, Hey Willis, this kid, I really love him, he's going to be a great player and we really want to recruit him and I need your help. So I invited Julius over. And you know he was all, Yes sir, and No sir, had a nice little bow tie on, about six-three then, had a nice 'fro. But he goes on to Massachusetts. [Erving attended the University of Massachusetts before turning pro.] Next thing you know, a few years later, the guy's grown four inches and he's doing all these funny dunks. So I have a good friend in Westchester County that I go hunting with and Louie and I are going up there to do some pheasant hunting. I pick him up and we're driving along and I said, Louie, remember when you had me try to recruit Julius Erving? Yep, yep, yep, he said, and then he looks at me. You know, he says, he could have made me a great coach!"

His attitude differed sharply from the ones he heard expressed by his new colleagues. "A lot of coaches think their players are overpaid. I listen to them say that. I took notes at a coaches' meeting and I said to myself, I can't believe this! I can't believe a man would say such things about a man upon whom he is dependent on making his living! The man who provides him with bread and money so that he can do the things he wants to do! If you don't like your players get new ones. The people I was coaching were different from the ones I played with, and I accepted that and dealt with it."

The first player to go was Frazier. His trade was widely seen as a predictable move, Reed wanting to be the only veteran influence on the team. Accepting only partial responsibility for the decision, Reed believes he has been unfairly blamed for the deal. "People said the trade for Frazier was Willis's fault, that I wanted to get rid of him. Management wanted to get rid of him anyway—from the top man to the coach. You just read the papers before I arrived and you'll see they were very unhappy with Frazier. If I had that much influence and could walk in and tell Donovan and Werblin [the new owner] and Mike Burke what to do, I would still have the job." Another member of the team's front office essentially confirms Reed's story. "He [Willis] wanted either Frazier or Monroe out. He thought they weren't compatible and I agree: if you were going to bring someone else along. Because if you have the two of them you've got to stay with them."

The beneficiaries of his rule were rookies. Two of them, Ray Williams and Michael Ray Richardson, emerged as excellent guards, and another, Toby Knight, turned into a reliable, fluid forward. Reed is not bashful about this record of excellence. He is especially proud of Richardson, who played unpromisingly in his first year—the season Reed was fired—but bloomed as a sophomore, leading the league in steals and assists. Reed had used a valuable draft pick to acquire Richardson, and his judgment had been discredited by Richardson's poor first season. The player's sudden emergence as an unusually gifted athlete confirmed Reed's intelligence and daring. "I knew Richardson wasn't ready to play," he asserted to me. "I hoped he would come along sooner than he did. But I had faith in Richardson. I watched tapes and films of him. I couldn't have been wrong in his ability. I just knew it: This kid could play." To the detriment of the veterans he compared Richardson to Bradley and Russell. "Bill and Cazzie might be better shooters than Richardson but that's where it stops. After that Richardson is quicker, better with the ball, better rebounder, better defensive player. Bill's a nice passer. I respected his ability to pass the ball and I respected his ability to read the floor. But Richardson does all that. There's no comparison between him and them in quickness. I have never seen a guy his size do the things he does."

He also took pride in his style of coaching. He adopted a more personal manner than Holzman. In a fashion reminiscent of Eddie Donovan's, an admirer and in-house booster of Reed's, he frequently mentioned his interest in his young players. "I was concerned about Ray Williams," he told me while speaking of his coaching, "and about what would happen to him once he stopped playing basketball, because I have a feeling for him. I want him to be the best basketball player he could ever be and the best person he could ever be." Later, speaking about his hopes of coaching again, he said, "I want to touch the lives of the kids who are coming up on a different level." At the same time, he viewed the players he selected as representative of him, wanting them to express the determination, talent, and sacrifice that had marked his own performances—a vanity Holzman lacks entirely. "Coaching is a matter of teaching and spending time. You don't just go out and play basketball because you have ability—you've got to get a person emotionally and mentally ready to play. My way of coaching is that I need to understand the kid—their family, their personality, their background. These are all things that are very important when you're dealing with a kid, and you've got a problem with him. Sometimes you're sympathetic. Sometimes you kick him in the ass too—that's not against the rules. The first thing about a coach is to know what a player's capable of giving me. Then I can say he's busting his hump, but he's having a bad night. But if I see him out there and he thinks he's fooling me and himself and giving something poor as his best effort, then I'm going to be upset. I'll give you an instance of knowing your players. Sometimes kids who grew up without fathers think they're going to get special treatment because most women raising a child by themselves are very worried about being liked by him. And the same can be true for college coaches: They give these kids everything. And that affects how the kids will play as a pro. Things don't go the way they want to, they don't get the kind of time they want, and they get upset. So in order for a coach to be good, he must understand his players, know what motivates them, and makes them good people. I don't care if you give a guy a million dollars. If he's stubborn and lackadaisical, the money's not going to change him. The money's not going to make him what he's not. And if you want to stay in the business and build a team you want to get the kid who comes to practice at nine-thirty when it's called for ten and not the kid who shows up at nine fifty-nine. You want people who are more concerned about the team than themselves."

But Reed's warmest feelings are reserved for the players like himself: the big men. I asked how he judged Bill Cartwright, the present center for the Knicks who then was establishing himself as an offensive threat in the league. The assumption that Cartwright had already proved himself as a player annoyed Reed, and at my occasional urging he spoke about the training he believed necessary for centers. "Cartwright has got to learn all the little tricks that make you good," he said. "He doesn't know them. He's raw talent. Let me tell you something. You play against guys like Wilt and Russell, you learn things. I mean maybe I can just overpower you and shoot the ball, but you're not going to do that with Wilt or Russell. You're going to have to show them something else because they're going to miss that ball by maybe just that much and that's all you're going to have to get it past them to score. That's no great room for error. And that's the game. You see, guys say, Let's go out and play some ball. But learning basketball is working on your fundamentals. I spent a lot of days, a lot of hours, a lot of nights working, working by myself in the gym. You see, I didn't shoot a hook much in college. I didn't have to. I shot a jump shot. Then I came into the pros and I was shooting against seven-footers who could block my jumper. So I needed to mix my game up so I could trick them and they wouldn't know what I was doing all the time. In other words, you had to keep learning things. I learned to drive on them, and then shoot my hook off the drive. I learned to shoot my jumper off one foot—you know, come across, make the dribble, and instead of planting both feet on the floor, just come off of one foot. I learned to go under the basket and to the other side and use the rim and net as a protection to keep from getting the shot blocked. You've got to learn these things: If you don't learn when you're playing guys bigger and better than you—and let's be real factual, they were bigger and they were better—you'll lose. Or learning to shoot the jumper and make it and set the guy up. See, I'd go down two or three times and hit the open jumper. But my man's not coming out from around the basket. Now I come down and the crowd is roaring because I've hit two or three consecutive times and now I know when I get in my position that my man is going to have to come out. So I drive on him and I jam the ball. Now I'm going to really screw him up. I've embarrassed him because first I make three jumpers in a row and then I drove and dunked it on him. So he doesn't know what to do now. So the game is strategy—it's not just to play. You see, if I go out there and make a hell of a move to the hoop and get it blocked, I've got to get that block to work to my advantage. The next time I come down, I'll come down under control, make a strong drive, make like I'm going to shoot the lay-up, pull it back, under control, and come back this way"—Reed stretched his arm out, tossing the imaginary ball off his fingertips—"and then lay it up on the guy. You see, that's all knowing the game. A lot of my moves I could start and stop, and that was important. Or a lot of players can't pivot off their left and right feet. They can only pivot off of one. That's a little thing, but I would pivot off a different foot every time. And all this took a long time to learn. How good could Cartwright be? It depends on how good he wants to be and whether someone can impress on him the things he needs to know."

His proclivity for big men sparked his first trouble with the team's management. In Reed's rookie season as coach Bob McAdoo played center for the team. Reed relied on McAdoo and praises him unstintingly. Still, he considers McAdoo more a forward than a center and believes champion squads demand defensive players in the pivot. "Your successful teams in pro ball are the ones in which the center is defensively orientated, not offensively. The only team that had a leading scorer and won was Jabbar's. But you go back to Chamberlain and the year he won with Philly, he led the league in assists." [Not quite: He was the third best scorer, highest field-goal-percentage shooter, leading rebounder, and third best in assists.] "You go to Bill Walton, and Philadelphia was a great team, but he knocked them off with passing and defense, and got his points too. That's the kind of center I like because you can always get a guy to put the ball in the basket, but the things a center has got to do to get a team to win are different things."

Anxious to acquire a true center, Reed announced publicly that he probably wouldn't return to coach the team unless the Knicks got a true big man. Reed insisted to me that he intended the petulant-sounding comment merely as a realistic appraisal of the team's chances for success. "Management just didn't understand what I was saying. I was saying, If I don't have a center, I'm going to lose anyway and I'm not going to have a job so I'll just resign and save myself the agony of being fired. I've been around basketball long enough to know you can't win with forwards. The big man is dominant."

The management actually obliged Reed, acquiring the services of Marvin Webster, who had helped lead the Seattle SuperSonics to the championship round in the '78–'79 season. Upon his arrival in New York, however, Webster appeared diffident and moody—a free agent, he had wanted to stay in Seattle, but couldn't agree with the SuperSonics on a contract —and the team posted a mediocre record at the start of the season. Reed's demands about obtaining a center now seemed suspect and there were press stories about his imminent dismissal. Under attack, Reed, true to his combative nature, fought back. He demanded the management announce he would remain the coach. The ultimatum was a miscalculation. Since Reed was hired, the ownership of the Garden had changed, and the team was now being run by Sonny Werblin, a longtime sports entrepreneur who, reportedly, believed Reed was acting in an amateurish fashion and wanted to make an example of him. Consequently, when Reed refused to back down from his challenge, Werblin took him at his word. He fired him.

As a coach, Reed aroused a considerable amount of animosity. This hostility can't be attributed to his performance. Indeed, measured by any objective standard, Reed's rookie year as coach matched his admirable one as a player. He guided the team into the play-offs for their first appearance in three seasons; he picked excellent players; his judgments about the team proved correct—though they were acted upon only after he left. And he accomplished these things against formidable odds. Werblin didn't plot Reed's usurpation, but he offered the big man no support against his detractors. The press —always a personal fan club of Reed's—treated him rudely. The team itself was a mishmash of veterans, rookies, and journeymen, a squad for whom the only logical system was chaos. Still, practically no fans or sportswriters can find nice words for Reed as a coach. His firing is seen almost universally as an act of self-destruction, the same stubbornness and pride that had helped make him such a formidable player on court now turning him into a foolish and unpleasant man. "Willis said things at the end of this first season that set up things later," Larry Fleisher told me, referring to Reed's comments about needing a center and his eventual firing. "I told Willis a lot of things but he's a stubborn guy. He thought [these statements] would help him—help him with the players to show them that he was the guy to respect." Fleisher also couldn't persuade him to change his relations with the players. "I tried to talk to Willis a number of times. I represented a lot of the players and knew them, and I told him I thought he was being too autocratic. They hadn't been complaining, just discussing things with me. Most of the guys on the team, especially the veterans, wanted Willis to succeed, they were looking forward to it. He came up the first year he was coaching for Christmas. He brought a date and had dinner. We finished a bottle of brandy and talked, discussing his relations with the players and everyone else. I wasn't telling him he should be playing X instead of Y, but his reaction was very defensive and that's not part of Willis, it never was: We were always able to talk.

Now he justified everything." In Fleisher's view, the end was entirely predictable. "I did everything I could to tell him not to be a coach in pro ball. I think it's impossible to come out ahead. You think of the people and how many have been a coach and come out on the up, and here's Willis, who has been loved by the whole world and what is he going to get? At some point, he's going to be a loser."

Willis views the episode differently. He agrees he is stubborn—"I am a stubborn guy to a certain extent about certain things"—but believes he was a victim. "I don't think that a lot of what happened to me was a judgment of my ability. I think a lot of what happened was because of the media. Most of the stuff that was written—you read it: We never won because we beat the other team, but because they played badly. Willis Reed was always in the hot seat. That's the way the media writes. I won't pinpoint anybody especially. But I was depicted as not being this, that, or everything else. And I agree—someone getting into a business is not going to be as good as someone else in it. But one thing was certain: Any player who played for me knew he came to work because I didn't accept mediocrity based on the fact that you don't give me one hundred percent. And I think we got that. But I also think there were other things. I got hired by one management and fired by another and there were a lot of changes going on, lots of high corporate stuff that I don't even know or understand and I don't think there was anything I ever could have done to change my situation. Take management criticizing me for saying our team was not so good. They asked me why. I said, Because we're not. If you tell the fans you're going to be a championship team and then you're not, you're lying to them. Instead I said, We can make the play-offs, that's as good as we can be. And we did that and got to the second round. A goal was set and met. As far as my interaction with players, they said, Well, it's not the best. I said, Let me tell you something, guys will never be happy. Give them everything they want and they still won't be happy."

He is especially bitter toward the press. "There were internal problems on that team before I came and they traded some people and solved some of the problems. But when I was there if there were any problems in the team, I was faulted. But after I left, they didn't blame Holzman—they blamed the players, even though the players were the same." I asked if he thought the sportswriters criticized him more than Holzman because he was black. "It could be," he answered, adopting a Cazzie Russell-like caution. "Let me tell you something," he continued, "I've probably lived in more situations than you ever will and the one thing I've learned is that it don't make any difference to anybody else in the world but you whether or not you survive. Everybody makes guys fall guys. There are a lot of things that went down that I don't want to speak about. You go back and get every paper of the day I got fired and you go back and get tapes of every guy on television: Ain't nobody saying shit that was good. And there's a possibility that was because I was black."

Reed's hesitation to consider himself a victim of prejudice in this instance comes from his basic attitude toward people. "I'm not a small person when it comes to human nature," he told me. For him, racism is primarily caused by economics. "I don't think you can make any strict rules about whites coaching whites or blacks coaching blacks," he answered when I asked whether he thought he enjoyed an easier rapport with the players than Holzman because he was black. "You got blacks who grew up in white society and whites who grew up in black society. You can't group all black people as having the same experience. If you grew up in New York you don't have the same experience I had in Louisiana and there are white kids who grew up on the fringes of Harlem and have been relating to black kids all their lives and they don't have the same experience of white kids growing up in Westchester who only saw black people as maids and butlers. I think prejudice comes more from economics than color. Most things in our country are economic, not social, though people try to make it look social. You see, if I keep you down then I don't have to worry about you; but if you're up here, then I'm competing with you for the same job. A lot of times things are presented to us, the masses, as being racial, but it's economic. A little old lady buys a house out on the Island and everybody protests. Why? Because the value of their house is going to go down. So it's economical."

In a way, this attitude shelters him from the possibility that there may be people who don't like him simply because he is black. Instead, he views people as either good or bad. I asked him about a scary incident that had happened to him in the early '70s. Driving his car, Reed was stopped by a white cop, who drew a gun on him and ordered him out of the vehicle. The story goes that the cop blanched as Reed unwound himself from the car, and, holding an umbrella in his hand, offered the officer the alternative of letting him go and meeting him in court, or persisting and fighting with him. The cop chose the former and Reed pursued the case, finally winning it. Reed resisted talking about the matter. "Yeah, I had that situation," he told me, "but I survived it. I don't want to talk about it." I asked him why, and he challenged me. "Let me ask you a question. If someone came up to you and held a gun to your head and said he was going to blow your fucking brains out, would you want to talk about it? Because the difference as to whether or not I'm sitting here right now is whether or not he pulls the trigger." But he did pass judgment on the man. "Bad folks, bad people. I don't give a damn if you're black or white or part of any system, if you're bad, you're bad and you've got to take those bad people out of the system."

But if you're good you are excused your failings: Reed's more constant tendency. "There are a lot of small people in the world," he said while we were talking about the bad treatment he received from the press, "and I won't subject myself to that. I go to a friend's house and hunt with him and everything else, and we're good friends, close friends. But I don't think he would approve of my marrying his daughter. But I don't dislike him for that. He's looking at all the problems that could occur out of the fact that she's white and I'm black. This society sees color, man, and if you don't believe that, then you don't believe anything exists. So he doesn't think it will be the best thing for his daughter. He could be wrong. But I've got to respect his opinion."

He tried to adopt the same broad view toward the unpleasant memory of his dismissal. "I'm not a small person when it comes down to me and my coaching experience," he said. He told me Mike Richardson had called him recently to say things were different without him. "I said, Hey Sugar, things are always different—that's part of growing up and you've got to survive."

Still, he can't be content without the game. "I played some nights when I shouldn't have played," he told me. "All players do. Because they want to play. Maybe that's the reason I have a bad knee now. But if you're a player, a competitor, you want to be out there every night. Shit—you don't want the ball to go up and the whistle blow and you're not there—and that's the way you feel about it." Coaching only deepened this love. "The thing is that fans see a game and it's over or you see it on television and it's finished," he said while we spent some minutes discussing passing. "But I would watch games two or three times. You start looking at slow mo at certain things and you start looking at what was going on and you start seeing what players were doing and you can see things that were happening which you didn't see when you were right there on the floor. That's why coaching, to me, was tremendous. I was talking to some people tonight about doing some things, outside basketball, business things. Well, I would enjoy doing them, but obviously I wouldn't give them the total involvement I gave to basketball as a player or a coach. All that time I spent putting that team together, working with kids, even when they'd get huffy—I loved that."

In the profession, people say that Reed is obsessed with getting back to coaching. He doesn't deny it. "I've always been obsessed with basketball," he said. "I played basketball obsessively—that's the way I am. I tell you I'm going to do something and I do it. I'm not going to be halfway doing anything. I've never done things that way." For him, the pursuit is a matter of fate and necessity. "You must survive," he said. "Socially, economically. You've got to learn to take care of yourself. And it's amazing because I find a lot of brilliant people who don't survive. The guys that make it are the guys who go out and face the world. I don't know what my son wants to do, but I know, goddamn! that as hard a world as I faced, this one is tougher. And it don't mean shit that he has a better education or that I can say things to him or share his experiences with him. I paid a price for him to be where he is and he's going to have to pay a price. I chopped cotton and picked watermelons and those were good experiences. Now my son won't do them—the society has changed—but my son will be very lucky if he makes as much money as I made because I was in a unique profession and I was a very very lucky man. But he won't have to worry about taking care of his parents like I did, he just has to worry about himself. And I would hope that the Reed family and the Reed generations to come would be better off because my son had a chance to do certain things that his father couldn't, and if he does, then I've helped contribute to that—just as my parents helped me, though they didn't graduate from college but I did. But I believe people are put in the world to do things."

He is here to play basketball. "I love basketball. There's no way you know what's going to happen until the game starts. You can't predict what the end's going to be until it's over. That's a tremendous excitement. You're playing the game and trying to ensure the outcome of it and you don't know what it will be. And I don't care how many games you've played —there are no two games alike. They won't be the same. One night you miss your free throws, the next you miss your guy on a block-out and he gets a tip-in. It goes on and on and on. The limits of what you can do as a player are only limited by the bounds of your imagination. The best move hasn't been developed, and the best play hasn't been invented, and the best player hasn't been born. I can't imagine getting the satisfaction basketball gives me from anything else. There are three things I do: I like to hunt and fish, and I love basketball, and I love chasing girls. Maybe not in that order, but that depends on the situation. But that's it. I didn't know that when I played, but I'll tell you this: Some guys when they played hated to go to practice or a game, but I couldn't wait to go to the game, and I totally enjoyed going to practice. I enjoyed the whole process. That's where I was. I knew it was hard. But the process of obtaining things is life. And people don't understand that. You know the thrill of winning the championship isn't the championship: It's the action and process of doing it, starting in training camp, the exhibition season, practices, the ups and downs of the whole year. The process is more important than the climax. The climax is that you win the championship and a lot of guys say, Give me the championship. But you know, I know the sweat and the anxiety and excitement and depression, all the different states you go through in getting ready to win. Some years we went through the same thing and we didn't win, but still the game was enjoyable because the championship itself was never the real important thing to me: To me, it was the whole trip of getting there."

# EPILOGUE

In December, 1979, the Knick management planned to honor Frazier on his retirement: prior to a game against the Boston Celtics, they would hold a public reunion of the team. They had already hosted several other public memorial parties. At the start of the '77 season, they had retired Willis's number, a standard devotion reserved for basketball heroes in which their jerseys are hung from the ceiling. Two years later they sponsored an old-timers' night, introducing several veterans to the obliging applause of the fans. Both nights had been essentially ragged affairs. Playing poorly, the team didn't attract large audiences and for Willis's night, the arena was only half filled, the house lights dimmed during the ceremony to make the rings of empty seats less conspicuous. Now the team was playing better and Frazier did draw a crowd. Still, although I usually am a sucker for these kinds of events—my imagination investing them with meanings and drama, a satisfying sentimental and emotional indulgence—I wasn't excited by this one. A controversy compromised the occasion, it's true: The management had first announced it wouldn't retire Frazier's number until next season, a needless, graceless, and insulting delay they retracted several hours before the ceremony began. Still, my coolness wasn't due to the festivity, but my general mood. Although I was loyally wedded to the game, my romance with it had ended. Contests lacked their former excitement. Having watched hundreds of them, I imagined, rightly or wrongly, some ability to forecast accurately their conclusions. My team disappointed me: When would their lessons on success match the thoroughness of their instruction about failure? Even some of the people in the business annoyed me. I approached most players respectfully, but encountered any number of difficulties and delays in setting up interviews and at times felt the victim of a thoughtless manner. I considered my feeling a privileged world-weariness, a surfeit of delight. But the fatigue colored my mood and I approached Walt Frazier Night with a measured tread. I didn't anticipate a memorable evening, but a packaged ritual, history wrapped in plastic, and simply wanted to get my story and go.

Not all the members of the team could make the date. Bill Hosket, Donnie May's friend from Ohio, and Dave Stallworth, the exuberant young player whose recovery from a heart seizure had helped symbolize the team's good fortunes during the championship year, both didn't show, and I'll use this occasion to fill in the blanks of their personal histories. Hosket played unexceptionally in Buffalo until knee injuries finally forced him to retire. Like Donnie May, he returned to Ohio. "We don't see each other that much," May told me. "He's got his own busy world and I've got mine. We don't get to each other's towns that often. At the same time, when you do get together it's all back to the way it was—there's no pretension, you just have a good time." Traded to the Bullets with Mike Riordan, Dave Stallworth had played for several years, his p.t. steadily diminishing until the team cut him. He tried out again for the New York squad, appearing in several games, but was released and went back to the West and worked for a large company. Still, he didn't leave New York easily: During the summers when I first attended semipro games, I noticed a tall, distinguished player with spots of gray in his hair who was treated with a friendly deference by the younger athletes and the knowledgeable crowd. The athlete was Stallworth.

Barnett, the veteran guard of the team, also didn't come. His absence was predictable. The acerb, stylish guard had kept out of the public eye since 1974 after he worked for a while as assistant coach of the team. Later it was reported in the papers that he was charged with mishandling funds for a poverty agency. By the time I began talking to the players he had been cleared of these charges, but had also covered all his tracks—he had no address, telephone number, post-office box. There were hints of him. The secretary in the Garden told me he called occasionally asking for tickets and sometimes showed up for boxing matches. DeBusschere told me Barnett was writing a book about Reggie Harding, a center who had played in Detroit and died from drugs; DeBusschere said he had received a phone call one night, Barnett casually inquiring whether they could talk about the Pistons, then never calling again. He was seen playing in a gym on Fourteenth Street, and a pleasant woman I met one night at a Knick game told me he frequently showed up for a poker game that she sometimes hosted. Finally, I spoke to Bowman. He told me he could definitely contact Barnett. I explained to Bowman that I respected Barnett's desire for privacy—I kept remembering his cutting comment to Berger that what writers do is get anecdotes about you so that you come out "like one big ancedote, like a clown"—but would be obliged to mention the public facts of his career and wanted to make sure he had a chance to reply. Bowman accepted the assignment and several days later a deep, scratchy voice spoke on my answering machine: "This is Dick Barnett. I have no interest in being interviewed. Thank you for your concern."

Those who came also included some whose stories I haven't told.

Mike Riordan, the nervous New Yorker who read every

paper and was famous for strong moves to the hoop, arrived from Maryland. He had met some success after being traded to the Bullets, winning himself a starting position as a small forward. In '74–'75 the team had a glorious regular season and met the Golden State Warriors in the championship round, the team Cazzie Russell, to his eternal regret, had elected to leave the season before. Favored to win, the Bullets lost four games straight and Riordan's chance at another championship was over. His p.t. was cut back over the next several seasons, and in the '78–'79 season, the team considered him expendable. Instead, he did television color commentary for the team, chronicling their surprising conquest of the championship the next year, and, scrappy and affable, retired to run a bar in Annapolis that was happily named after himself.

Phil Jackson drove in from New Jersey. In the '79 season, he had been waived by the Knicks and signed by the New Jersey Nets. Now he worked as an assistant coach for the suburban counterpart of his old team. He remained thin and angular, his brow so pronounced and his expression so skeptical that when he craned his neck upward to see the scoreboard he looked like a farmer peering out from under the roof of his porch for rain.

He had an admirable gentleness of spirit. A month before Frazier Night, I spoke to Jackson for an afternoon. His wife had recently given birth to twins, and we talked while Phil stretched out on a chaise-longue, cradling one baby in his arm, the other infant lying with its head on his thigh. As he spoke he periodically wet his pinkie and put it to the mouth of one of his two charges, who happily mistook it for a milk-giving nipple. "Coaches control the game more," he told me, dismayed at the lack of independence and character among new players. "They do a lot more talking, a lot more demonstration, a lot more drill activity. We [the old Knicks]never had a situation in which we worked off a board—either a blackboard before the game or during half time or a clipboard with X's and O's. We used to watch films and that was it. I think that has made the players less secure in their own talents. Two things have happened in general. One is that coaches get to ballplayers very, very young—as soon as a kid shows any kind of physical ability he starts getting dragged into situations where he is recruited and taken and bought. And because of this kind of prostitution—and it wasn't that way with Willis or DeBusschere or me—there's a kind of usury that goes on. I think ninety percent of the people in the pros have been paid to play before they left school: They are coerced or bought out to come to a school. The coaches are the johns and the kids the prostitutes, and the basis of the relationship is: We're going to buy you so you're going to do what we tell you to —not because you want to or because you have an understanding of it. The kids learn early that they have to be bought out to play—what are you going to do for me? And in about every level of ballplayer you can see the difference. There are very few kids who stay late to practice—at least after training camp. It becomes such a business with everybody thinking they won't do anything unless they get paid for it that the game's lost a lot of its fun and flair." Later he spoke about relations on the championship team. "There were periods and times when there were hassles—Clyde taking too many shots or Willis not getting enough. One would say, Hey, let's talk about this. They were difficult problems to talk about—it always is—but I think most of the guys were behind the fact that, hey, we've got to get a certain amount of shots from Willis from inside if we want to win. After the first championship it got harder to talk about those things. We split up after a while. We got so close. From '68 on we had five iron men who went out there every night and worked and they knew they would play forty or forty-four minutes and they just played so much together that they got really into a very precise team: Even the second team really knew very little of what the first team was doing. But after the championship we didn't get any closer. You couldn't get any closer. Everybody knew each other. How many times can you go to the same party? We had fun at the party, but then it got to be that other people had to come to the parties we had—Howard Cosell and other sports figures and ABC and television crews—and it got to be a drag. A lot of times you went to be with the guy you knew, your team, and you ended up with the other people. And, besides, we just knew each other so well—we had been with each other for three or four years."

Finally, there was Danny Whelan, the trainer of the team. He had suffered a stroke the year before, but made an astonishing, rapid recovery, slowly working his muscles back into shape. The Knicks had hired a new, younger trainer to replace him, but Whelan, a Knick emeritus, was still welcomed daily at the Garden, supervising the team's supplies. A handsomely white-haired man who carries himself with a dapper air, Whelan is famous as an oral historian of the sports scene, a prodigious story-teller who recounts tales of the past with a naïve flair, a talent for which Nate Bowman awarded him the nickname "Big-time." One young player I knew was happy after a Knick tryout because although the team hadn't taken him, Danny Whelan had at least wrapped his ankles, and encouraged him with some of his famous gab.

Whelan left the Pittsburgh Pirates in 1967 to come to the Knicks. He had two impressions of the team upon his arrival. He thought they weren't champions—"they weren't good enough—they just weren't good enough"—but were more adult than the baseball players he was used to. "They were real grown-up men. They went day by day. Baseball players said, Oh we're going to win the pennant, we're going to do this or that and then they come in last. But these guys were much more mature. They didn't talk about winning. They were good kids. The only peculiarity was that DeBusschere took Juicy Fruit gum to go out when he was warming up and Doublemint when the game started. I don't know why."

The rest too were in perfect form. John Warren came in from Rockaway, after studying for his upcoming C.P.A. test.

Donnie May flew in from Ohio with his wife; always ambivalent toward New York, he planned a festive weekend and quick return to Dayton. Nate Bowman thought the management had acted with predictable meanness by not retiring Frazier's number, but, like Warren and May, was looking forward to the party, the second one he had attended at the Garden in the past couple of years. The day before the celebration, I invited him to join me at my gym, where a young attendant immediately recognized the dramatically tall man wearing a sheepskin coat, cowboy boots, and Stetson hat and addressed Nate by his first name as though they were acquaintances of long standing. Cazzie Russell flew in from California. The afternoon of the game, he strolled over to the Garden, shot around the baskets, showered in the old locker room, and watched a college basketball game in the players' lounge. Bill Bradley didn't come, begging off because of senatorial obligations. Holzman and Donovan followed their regular schedule, leaving their offices to join the festivities. DeBusschere and Reed came from home looking even more commanding than usual, veterans ready for honor. They gathered in the press room before the game, and one reporter, who covered the team during its glorious year, lamented the present state of the game as he observed them leaving to go downstairs where they would prepare for the ceremony: "There are no personalities in the game today, anymore," he said. "Look at Reed, DeBusschere, Frazier—those guys were personalities."

And Frazier. A day earlier, I had attended a press conference he held in the Garden press room. Dressed in casually resplendent attire, an oatmeal wool suit, brown turtleneck, gold medallion, and plaid wool blanket coat, he had conducted himself with extreme modesty. He joked with the reporters who greeted him with genuine affection, and fooled with Sam Goldaper, a grandfatherly man with a limp who covers the team for the *Times*. "You ready to talk?" Goldaper demanded. Frazier smiled as though he were returning to a childhood haunt. "I'm ready to talk. I haven't talked in a long time." Jim Wergeles, one of the PR men for the Garden, who had worked with the team during its glory years, walked up. "There's Walter," he exclaimed, clapping Frazier on the arm. "He's come a long way since he was a little kid, hasn't he, Sam?" Wergeles asked Goldaper. "You were a little scared jackrabbit," Wergeles told Frazier. "You came up to me your first game and asked me if you should speak to this guy with the bad leg. Remember?"

For the next forty-five minutes, Frazier spoke about himself in an almost diffident tone of voice. He was proud of the opinion others had of him—and shared it—but was ready to move on. Being waived wasn't a disgrace, though he had sometimes wanted a storybook ending to his career. He believed his banishment from New York was part of destiny. During his exile in Cleveland, he had done a lot of soul-searching and found that life was mostly ego and, though he knew he could still play, other people wouldn't be satisfied with him just scoring twelve points and helping his team to win. He thanked the press—you guys—for making him grow up and apologized for not talking to them during his last years. Someone asked if he wanted to see his number retired—the management had yet to make their about-face. After Frazier answered yes, someone commented that he thought the management had done a classy thing by scheduling Frazier night for the Celtic game. Frazier laughed. Either they were classy, he joked, or they thought I couldn't sell the joint out.

The press conference broke up. Followed by a squadron of reporters, Frazier went down to the court. The vast arena was empty and still except for two young members of the team who were shooting around the basket, warming up, the balls thumping rhythmically on the floor. Frazier gave some more interviews and a young man who helped set up the celebration came over and told him the schedule for the next day. After getting Frazier's okay, he broke the businesslike formality of the occasion and told Frazier he had been in high school when the team won the championship, and he wanted to tell him he admired him a lot. Frazier thanked him for the compliment, but the appreciation seemed poignantly insufficient—this man had never figured in Frazier's inner life as the star had in his. After an uncomfortable moment the young man simply repeated his praise and left. Another member of the front office came over. "Come on, Clyde," he urged, "I'll show you the new locker room: You won't recognize it." But Frazier begged off; he would see it tomorrow. These private testimonials gave no one satisfaction.

Now, with the ceremony about to begin, I wondered how he would conduct himself publicly. Walt Frazier or Clyde? A red ribbon cordoned off a section of the court where photographers and officials waited to take pictures and make presentations. At the press table Marv Albert prepared his introductions. I sat in a gondola above the court and watched the crowd that already filled the arena. A banner hung from a balcony—Clyde, Naturally—and people held up large poster-size photos of the star. The festival-like atmosphere reminded me of rallies: The shared purpose of the occasion seemed to make everyone happier, prettier, funnier. I took notes, the excitement overcoming my indifference. A blonde wearing a white cashmere sweater and a red fox coat brushed her hair vigorously and shook it back, making herself beautiful for the coming minutes. A black kid in a green sweat shirt walked up and down the aisles telling people he was Clyde's nephew. A man my age dressed in expensive sports clothes rubbed his hands on his pants legs, ready to applaud. Tonight they too would perform. Then the PA announcer gave the inimitable introduction—"Good evening, ladies and gentlemen, and welcome to Madison Square Garden!" From the balcony there was a rumble of noise, shouts, and applause, and spotlights lit the court as the house went black.

One by one, the players walked onto the court, Albert introducing them with a flair, giving their schools and nicknames, identifying them for the crowd: Johnny Warren, Donnie May, Nate—Nate the Snake—Bowman, Danny Whelan. The applause and cheers never stopped, only modulating during the moments between entrances, and the players turned delightedly to each other, shaking hands and joking as they were joined by each new comrade. Mike Riordan's name was greeted with a percussive cheer. Cazzie Russell, the man of "instant offense, who could hit from all angles and was one of the all-time great Knick players," received a standing ovation. Phil "Action" Jackson strode out as a group of fellows near courtside waved their arms like semaphores, imitating the famous air-flailing gesture the player used when guarding a man making an inbounds pass. Then, gloriously white-haired, fists high in the air, DeBusschere came out, and the cheers changed to the old watchword cry: Dee-fense! Dee-fense! Willis followed, people shouting his name as the captain made his first appearance since being fired, Earl Monroe joined the squad from off the bench, and only Frazier was left. DeBusschere began to clap in time with the organ as it played "For He's a Jolly Good Fellow," and the electric lights of the scoreboard blinked:

WELCOME HOME
CLYDE

And Clyde came on stage, gray suit, black shirt, white tie, white shoes, a dazzling display. He stood mutely, his arms at his side, humbled and glorious as the fans honored him with an ovation that renewed itself every time it died down. Finally the organ and applause stopped and just whistles filled the arena, shrill sweeps of sound at once congratulatory and commanding. Frazier received the testimonials, and Reed gave him the jersey with No. 10, which would now be retired. Then he spoke. "This is a proud moment," he told the loving crowd, "and I'll never forget it. It ranks along with the '69–'70 year." He thanked his mother: "She always taught me to treat people the right way and that if I wanted something I could do it. I just had to work hard for it." Then he thanked the Knick management for drafting him—"they knew they had talent"—and Holzman and Irish, and the timekeeper, announcer, Danny Whelan, the PR men, the secretaries (who got a big cheer from the balcony), and a ballboy named Randy, who kept him in clean socks and a jock. Most of all, he said, he wanted to thank his teammates. Without them he would have been good, but because of them he was great. Finally, he wished to thank the fans—the greatest fans in the world. "I know that there were nights on this floor that I thought I could conquer anything," he said and waited before delivering the inevitable, glorious assertion we all wanted to hear because it celebrated us and the team as well as him: "and I often did." Then the magic worked once more, the presence of him and his teammates causing us all to express our gratitude and joy, and he turned and walked off court, the rest of the old team following him as the new one began its warmups.

The game itself was exciting but disappointing, the Knicks blowing a lead in the last minute. Still, the team was promising: A year before, they would have been out of the contest from the third quarter. Afterward I walked downstairs to the locker room, where Holzman studied the stat sheet. After five minutes he looked up and announced that he had discovered the reason for the loss, but refused to disclose it. Upstairs the players, old and young, were gathering in Harry M. Stevens, the restaurant on the street level of the Garden with large glass windows where, on cold nights, the pleased and jovial crowd inside always exudes a festive air. I walked toward the players' entrance, going through the complicated underground passageways of the arena: When I had first come to games, they seemed impossible to know. Outside the doorway kids were lined up as usual wanting autographs, and as I entered the bitterly chilled air one yelled I was a Boston Celtic. I could enjoy the mistake for only a minute. Willis Reed and some of the young Knicks emerged right after me, and the kids swarmed over them, chasing them to the restaurant, a flurry of corduroy and dungarees. Willis and the rest paused before the restaurant, fulfilling all the requests. Then they went inside, joining the party. Huge, handsome, accomplished, they passed before the window, drinking and dining, while outside, fascinated and eager, the kids watched them, their noses pressed to the glass.